NEWS OF A KIDNAPPING

OTHER BOOKS IN ENGLISH TRANSLATION
BY GABRIEL GARCÍA MÁRQUEZ

No One Writes to the Colonel and Other Stories   (1968)

One Hundred Years of Solitude   (1970)

The Autumn of the Patriarch   (1976)

Innocent Eréndira and Other Stories   (1978)

In Evil Hour   (1979)

Leaf Storm and Other Stories   (1979)

Chronicle of a Death Foretold   (1982)

The Story of a Shipwrecked Sailor   (1986)

Clandestine in Chile: The Adventures of Miguel Littín   (1987)

Love in the Time of Cholera   (1988)

The General in His Labyrinth   (1990)

Strange Pilgrims   (1993)

Of Love and Other Demons   (1995)

NEWS OF A KIDNAPPING

GABRIEL GARCÍA
MÁRQUEZ

TRANSLATED FROM THE SPANISH

BY EDITH GROSSMAN

JONATHAN CAPE
LONDON

First published 1997

1 3 5 7 9 10 8 6 4 2

© Gabriel García Marquez 1997
© Mondadori (Grijalbo Comercial, S.A.)

Gabriel García Marquez has asserted his right
under the Copyright, Designs and Patents Act 1988
to be identified as the author of this work

Originally published in Spain as *Noticia de un secuestro*
by Mondadori (Grijalbo Comercial, S.A.), Barcelona, in 1996.

First published in the United Kingdom in 1997 by Jonathan Cape,
Random House, 20 Vauxhall Bridge Road, London SW1V 2SA

Random House Australia (Pty) Limited
20 Alfred Street, Milsons Point, Sydney,
New South Wales 2061, Australia

Random House New Zealand Limited
18 Poland Road, Glenfield,
Auckland 10, New Zealand

Random House South Africa (Pty) Limited
Endulini, 5A Jubilee Road, Parktown 2193, South Africa

Random House UK Limited Reg. No. 954009

A CIP catalogue record for this book is available from the British Library

Papers used by Random House UK Limited are natural,
recyclable products made from wood grown in sustainable forests.
The manufacturing processes conform to the environmental
regulations of the country of origin.

ISBN 0-224-05002-8

Printed and bound in Great Britain
by Mackays of Chatham PLC

ACKNOWLEDGMENTS

IN OCTOBER 1993, Maruja Pachón and her husband, Alberto Villamizar, suggested I write a book about her abduction and six-month captivity, and his persistent efforts to obtain her release. I was already well into the first draft when we realized it was impossible to separate her kidnapping from nine other abductions that occurred at the same time in Colombia. They were not, in fact, ten distinct abductions—as it had seemed at first—but a single collective abduction of ten carefully chosen individuals, which had been carried out by the same group and for only one purpose.

This belated realization obliged us to begin again with a different structure and spirit so that all the protagonists would have their well-defined identities, their own realities. It was a technical solution to a labyrinthine narrative that in its original form would have been confused and interminable. But this meant that what had been foreseen as a year's work extended into almost three, even with the constant, meticulous assistance and collaboration of Maruja and Alberto, whose personal stories are the central axis, the unifying thread, of this book.

I interviewed all the protagonists I could, and in each of them

ACKNOWLEDGMENTS

I found the same generous willingness to root through their memories and reopen wounds they perhaps preferred to forget. Their pain, their patience, and their rage gave me the courage to persist in this autumnal task, the saddest and most difficult of my life. My only frustration is knowing that none of them will find on paper more than a faded reflection of the horror they endured in their real lives—above all, the families of Marina Montoya and Diana Turbay, the two hostages who were killed, and in particular Diana Turbay's mother, doña Nydia Quintero de Balcázar, whose interviews were a heartrending, unforgettable human experience for me.

I share this sense of inadequacy with the two people who suffered along with me through the intimate hammering out of the book: the journalist Luzángela Arteaga, who tracked down and captured innumerable impossible facts with the tenacity and absolute discretion of a crafty hunter, and Margarita Márquez Caballero, my first cousin and private secretary, who took care of the transcription, verification, and confidentiality of the intricate raw material that we often thought would overwhelm us.

To all the protagonists and all my collaborators, I offer my eternal gratitude for not allowing this gruesome drama to sink into oblivion. Sadly, it is only one episode in the biblical holocaust that has been consuming Colombia for more than twenty years. I dedicate this book to them, and to all Colombians—innocent and guilty—with the hope that the story it tells will never befall us again.

G. G. M.
Cartagena de Indias, May 1996

NEWS OF A KIDNAPPING

1

SHE LOOKED OVER her shoulder before getting into the car to be sure no one was following her. It was 7:05 in the evening in Bogotá. It had been dark for an hour, the Parque Nacional was not well lit, and the silhouettes of leafless trees against a sad, overcast sky seemed ghostly, but nothing appeared to be threatening. Despite her position, Maruja sat behind the driver because she always thought it was the most comfortable seat. Beatriz climbed in through the other door and sat to her right. They were almost an hour behind in their daily schedule, and both women looked tired after a soporific afternoon of three executive meetings—Maruja in particular, who had given a party the night before and had slept for only three hours. She stretched out her tired legs, closed her eyes as she leaned her head against the back of the seat, and gave the usual order:

"Please take us home."

As they did every day, they sometimes took one route, sometimes another, as much for reasons of security as because of traffic jams. The Renault 21 was new and comfortable, and the chauffeur drove with caution and skill. The best alternative that night was

Avenida Circunvalar heading north. They had three green lights, and evening traffic was lighter than usual. Even on the worst days it took only half an hour to drive from the office to Maruja's house, at No. 84A-42 Transversal Tercera, and then the driver would take Beatriz to her house, some seven blocks away.

Maruja came from a family of well-known intellectuals that included several generations of reporters. She herself was an award-winning journalist. For the past two months she had been the director of FOCINE, the state-run enterprise for the promotion of the film industry. Beatriz, Maruja's sister-in-law and personal assistant, had been a physical therapist for many years but had decided on a change of pace for a while. Her major responsibility at FOCINE was attending to everything related to the press. Neither woman had any specific reason to be afraid, but since August, when the drug traffickers began an unpredictable series of abductions of journalists, Maruja had acquired the almost unconscious habit of looking over her shoulder.

Her suspicion was on target. Though the Parque Nacional had seemed deserted when she looked behind her before getting into the car, eight men were following her. One was at the wheel of a dark blue Mercedes 190 that had phony Bogotá plates and was parked across the street. Another was in the driver's seat of a stolen yellow cab. Four of them were wearing jeans, sneakers, and leather jackets and strolling in the shadows of the park. The seventh, tall and well-dressed in a light-weight suit, carried a briefcase, which completed the picture of a young executive. From a small corner café half a block away, the eighth man, the one responsible for the operation, observed the first real performance of an action whose intensive, meticulous rehearsals had begun twenty-one days earlier.

The cab and the Mercedes followed Maruja's automobile, keeping a close distance just as they had been doing since the previous Monday to determine her usual routes. After about twenty minutes the three cars turned right onto Calle 82, less than two hundred meters from the unfaced brick building where Maruja lived with her husband and one of her children. They had just begun to drive up the steep slope of the street, when the yellow cab passed Maruja's car, hemmed it in along the left-hand curb, and forced the driver to slam on the brakes to avoid a collision. At almost the same time, the Mercedes stopped behind the Renault, making it impossible to back up.

Three men got out of the cab and with resolute strides approached Maruja's car. The tall, well-dressed one carried a strange weapon that looked to Maruja like a sawed-off shotgun with a barrel as long and thick as a telescope. It was, in fact, a 9mm Mini-Uzi equipped with a silencer and capable of firing either single shots or fifteen rounds per second. The other two were armed with submachine guns and pistols. What Maruja and Beatriz could not see were the three men getting out of the Mercedes that had pulled in behind them.

They acted with so much coordination and speed that Maruja and Beatriz could remember only isolated fragments of the scant two minutes of the assault. With professional skill, five men surrounded the car and at the same time dealt with its three occupants. The sixth watched the street, holding his submachine gun at the ready. Maruja's fears had been realized.

"Drive, Angel," she shouted to the driver. "Go up on the sidewalk, whatever, but drive."

Angel was paralyzed, though with the cab in front of him and the Mercedes behind, he had no room to get away in any case. Fearing the men would begin shooting, Maruja clutched at her handbag as if it were a life preserver, crouched down behind the driver's seat, and shouted to Beatriz:

"Get down on the floor!"

"The hell with that," Beatriz whispered. "On the floor they'll kill us."

She was trembling but determined. Certain it was only a holdup, she pulled the two rings off her right hand and tossed them out the window, thinking: "Let them earn it." But she did not have time to take off the two on her left hand. Maruja, curled into a ball behind the seat, did not even remember that she was wearing a diamond and emerald ring and a pair of matching earrings.

Two men opened Maruja's door and another two opened Beatriz's. The fifth shot the driver in the head through the glass, and the silencer made it sound no louder than a sigh. Then he opened the door, pulled him out, and shot him three more times as he lay on the ground. It was another man's destiny: Angel María Roa had been Maruja's driver for only three days, and for the first time he was displaying his new dignity with the dark suit, starched shirt, and black tie worn by the chauffeurs who drove government ministers. His predecessor, who had retired the week before, had been FOCINE's regular driver for ten years.

Maruja did not learn of the assault on the chauffeur until much later. From her hiding place she heard only the sudden noise of breaking glass and then a peremptory shout just above her head: "You're the one we want, Señora. Get out!" An iron hand grasped her arm and dragged her out of the car. She resisted as much as she could, fell, scraped her leg, but the two men picked her up and carried her bodily to the car behind the Renault. They did not notice that Maruja was still clutching her handbag.

Beatriz, who had long, hard nails and good military training, confronted the boy who tried to pull her from the car. "Don't touch me!" she screamed. He gave a start, and Beatriz realized he was just as nervous as she, and capable of anything. She changed her tone.

"I'll get out by myself," she said. "Just tell me what to do."

The boy pointed to the cab.

"Into that car and down on the floor," he said. "Move!" The doors were open, the motor running, the driver motionless in his seat. Beatriz lay down in the back. Her kidnapper covered her with his jacket and sat down, resting his feet on her. Two more men got in: one next to the driver, the other in back. The driver waited for the simultaneous thud of both doors, then sped away, heading north on Avenida Circunvalar. That was when Beatriz realized she had left her bag on the seat of the Renault, but it was too late. More than fear and discomfort, what she found intolerable was the ammonia stink of the jacket.

They had put Maruja into the Mercedes, which had driven off a minute earlier, following a different route. They had her sit in the middle of the back seat, with a man on either side. The one on the left forced Maruja's head against his knees, in a position so uncomfortable she had difficulty breathing. The man beside the driver communicated with the other car by means of an antiquated two-way radio. Maruja's consternation was heightened because she could not tell which vehicle she was in—she had not seen the Mercedes stop behind her car—but she did know it was comfortable and new, and perhaps bulletproof, since the street noises sounded muted, like the whisper of rain. She could not breathe, her heart pounded, and she began to feel as if she were suffocating. The man next to the driver, who seemed to be in charge, became aware of her agitation and tried to reassure her.

"Take it easy," he said, over his shoulder. "We only want you to deliver a message. You'll be home in a couple of hours. But if you move there'll be trouble, so just take it easy."

The one who held her head on his knees also tried to reassure her. Maruja took a deep breath, exhaled very slowly through her mouth, and began to regain her composure. After a few blocks the situation changed because the car ran into a traffic jam on a steep incline. The man on the two-way radio started to shout impossible orders that the driver of the other car could not carry out. Several ambulances were caught in traffic somewhere along the highway, and the din of sirens and earsplitting horns was maddening even for someone with steady nerves. And for the moment, at least, that did not describe the kidnappers. The driver was so agitated as he tried to make his way through traffic that he hit a taxi.

It was no more than a tap, but the cab driver shouted something that made them even more nervous. The man with the two-way radio ordered him to move no matter what, and the car drove over sidewalks and through empty lots.

When they were free of traffic, they were still going uphill. Maruja had the impression they were heading toward La Calera, a hill that tended to be very crowded at that hour. Then she remembered some cardamom seeds, a natural tranquilizer, in her jacket pocket, and asked her captors to let her chew a few. The man on her right helped her look for them, and this was when he noticed she was still holding her handbag. They took it away but gave her the cardamom. Maruja tried to get a good look at the kidnappers, but the light was too dim. She dared to ask a question: "Who are you people?" The man with the two-way radio answered in a quiet voice:

"We're from the M-19."

A nonsensical reply: The M-19, a former guerrilla group, was legal now and campaigning for seats in the Constituent Assembly.

"Seriously," said Maruja. "Are you dealers or guerrillas?"

"Guerrillas," said the man in front. "But don't worry, we just want you to take back a message. Seriously."

He stopped talking and told the others to push Maruja down on the floor because they were about to pass a police checkpoint. "Now if you move or say anything, we'll kill you." She felt the barrel of a revolver pressing against her ribs, and the man beside her completed the thought:

"That's a gun pointing at you."

The next ten minutes were eternal. Maruja focused her energy, chewing the cardamom seeds that helped to revive her, but her position did not let her see or hear what was said at the checkpoint, if in fact anything was said. Maruja had the impression that they went through with no questions asked. The suspicion that they were going to La Calera became a certainty, and the knowledge brought her some relief. She did not try to sit up because she felt more comfortable on the floor than with her head on the man's knees. The car drove along a dirt road for about five minutes, then stopped. The man with the two-way radio said:

"This is it."

No lights were visible. They covered Maruja's head with a jacket and made her look down when she got out, so that all she saw was her own feet walking, first across a courtyard and then through what may have been a kitchen with a tile floor. When they uncovered her head she found herself in a small room, about two by three meters, with a mattress on the floor and a bare red light-bulb hanging from the ceiling. A moment later two men came in, their faces concealed by a kind of balaclava that was in fact the leg of a pair of sweatpants with three holes cut for the eyes and mouth. From then on, during her entire captivity, she did not see her captors' faces again.

She knew that these two were not the same men who had abducted her. Their clothes were shabby and soiled, they were shorter than Maruja, who is five feet, six inches tall, and they had the voices and bodies of boys. One of them ordered Maruja to hand over her jewelry. "For security reasons," he said. "It'll be safe here." She gave him the emerald ring with the tiny diamonds, but not the earrings.

In the other car, Beatriz could draw no conclusion regarding their route. She lay on the floor the entire time and did not recall driving up any hill as steep as La Calera, or passing any check-points, though the cab might have had a special permit that allowed it through without being stopped. The atmosphere in the car was very tense because of the heavy traffic. The man at the wheel shouted into the two-way radio that he couldn't drive over the other cars and kept asking what to do, which made the men in the lead car so nervous they gave him different, and contradictory, instructions.

Beatriz was very uncomfortable, with one leg bent under her and the stink of the jacket making her dizzy. She tried to find a less painful position. Her guard thought she was struggling and attempted to reassure her: "Take it easy, sweetheart, nothing's going to happen to you. You just have to deliver a message." When he realized at last that the problem was her leg, he helped her straighten it and was less brusque with her. More than anything else, Beatriz could not bear the "sweetheart," a liberty that offended her almost more than the stench of the jacket. But the more he tried to reassure her, the more convinced she became that they were going to kill her. She estimated the trip as taking no more than forty minutes, so it must have been about a quarter to eight when they reached the house.

Her arrival was identical to Maruja's. Her head was covered by the foul-smelling jacket, and they led her by the hand, warning her not to look anywhere but down. She saw what Maruja had seen: the courtyard, the tile floor, and two steps. They told her to move left, and then they removed the jacket. There was Maruja, sitting on a stool, looking pale in the red glow of the only light in the room.

"Beatriz!" said Maruja. "You're here too?"

She did not know what had happened to Beatriz, but thought they had let her go because she was not really involved in anything. When she saw her she felt great joy at not being alone, and at the same time immense sadness because she had been kidnapped too. They embraced as if they had not seen each other for a long time.

It was inconceivable that the two of them could survive in that squalid room, sleeping on a single mattress on the floor, with two masked guards who did not take their eyes off them for an instant. Then another man in a mask—elegant, well built, at least five feet, ten inches tall—whom the others called "Doctor," the title used for any professional, took charge with the air of someone who had great authority. The rings were removed from Beatriz's left hand, but they did not notice that she was wearing a gold chain with a medal of the Virgin.

"This is a military operation, and nothing's going to happen to you," he said, and repeated: "We've only brought you here so that you can deliver a communiqué to the government."

"Who's holding us?" Maruja asked.

He shrugged. "That doesn't matter now," he said. He raised the machine gun so they had a clear view of it, and went on: "But I want to tell you one thing. This machine gun has a silencer, nobody knows where you are, or who you're with. The minute you scream or do anything else, we'll get rid of you and nobody will ever see you again." They held their breath, expecting the worst. But when he had finished his threats, the boss turned to Beatriz.

"Now we're separating you, we're going to let you go," he said. "We took you along by mistake."

Beatriz's response was immediate.

"Oh, no," she said without any hesitation. "I'm staying with Maruja."

Her decision was so brave and generous that even her abductor exclaimed in amazement, without a shred of irony: "What a loyal friend you have, doña Maruja!" And she, grateful despite her consternation, agreed and thanked Beatriz. Then the "Doctor" asked if they wanted anything to eat. They refused but asked for water since their mouths were bone dry. Maruja, who always has a cigarette lit and keeps the pack and lighter in easy reach, had not smoked during the trip. She asked for her bag, where she kept her cigarettes, and he gave her one of his.

Both women asked to use the bathroom. Beatriz went first, her head covered by a torn, dirty cloth. "Keep your eyes on the floor," someone ordered. She was led by the hand along a narrow hall to a tiny, filthy lavatory with a sorry little window looking out on the night. The door had no inside lock, but it did close, and so Beatriz climbed up on the toilet and looked out the window. In the light of a streetlamp all she could see was a small adobe house with red roof tiles and a patch of grass in front, the kind of house seen all along the roads through the savanna.

When she returned to the room, she found a drastic change in circumstances. "We know who you are now, and we can use you, too," the "Doctor" said. "You'll stay with us." They had found out on the radio, which had just announced the kidnapping.

Eduardo Carrillo, who reported on legal issues for the National Radio Network (RCN), had been discussing another matter with one of his sources in the military when the officer received a report of the abduction on his two-way radio. The news was announced without delay, or further details. That was how the kidnappers learned Beatriz's identity.

The radio also said that the cab driver could remember two numbers on the license plate, and had given a general description of the car that had bumped into his taxi. The police had determined their escape route. The house had become dangerous for everyone, and they had to leave right away. Even worse: They were going to use a different car, and the two women would have to be put in the trunk.

They protested but to no avail because their kidnappers seemed as frightened as they were, and made no effort to conceal it. Maruja asked for a little rubbing alcohol, terrified at the thought they would suffocate in the trunk.

"We don't have any alcohol," said the "Doctor" in a harsh voice. "You'll ride in the trunk and that's all there is to it. Hurry up."

They were obliged to take off their shoes and carry them as they were led through the house to the garage. There their heads were uncovered, and they were put into the trunk of the car in a fetal position. No force was used. The space was big enough, and it was well ventilated because the rubber seals had been removed. Before he closed the trunk, the "Doctor" filled them with dread. "We're carrying ten kilos of dynamite," he said. "At the first shout, cough, cry, whatever, we'll get out of the car and blow it up."

To their relief and surprise, a breeze as cold and pure as air-conditioning came in the sides of the trunk. The desperate anguish disappeared, leaving only uncertainty. Maruja turned inward, an attitude that could have been confused with complete withdrawal but was in fact her magic formula for dealing with anxiety. Beatriz, on the other hand, driven by an insatiable curiosity, looked through the illuminated opening of the poorly sealed trunk. She could see the passengers through the back window: two men in the back seat, and next to the driver a woman with long hair, holding a baby about two years old. To her right she saw the yellow lights of the huge sign for a well-known shopping center. There could be no doubt: They were on the highway heading north. It was well lit for a long time, then they were in total darkness on an unpaved road, and the car slowed down. After about fifteen minutes, it stopped.

It must have been another checkpoint. Beatriz heard indistinct voices, the sound of other cars, music, but it was too dark to see anything. Maruja roused herself and became alert, hoping it was an inspection station where the men would be obliged to show what they were carrying in the trunk. After about five minutes the car pulled away and drove up a steep incline, but this time they could not determine the route. Some ten minutes later the automobile stopped, and the trunk was opened. Again their heads were covered, and their captors helped them out into darkness.

Together this time, Maruja and Beatriz walked as they had in the other house, looking down, and were led by their kidnappers along a hall, through a small living room where other people were speaking in whispers, until they came to a room. Before they went in, the "Doctor" prepared them:

"Now you're going to see a friend of yours," he said.

The light in the room was so dim it took a moment for their eyes to adjust. It was a space no larger than the other room, with one boarded-up window. Two men, sitting on a single mattress on the floor and wearing hoods like the ones in the first house, were absorbed in watching television. Everything was dismal and oppressive. In the corner, to the left of the door, on a narrow bed with iron posts, sat a spectral woman with limp white hair, dazed eyes, and skin that adhered to her bones. She gave no sign of having heard them come in: not a glance, not a breath, nothing. A corpse could not have seemed so dead. Maruja had to control her shock.

"Marina!" she whispered.

Marina Montoya, kidnapped three months earlier, was thought to be dead. Her brother, don Germán Montoya, had been secretary general to the presidency and a powerful figure in the Virgilio Barco government. His son, Alvaro Diego, the director of an important insurance company, had been abducted by the narco-traffickers to put pressure on their negotiations with the government. The accepted story, which was never confirmed, was that he had been released following a secret agreement that the government had not lived up to. The kidnapping of his aunt Marina nine months later could only be interpreted as a brutal reprisal because by then she no longer had exchange value. The Virgilio Barco government was out of office, Germán Montoya was Colombia's ambassador to Canada, and the thought in everyone's mind was that Marina had been kidnapped for the sole purpose of killing her.

After the initial outcry over her abduction, which had mobilized both national and international opinion, Marina's name had disappeared from the papers. Maruja and Beatriz knew her well, but it was difficult for them to recognize her. As far as they were concerned, the fact that they had been brought to the same room could only mean that they were in the cell for prisoners condemned to death. Marina did not move a muscle. Maruja squeezed her hand, then shuddered. Marina's hand was neither cold nor warm; it conveyed nothing.

The theme music for the television newscast brought them out of their stupor. It was nine-thirty on the night of November 7, 1990. Half an hour earlier, Hernán Estupiñán, a reporter for the program "National News," had been informed of the kidnapping by a friend at FOCINE and had hurried to the site of the abduction. He had not yet returned with complete details, but Javier Ayala, the director and announcer, began the program by reading an emergency bulletin before the credits came on: "The director of FOCINE, doña Maruja Pachón de Villamizar, wife of the well-known politician Alberto Villamizar, and his sister, Beatriz Villamizar de Guerrero, were kidnapped at seven-thirty this evening." The purpose seemed clear: Maruja was the sister of Gloria Pachón, the widow of Luis Carlos Galán, the young journalist who, in 1979, had founded the New Liberalism in an effort to revitalize and modernize the corrupt Liberal Party; the New Liberalism was the most serious and energetic force that opposed drug trafficking and supported the extradition of Colombian nationals.

2

THE FIRST FAMILY member to learn about the abduction was Dr. Pedro Guerrero, Beatriz's husband. He was at the Clinic for Psychotherapy and Human Sexuality—about ten blocks away—preparing a lecture on the evolution of animal species from the elementary functions of single-celled organisms to human emotions and affections. He was interrupted by a phone call from a police officer who asked in a cold, professional way if he was acquainted with Beatriz Villamizar. "Of course," Dr. Guerrero replied, "she's my wife." The officer was silent for a moment and then, in a more human tone, said, "All right, try to stay calm." Dr. Guerrero did not need to be a distinguished psychiatrist to understand that those words were the preamble to something very serious.

"What's happened?" he asked.

"A driver was murdered at the corner of Carrera Quinta and Calle 85," said the officer. "The car's a Renault 21, light gray, Bogotá license plate PS-2034. Do you know the number?"

"I have no idea," said Dr. Guerrero in an impatient voice. "Just tell me what happened to Beatriz."

"The only thing we can tell you now is that she's missing," the officer said. "We found her handbag on the seat, and a notebook where it said to call you in case of emergency."

There could be no doubt. Dr. Guerrero was the one who had advised his wife to put an emergency number in her datebook. Although he did not know the license number, the description matched Maruja's car. The corner where the crime occurred was just a few steps from Maruja's house, their first stop before Beatriz was driven home. Dr. Guerrero canceled his lecture with a hurried explanation. His friend, the urologist Alonso Acuña, drove him to the crime scene, through the heavy seven o'clock traffic, in fifteen minutes.

Alberto Villamizar, Maruja Pachón's husband and Beatriz's brother, was only two hundred meters from the corner where the abduction took place, but heard about it when the doorman called him on the house phone. He had come home at four, after spending the afternoon at the offices of the newspaper *El Tiempo*, working on the campaign for the Constituent Assembly whose members were to be elected in December, and he had fallen asleep fully dressed, exhausted by the previous night's party. His son Andrés came in a little before seven, accompanied by Beatriz's son Gabriel, who had been his best friend since childhood. Andrés looked for his mother in the bedroom and woke Alberto, who was surprised to see that it was already dark. Still half asleep, he turned on the light and checked the time. It was almost seven, and Maruja was not back yet.

The delay was unusual. She and Beatriz were always home earlier than this, regardless of traffic, or called if they were detained for some reason. And Maruja and he had both arranged to be at home by five. Alberto was worried and asked Andrés to call FOCINE. The watchman said that Maruja and Beatriz had left a little later than normal and would be there any minute. Villamizar had gone to the kitchen for a glass of water when the telephone rang. Andrés answered. Just by the sound of his son's voice, Alberto could tell it was an alarming call. He was right. Something had happened on the corner, and the car seemed to be Maruja's. The doorman's account was confused.

Alberto asked Andrés to stay home in case anyone called, then raced out. Gabriel ran after him. They were too impatient to wait for the elevator, and they dashed down the stairs. The doorman shouted after them:

"I think somebody was killed."

The street looked as if a celebration were in progress. The neighbors were at the windows of the residential buildings, and the horns of cars stalled on the Circunvalar were blaring. At the corner a squad car attempted to keep a curious crowd away from the abandoned automobile. It surprised Villamizar to see Dr. Guerrero there before him.

It was, in fact, Maruja's car. At least half an hour had gone by since the kidnapping, and all that was left were the remains: bullet-shattered glass on the driver's side, blood and broken glass on the seat, and the dark wet stain on the asphalt where the driver had been lying. He had just been taken away, still alive. Everything else was clean and in order.

An efficient, well-mannered policeman gave Villamizar the details provided by the few witnesses. They were fragmentary, imprecise, sometimes contradictory, but left no doubt that it had been an abduction, and that the driver was the only one wounded. Alberto wanted to know if he had said anything, given any clues. But that had been impossible: The driver was in a coma, and no one had said where he had been taken.

Dr. Guerrero, on the other hand, seemed anesthetized by shock, incapable of assessing the gravity of the situation. When he arrived he had identified Beatriz's bag, her cosmetic case, her date-book, a leather cardcase that held her identity card, her wallet containing twelve thousand pesos and a credit card, and concluded that only his wife had been abducted.

"See, Maruja's bag isn't here," he said to his brother-in-law. "She probably wasn't even in the car."

Perhaps this was a kind of professional delicacy intended to distract him while they both caught their breath. But Alberto was beyond that. What interested him now was to find out if the only blood in and around the car was the driver's, to be certain neither woman had been wounded. Everything else seemed clear to him, and what his feeling most resembled was guilt at never having foreseen that this kidnapping might happen. He had the absolute conviction that it was a personal act directed at him, and he knew who had done it, and why.

He had just left the house when radio programs were interrupted by the announcement that Maruja's driver had died in the private car that was taking him to the Clínica del Country. A short while later Guillermo Franco, the crime reporter for Caracol Radio, came on the scene, alerted by the report of a shooting, but all he found was the abandoned car. He picked up glass fragments and a blood-stained cigarette paper from the driver's seat and placed them in a small, transparent box that was numbered and dated. That same night the box joined the extensive collection of artifacts in the chronicle of crime created by Franco during his long years in the profession. The police officer accompanied Villamizar back to his house, asking a series of informal questions that might prove helpful to his investigation, but Alberto responded without thinking of anything but the long, difficult days that lay ahead of him. The first thing was to tell Andrés about the decision he had made. He asked him to see to the people who were beginning to come to the house, while he made some urgent phone calls and put his ideas in order. He went to the bedroom, closed the door, and called the presidential palace.

He had a very good political and personal relationship with President César Gaviria, and Gaviria knew Alberto as an impulsive but cordial man capable of maintaining his sangfroid under the most stressful circumstances. He was struck, therefore, by the abrupt vehemence with which Villamizar informed him that his wife and sister had been abducted, concluding with a brusque:

"I'm holding you responsible for their lives."

César Gaviria can be the harshest of men when he believes he should be, and this was one of those times.

"You listen to me, Alberto." His tone was curt. "Everything will be done that can be done."

And then, with the same coldness, he said he would immediately instruct his adviser on security, Rafael Pardo Rueda, to take charge of the matter and keep him up-to-date regarding the situation. Subsequent events would prove that his decision was the correct one.

The media arrived en masse. Villamizar knew that other kidnapping victims had been allowed to listen to the radio and television, and he improvised a message in which he demanded that Maruja and Beatriz be treated with the respect they deserved as honorable women who had nothing to do with the war, and announced that from this moment on he would devote all his time and energy to obtaining their release.

One of the first to come to the house was General Miguel Maza Márquez, head of the Administrative Department for Security (DAS), whose responsibility it was to investigate the abduction. The general had held this position for seven years, since the days of the Belisario Betancur government; he had continued in office under President Virgilio Barco, and had just been confirmed by César Gaviria—unprecedented longevity in a post from which it is almost impossible to emerge unscathed, above all during the most difficult days in the war against the drug traffickers. Compact and hard, as if forged in steel, with the bull neck typical of the warlike people from La Guajira, the general is a man of long, gloomy silences, and at the same time capable of openhearted intimacy with friends: He is pure Guajiran. But in his work there were no nuances. To his mind, the war against the drug dealers was a personal struggle to the death with Pablo Escobar. And the feeling was more than mutual. Escobar had used 2,600 kilos of dynamite in two successive attempts against his life: the highest distinction Escobar had ever granted to an enemy. Maza Márquez escaped unharmed on both occasions, attributing this to the protection of the Holy Infant—the same saint, of course, to whom Escobar attributed the miracle of his not being killed by Maza Márquez.

President Gaviria had made it a matter of policy that no armed force was to attempt a rescue without the prior agreement of the kidnap victim's family. But the political rumor mill produced a good deal of talk regarding procedural differences between the president and General Maza. Villamizar was taking no chances.

"I want you to know that I'm opposed to an armed rescue," he told General Maza. "I want to be sure it won't happen, and that I'm consulted before any decision is reached."

Maza Márquez agreed. At the end of their long, informative talk, he ordered a tap on Villamizar's telephone in the event the kidnappers attempted to communicate with him at night.

That same evening Villamizar had his first conversation with Rafael Pardo, who informed him that the president had appointed him mediator between the government and the family, and that he, Pardo, was the only one authorized to make official statements regarding the case. It was clear to both men that Maruja's abduction was a move by the drug dealers to exert pressure on the government through her sister, Gloria Pachón, and they decided to proceed on that assumption without hypothesizing any further.

Colombia had not been aware of her own importance in the international drug trade until the traffickers invaded the country's highest political echelons through the back door, first with their increasing ability to corrupt and suborn, and then with their own ambitions. In 1982 Pablo Escobar had tried to find a place in the New Liberalism movement headed by Luis Carlos Galán, but Galán removed his name from the rolls and exposed him before a crowd of five thousand people in Medellín. A short while later Escobar was in the Chamber of Deputies as a representative of a marginal wing of the official Liberal Party, but he had not forgotten the insult and unleashed an all-out war against the state, in particular against the New Liberalism. Rodrigo Lara Bonilla, who represented the New Liberalism as justice minister in the Belisario Betancur government, was murdered in a drive-by shooting on the streets of Bogotá. His successor, Enrique Parejo, was pursued all the way to Budapest by a hired assassin who shot him in the face with a pistol but did not kill him. On August 18, 1989, Luis Carlos Galán, who was protected by eighteen well-armed bodyguards, was machine-gunned on the main square in the municipality of Soacha, some ten kilometers from the presidential palace.

The main reason for the war was the drug traffickers' fear of extradition to the United States, where they could be tried for crimes committed there and receive extraordinarily harsh sentences, like the one given Carlos Lehder, a Colombian drug dealer who had been extradited to the United States in 1987 and sentenced to life imprisonment plus 130 years. This was possible because a treaty signed during the presidency of Julio César Turbay allowed the extradition of Colombian nationals for the first time. After the murder of Lara Bonilla, President Belisario Betancur applied its provisions with a series of summary extraditions. The traffickers—terrified by the long, worldwide reach of the United States—realized that the safest place for them was Colombia, and they went underground, fugitives inside their own country. The great irony was that their only alternative was to place themselves under the protection of the state to save their own skins. And so they attempted—by persuasion and by force—to obtain that protection by engaging in indiscriminate, merciless terrorism and, at the same time, by offering to surrender to the authorities and bring home and invest their capital in Colombia, on the sole condition that they not be extradited. Theirs was an authentic shadow power with a brand name—the Extraditables—and a slogan typical of Escobar: "We prefer a grave in Colombia to a cell in the United States."

President Betancur kept up the war. His successor, Virgilio

Barco, intensified it. This was the situation in 1989 when César Gaviria emerged as a presidential candidate following the assassination of Luis Carlos Galán, whose campaign he had directed. In his own campaign, he defended extradition as an indispensable tool for strengthening the penal system, and announced an unprecedented strategy against the drug traffickers. It was a simple idea: Those who surrendered to the judges and confessed to some or all of their crimes could obtain non-extradition in return. But this idea, as formulated in the original decree, was not enough for the Extraditables. Through his lawyers, Escobar demanded that non-extradition be made unconditional, that confession and indictment not be obligatory, that the prison be invulnerable to attack, and that their families and followers be guaranteed protection. Holding terrorism in one hand and negotiation in the other, he began abducting journalists in order to twist the government's arm and achieve his demands. In two months, eight had been kidnapped. The abduction of Maruja and Beatriz seemed to be one more in that ominous series.

Villamizar thought this was the case as soon as he saw the bullet-riddled car. Later, in the crowd that invaded his house, he was struck by the absolute certainty that the lives of his wife and sister depended on what he could do to save them. Because this time, as never before, the war was being waged as an unavoidable personal challenge.

Villamizar, in fact, was already a survivor. When he was a representative in the Chamber, he had achieved passage of the National Narcotics Statute in 1985, a time when there was no ordinary legislation against drug trafficking but only the scattershot decrees of a state of siege. Later, Luis Carlos Galán had told him to stop passage of a bill introduced in the Chamber by parliamentarians friendly to Escobar, which would have removed legislative support for the extradition treaty then in effect. It was nearly his death sentence. On October 22, 1986, two assassins in sweatsuits who pretended to be working out across from his house fired submachine guns at him as he was getting into his car. His escape was miraculous. One assailant was killed by the police, and his accomplices arrested, then released a few years later. No one took responsibility for the attempt, but no one had any doubt as to who had ordered it.

Persuaded by Galán himself to leave Colombia for a while, Villamizar was named ambassador to Indonesia. After he had been there for a year, the U.S. security forces in Singapore captured a Colombian assassin traveling to Jakarta. It was never proved that he had been sent to kill Villamizar, but it was established that in the United States a fake death certificate had declared him dead.

On the night that Maruja and Beatriz were abducted, Villamizar's house was filled to overflowing. There were people in politics and the government, and the families of the two victims. Aseneth Velásquez, an art dealer and close friend of the Villamizars, who lived in the apartment above them, had assumed the duties of hostess, and all that was missing was music to make the evening seem like any other Friday night. It can't be helped: In Colombia, any gathering of more than six people, regardless of class or the hour, is doomed to turn into a dance.

By this time the entire family, scattered all over the world, had been informed. Alexandra, Maruja's daughter by her first marriage, had just finished supper in a restaurant in Maicao, on the remote Guajira peninsula, when Javier Ayala gave her the news. The director of "Enfoque," a popular Wednesday television program, she had gone to Guajira the day before to do a series of interviews. She ran to the hotel to call her family, but all the telephones at home were busy. By a lucky coincidence, on the previous Wednesday she had interviewed a psychiatrist who specialized in treating cases of clinical depression brought on by imprisonment in high-security institutions. When she heard the news in Maicao, she realized that the same therapy might be useful for kidnapping victims as well, and she returned to Bogotá to start to apply it, beginning with the next program.

Gloria Pachón, Maruja's sister, who was then Colombia's representative to UNESCO, was awakened at two in the morning by Villamizar's words: "I have something awful to tell you." Maruja's daughter Juana, who was vacationing in Paris, learned the news a moment later in the adjoining bedroom. Maruja's son Nicolás, a twenty-seven-year-old musician and composer, was in New York when he was awakened by a phone call.

At two o'clock that morning, Dr. Guerrero and his son Gabriel went to see the parliamentarian Diego Montaña Cuéllar, president of the Patriotic Union—a movement linked to the Communist Party—and a member of the Notables, a group formed in December 1989 to mediate between the government and the kidnappers of Alvaro Diego Montoya. They found him not only awake but very dejected. He had heard about the abduction on the news that night and thought it a demoralizing symptom. The only thing Guerrero wanted to ask was if he would act as mediator with Pablo Escobar and persuade him to hold Guerrero hostage in exchange for Beatriz. Montaña Cuéllar's answer was typical of his character.

"Don't be an ass, Pedro," he said. "In this country there's nothing you can do."

Dr. Guerrero returned home at dawn but did not even try to sleep. His nerves were on edge. A little before seven he received a call from Yami Amat, the news director at Caracol, and in the worst state of mind responded with a rash challenge to the kidnappers.

At six-thirty, without any sleep, Villamizar showered and dressed for his appointment with Jaime Giraldo Angel, the justice minister, who brought him up-to-date on the war against narcoterrorism. Villamizar left the meeting convinced that his struggle would be long and difficult, but grateful for the two hours he had spent finding out about recent developments, since for some time he had paid little attention to the issue of drug trafficking.

He did not eat breakfast or lunch. By late afternoon, after various frustrating errands, he too visited Diego Montaña Cuéllar, who surprised him once again with his frankness. "Don't forget that this is for the long haul," he said, "at least until next June, after the Constituent Assembly, because Maruja and Beatriz will be Escobar's defense against extradition." Many of his friends were annoyed with Montaña Cuéllar for not disguising his pessimism in the press, even though he belonged to the Notables.

"Anyway, I'm resigning from this bullshit," he told Villamizar in his florid language. "We don't do anything but stand around like assholes."

Villamizar felt drained and alone when he returned home after a fruitless day. The two neat whiskeys he drank one after the other left him exhausted. At six in the evening his son, Andrés, who from then on would be his only companion, persuaded him to have breakfast. They were eating when the president telephoned.

"All right, Alberto," he said in his best manner. "Come over and we'll talk."

President Gaviria received him at seven in the library of the private wing in the presidential palace, where he had lived for the past three months with his wife, Ana Milena Muñoz, and his two children, eleven-year-old Simón, and María Paz, who was eight. A small but comfortable refuge next to a greenhouse filled with brilliant flowers, it had wooden bookshelves crowded with official publications and family photos, a compact sound system, and his favorite records: the Beatles, Jethro Tull, Juan Luis Guerra, Beethoven, Bach. After long days of official duties, this was where the president held informal meetings or relaxed with friends at nightfall with a glass of whiskey.

Gaviria greeted Villamizar with affection and spoke with solidarity and understanding, and with his rather abrupt frankness as well. But Villamizar was calmer now that he had recovered from the initial shock, and he had enough information to know there was very little the president could do for him. Both men were sure the abduction of Maruja and Beatriz had political motivations, and they did not need to be fortune-tellers to realize that Pablo Escobar was behind it. But the essential thing, Gaviria said, was not knowing it but getting Escobar to acknowledge it as a first important step in guaranteeing the safety of the two women.

It was clear to Villamizar from the start that the president would not go beyond the Constitution or the law to help him, nor stop the military units that were searching for the kidnappers, but it was also clear he would not attempt any rescue operations without the authorization of the families.

"That," said the president, "is our policy."

There was nothing else to say. When Villamizar left the presidential palace, twenty-four hours had passed since the kidnapping, and he felt like a blind man facing the future, but he knew he could count on the government's cooperation to undertake private negotiations to help his wife and sister, and he had Rafael Pardo, the president's security adviser, ready to assist him. But what seemed to deserve his deepest belief was Diego Montaña Cuéllar's crude realism.

THE FIRST IN that unprecedented series of abductions—on August 30, 1990, a bare three weeks after President César Gaviria took office—was the kidnapping of Diana Turbay, the director of the television news program "Criptón" and of the Bogotá magazine *Hoy x Hoy*, and the daughter of the former president and leader of the Liberal Party, Julio César Turbay. Four members of her news team were kidnapped along with her—the editor Azucena Liévano, the writer Juan Vitta, the cameramen Richard Becerra and Orlando Acevedo—as well as the German journalist Hero Buss, who was stationed in Colombia. Six in all.

The trick used by the kidnappers was a supposed interview with Manuel Pérez, the priest who was supreme commander of the guerrilla group called the Army of National Liberation (ELN). Few people knew about the invitation, and none thought Diana should accept it. Among them were the defense minister, General Oscar Botero, and Rafael Pardo, who had been informed of the danger by the president so that he could communicate his concerns to the Turbay family. But anyone who thought Diana would cancel the trip did not know her. In fact, the press interview with Father Manuel Pérez probably did not interest her as much as the possibility of a dialogue on peace. Years earlier, in absolute secret, she had traveled on muleback to talk to armed self-defense groups in their own territory, in a solitary attempt to understand the guerrilla movements from a political and journalistic point of view. The news had no relevance at the time, and the results were not made public. Later, despite her long-standing opposition to the M-19, she became friends with Commander Carlos Pizarro, whom she visited in his camp to search for peaceful solutions. It is clear that the person who planned the deception in order to abduct her must have known her history. At that time, no matter what the reason, no matter what the obstacle, nothing in this world could have stopped Diana from talking to Father Pérez, who held another of the keys to peace.

A variety of last-minute problems had postponed the appointment the year before, but on August 30, at five-thirty in the afternoon, and without informing anyone, Diana and her team set out in a battered van with two young men and a girl who passed themselves off as representatives of the ELN leadership. The drive from Bogotá was a faithful parody of the kind of trip real guerrillas would have organized. Their traveling companions must have been members of an armed group, or had been once, or had learned their lessons very well, because they did not make a single mistake, in speech or behavior, that would have betrayed the subterfuge.

On the first day they had reached Honda, 146 kilometers to the west of Bogotá, where other men were waiting for them in two vehicles that were more comfortable. They had supper in a roadside tavern, then continued along a dark, hazardous road under a heavy downpour, and dawn found them waiting for a landslide to be cleared. At last, weary from lack of sleep, at eleven in the morning they reached a spot where a patrol was waiting for them with five horses. Diana and Azucena rode for four hours, while their companions traveled by foot, first through dense mountain forest and then through an idyllic valley with peaceful houses among the coffee groves. People came out to watch them go by, some recognized Diana and called out greetings from their terraces. Juan Vitta estimated that no fewer than five hundred people had seen them along the route. In the evening they dismounted at a deserted ranch where a young man who looked like a student identified himself as being from the ELN but said nothing about their destination. They were all confused. No more than half a kilometer away was a stretch of highway, and beyond that a city that had to be Medellín. In other words: This was not ELN territory. Unless—it occurred to Hero Buss—this was a masterful move by Father Pérez to meet them in an area where no one expected to find him.

About two hours later they came to Copacabana, a municipality that had been devoured by the urban sprawl of Medellín. They dismounted at a little house with white walls and moss-covered roof tiles that seemed imbedded in a steep, overgrown slope. It had a living room, with a small room on either side. In one of them there were three double beds, which were taken by the guides. The other, with a double bed and a bunk bed, was for the men on the crew. Diana and Azucena had the best room, which was in the rear and showed signs of having been occupied before by women. The light was on in the middle of the day because all the windows were boarded over.

After waiting for about three hours, a man in a mask came in, welcomed them on behalf of the high command, and announced that Father Pérez was expecting them but for reasons of security the women should go first. This was the first time that Diana showed signs of uneasiness. Hero Buss took her aside and said that under no circumstances should she agree to break up their group. Because she could not prevent that from happening, Diana slipped him her identity card. She did not have time to explain why, but he understood it to be a piece of evidence in the event she disappeared.

Before daybreak they took away the women and Juan Vitta. Hero Buss, Richard Becerra, and Orlando Acevedo stayed in the room with the double bed and the bunk bed, and five guards. The suspicion that they had fallen into a trap grew as the hours passed. That night, while they were playing cards, Hero Buss noticed that one of the guards was wearing an expensive watch. "So now the ELN can afford Rolexes," he joked. But the man ignored him. Another thing that perplexed Hero Buss was that their guns were not typical guerrilla weapons but the kind used for urban operations. Orlando, who spoke little and thought of himself as the poor relation on this expedition, did not need as many clues to discover the truth, for he had an unbearable feeling that something very serious was going on.

The first change of house occurred in the middle of the night on September 10, when the guards burst in shouting: "It's the cops!" After two hours of a forced march through the underbrush, in a terrible storm, they reached the house where Diana, Azucena, and Juan Vitta were being held. It was roomy and well furnished, with a large-screen television set and nothing that could arouse any suspicions. What none of them imagined was how close they all were to being rescued that night through sheer coincidence. The stop there of a few hours allowed them to exchange ideas, experiences, plans for the future. Diana unburdened herself to Hero Buss. She spoke of how depressed she was because she had led them into the trap, and confessed that she was trying to push away the thought of her family—husband, children, parents—which did not give her a moment's peace, but her efforts always had the opposite result.

The following night, as Diana, Azucena, and Juan Vitta were walked to a third house, along a very rough path and under a steady rain, she realized that nothing they had been told was true. And that same night a new guard erased any final doubts she might have had.

"You're not with the ELN; you're being held by the Extraditables," he said. "But don't worry, because you're going to see something you won't forget."

The disappearance of Diana Turbay's team was still a mystery nineteen days later, when Marina Montoya was abducted. She had been dragged away by three well-dressed men carrying 9mm pistols and Mini-Uzis equipped with silencers, just as she was closing her restaurant, Donde las Tías, in the northern section of Bogotá. Her sister Lucrecia, who worked with her, was lucky enough to have her foot in a cast because of a sprained ankle, which kept her from going to the restaurant. Marina had already locked the doors but opened them again because she recognized two of the three men who were knocking. They had come in for lunch several times during the past week and impressed the staff with their amiability and Medellinese humor and the 30 percent tips they left the waiters. That night, however, they were different. As soon as Marina opened the door, they immobilized her with an armlock and forced her out of the restaurant. She managed to clutch at a lamppost and began to scream. One of them kneed her in the spine with so much force she could not catch her breath. She was unconscious when they put her into the trunk of a blue Mercedes 190, which had been prepared to allow her to breathe.

Luis Guillermo Pérez Montoya, one of Marina's seven children, was a forty-eight-year-old executive with the Kodak Company in Colombia. His interpretation of events was the same as everyone else's: His mother had been abducted in retaliation for the government's failure to comply with the agreements reached by her brother Germán Montoya and the Extraditables. Distrustful by nature of everything having to do with officialdom, he set himself the task of freeing his mother through direct negotiation with Pablo Escobar.

Without orientation, without prior contact with anyone, without even knowing what he would do when he got there, he left two days later for Medellín. At the airport he took a cab but had no address to give the driver and told him simply to take him into the city. Reality came out to meet him when he saw the body of a girl about fifteen years old lying by the side of the road, wearing an expensive party dress and very heavy makeup. There was a bullet hole and a trickle of dried blood on her forehead. Luis Guillermo, who could not believe his eyes, pointed at the corpse.

"There's a dead girl over there."

"Yes," said the driver without looking. "One of the dolls who party with don Pablo's friends."

This broke the ice. Luis Guillermo told the driver the reason for his visit, and he in turn told him how to meet with a girl who was supposed to be the daughter of one of Pablo Escobar's first cousins.

"Tonight at eight o'clock go to the church behind the market. A girl named Rosalía will be there."

And in fact she was there, waiting for him, sitting on a bench in the square. She was almost a child, but her demeanor and the assurance of her words were those of a mature woman who had been instructed with care. To begin negotiations, she said, he would need half a million pesos in cash. She told him the hotel where he should register the following Thursday and wait for a call at either seven in the morning or seven in the evening on Friday.

"The woman who'll call you is named Pita."

He waited in vain for two days and part of a third. At last he realized it was all a joke and was thankful Pita had not called to ask for the money. He behaved with so much discretion that not even his wife knew about these trips or their deplorable results until four years later, when he spoke about them for the first time for this report.

FOUR HOURS AFTER the kidnapping of Marina Montoya, on a side street in the Las Ferias district to the west of Bogotá, a Jeep and a Renault 18 hemmed in the car of Francisco Santos, nicknamed Pacho, the editor in chief at *El Tiempo*. His vehicle looked like an ordinary red Jeep, but it had been bulletproofed at the factory, and the four assailants who surrounded it were not only carrying 9mm pistols and Mini-Uzi submachine guns equipped with silencers, but one also held a special mallet for breaking glass. None of that was necessary. Pacho, an incorrigible talker, opened the door to speak to the men. "I preferred to die rather than not know what was going on," he has said. One of his abductors immobilized him with a pistol to the forehead and forced him to get out of the car with his head lowered. Another opened the front door and fired three shots: One hit the windshield, and two shattered the skull of Oromansio Ibáñez, the thirty-eight-year-old driver. Pacho was not aware of what had happened. Days later, as he was thinking about the attack, he recalled hearing the whine of three bullets muffled by the silencer.

The operation was so rapid that it attracted no attention in the middle of the busy Tuesday traffic. A police officer discovered the blood-soaked body in the front seat of the abandoned vehicle; he picked up the two-way radio and immediately heard on the other end a voice half-lost among distant galaxies.

"Hello."

"Who is this?" asked the officer.

"*El Tiempo.*"

The news was on the air in ten minutes. In reality, preparations for his abduction had been going on for close to four months but

almost failed because Pacho Santos's movements were so unpredictable and irregular. Fifteen years earlier the same reasons had
stopped the M-19 from kidnapping his father, Hernando Santos.

This time the smallest details had been taken into account.
The kidnappers' automobiles, caught in a traffic jam on Avenida
Boyacá at Calle 80, drove on the sidewalks to make their escape
and disappeared down the winding streets of a working-class
neighborhood. Pacho Santos sat between two of the kidnappers,
his eyes covered by glasses that had been painted over with nail
polish, but in his mind he followed all the car's turns until it
screeched to a stop in a garage. By the route and the length of time
they had been driving, he formed a tentative idea of the neighborhood they were in.

One kidnapper led him by the arm—he was still wearing the
painted glasses—to the end of a hall. They climbed to the second
floor, turned left, walked about five paces, and went into a place
that was icy cold. This is where they removed the glasses. Then he
saw that he was in a dismal bedroom with boarded-up windows
and a single bulb in the ceiling. The only furnishings were a double bed, whose sheets had seen too much use, and a table with a
portable radio and a television set.

Pacho realized that his abductors had been in a hurry not only
for reasons of security but in order to get back in time for the soccer game between Santafé and Caldas. To keep everybody happy,
they gave him a bottle of *aguardiente*, left him alone with the radio,
and went downstairs to watch the game. He drank half the bottle
in ten minutes and felt no effects, though it did put him in the
mood to listen to the game on the radio. A devoted Santafé fan
since his childhood, the tie—the score was 2–2—made him so
angry he could not enjoy the liquor. When it was over, he saw
himself on the nine-thirty news on file footage, wearing a dinner
jacket and surrounded by beauty queens. That was when he
learned his driver was dead.

At the end of the newscast, a guard wearing a heavy flannel

mask came in and had him remove his clothes and put on a gray sweatsuit, which seemed a requirement in the prisons of the Extraditables. He also tried to take the inhaler for asthma that was in his jacket pocket, but Pacho convinced him that keeping it was a matter of life and death. The guard explained the rules of his captivity: He could use the bathroom in the hall, listen to the radio, and watch television with no restrictions, but at normal volume. When he was finished, he made Pacho lie down, then used a heavy rope to tie him to the bed by his ankle.

The guard laid a mattress on the floor beside the bed, and a few moments later began to snore with an intermittent whistle. The night thickened. In the dark, Pacho became aware that this was the first night of an uncertain future in which anything could happen. He thought about María Victoria—her friends called her Mariavé—his pretty, intelligent, and strong-willed wife, and about their two sons, twenty-month-old Benjamín and seven-month-old Gabriel. A rooster crowed nearby, and Pacho was surprised at its mistaken timing. "A rooster that crows at ten at night must be crazy," he thought. He is an emotional, impulsive man, easily moved to tears: the image of his father. Andrés Escabi, his sister Juanita's husband, had died in a plane that had been blown up in midair by the Extraditables. In the midst of the family upheaval, Pacho said something that made all of them shudder: "One of us will not be alive in December." He did not think, however, that the night of his abduction would be his last. For the first time his nerves were calm, and he felt sure he would survive. Pacho knew the guard lying on the floor was awake by the rhythm of his breathing. He asked him:

"Who's holding me?"

"Who do you want to be held by," asked the guard, "the guerrillas or the drug dealers?"

"I think I'm being held by Pablo Escobar," Pacho replied.

"That's right," said the guard, and made an immediate correction, "the Extraditables."

The news was in the air. The switchboard operators at *El Tiempo* had notified his closest relatives, who had notified others, who called others, until everybody knew. Through a series of peculiar circumstances, one of the last in the family to find out was Pacho's wife. A few minutes after the abduction she had received a call from his friend Juan Gabriel Uribe, who still was not sure what had happened and could only ask if Pacho was home yet. She said no, and Juan Gabriel did not have the heart to tell her what was still an unconfirmed report. A few minutes after that she had a call from Enrique Santos Calderón, her husband's double first cousin and the assistant manager at *El Tiempo*.

"Have you heard about Pacho?" he asked.

María Victoria thought he was referring to another matter having to do with her husband, which she already knew about.

"Of course," she said.

Enrique said a quick goodbye so he could call other family members. (Years later, commenting on the mistake, María Victoria said: "That happened to me because I wanted to pass myself off as a genius.") Then Juan Gabriel called back and told her the whole story: They had killed the driver and taken Pacho.

PRESIDENT GAVIRIA and his closest advisers were reviewing television ads to promote the election campaign for the Constituent Assembly when his press adviser, Mauricio Vargas, whispered in his ear: "They've kidnapped Pachito Santos." The viewing was not interrupted. The president, who needs glasses to watch movies, took them off and looked at Vargas.

"Keep me informed," he told him.

He put on his glasses again and continued to watch the ads. His close friend Alberto Casas Santamaría, the communications minister, was sitting beside him and heard the news, and it was whispered from ear to ear along the row of presidential advisers. A shudder passed through the room. But the president did not blink, following a norm in his life that he expresses in a schoolboy's rule: "I have to finish this assignment." When the tape had ended, he took off his glasses again, put them in his breast pocket, and told Mauricio Vargas:

"Phone Rafael Pardo and tell him to call a meeting of the Council on Security right away."

Then he began the planned discussion of the ads. Only when a decision had been reached did he reveal the impact that the news of the abduction had on him. Half an hour later he walked into the room where most of the members of the Council on Security sat waiting for him. They had just started the meeting when Mauricio Vargas tiptoed in and whispered in his ear:

"They've kidnapped Marina Montoya."

It had, in reality, occurred at four o'clock, before Pacho's kidnapping, but the news did not reach the president until four hours later.

TEN THOUSAND kilometers away, in a hotel in Florence, Pacho's father, Hernando Santos Castillo, had been asleep for three hours. His daughter Juanita was in an adjoining room, and his daughter Adriana and her husband were in another. They had been informed by telephone and had decided not to disturb their father. But his nephew Luis Fernando called him direct from Bogotá, using the most cautious opening he could think of for waking his uncle, who was seventy-eight years old and had undergone five bypasses.

"I have some very bad news for you," he said.

Hernando, of course, imagined the worst, but he put on a good front.

"What happened?"

"They kidnapped Pacho."

News of a kidnapping, no matter how painful, is not as irremediable as news of a murder, and Hernando breathed a sigh of relief. "Thank God," he said, and then changed his tone:

"Okay. Don't worry. We'll see what we have to do."

An hour later, in the middle of a fragrant Tuscan autumn night, they began the long trip home to Colombia.

THE TURBAY FAMILY, distraught at having heard nothing from Diana in the week since her departure, requested the government to make official inquiries through the principal guerrilla organizations. A week after the date on which Diana was due back, her husband, Miguel Uribe, and Alvaro Leyva, a member of parliament, traveled in secret to Casa Verde, the general headquarters of the Revolutionary Armed Forces of Colombia (FARC) in the eastern mountains. There they were able to contact all the armed groups in an effort to determine if Diana was with any of them. Seven denied it in a joint communiqué.

Not knowing what to expect, the presidency alerted the public to a proliferation of false communiqués and asked the people not to put more faith in them than in announcements from the government. But the grave and bitter truth was that the public had implicit trust in the Extraditables' communiqués, which meant that on October 30—sixty-one days after the abduction of Diana Turbay, forty-two days after the kidnapping of Francisco Santos—everyone gave a sigh of relief when the last remaining doubts were dispelled by a single sentence from the Extraditables: "We acknowledge publicly that we are holding the missing journalists." Eight days later, Maruja Pachón and Beatriz Villamizar were abducted. There were plenty of reasons for assuming that this escalation had even broader implications.

On the day following the disappearance of Diana and her crew, when there was still no suspicion in anyone's mind that they had been kidnapped, Yami Amat, the distinguished news director at

Caracol Radio, was intercepted on a street in downtown Bogotá by a group of thugs who had been following him for several days. Amat slipped out of their hands with an athletic maneuver that caught them off guard, and somehow survived a bullet in the back. Just a few hours later, María Clara, the daughter of former president Belisario Betancur, and her twelve-year-old daughter Natalia, managed to escape in her car when another armed gang blocked her way in a residential neighborhood in Bogotá. The only explanation for these two failures is that the kidnappers must have had strict orders not to kill their victims.

THE FIRST PEOPLE to have definite knowledge of who was holding Maruja Pachón and Beatriz Villamizar were Hernando Santos and former president Julio César Turbay, because forty-eight hours after their abduction, Escobar himself informed them in writing through one of his lawyers: "You can tell them that the group is holding Pachón." On November 12, there was another oblique confirmation in a letter written on the Extraditables' stationery to Juan Gómez Martínez, director of the Medellín newspaper *El Colombiano*, who had mediated on several occasions with Escobar on behalf of the Notables. "The detention of the journalist Maruja Pachón," said the letter from the Extraditables, "is our response to the recent tortures and abductions perpetrated in the city of Medellín by the same state security forces mentioned so often in our previous communiqués." And once again they expressed their determination not to free any of the hostages as long as that situation continued.

Dr. Pedro Guerrero, Beatriz's husband, overwhelmed by his utter powerlessness in the face of these crushing events, decided to close his psychiatric practice. "How could I see patients when I was in worse shape than they were," he has said. He suffered attacks of anxiety that he did not want to impart to his children. He did not have a moment's peace, at nightfall he consoled himself with whiskey, and his insomnia was spent listening to tearful boleros of lost love on "Radio Recuerdo." "My love," someone sang, "if you're listening, answer me."

Alberto Villamizar, who had always known that the abduction of his wife and sister was one more link in a sinister chain, closed ranks with the families of the other victims. But his first visit to Hernando Santos was disheartening. He was accompanied by Gloria Pachón de Galán, his sister-in-law, and they found Hernando sprawled on a sofa in a state of total demoralization. "What I'm doing is getting ready to suffer as little as possible when they kill Francisco," he said when they came in. Villamizar attempted to outline a plan to negotiate with the kidnappers, but Hernando cut him off with irreparable despair.

"Don't be naive, my boy," he said, "you have no idea what those men are like. There's nothing we can do."

Former president Turbay was no more encouraging. He knew from a variety of sources that his daughter was in the hands of the Extraditables, but he had decided not to acknowledge this in public until he knew for certain what they were after. A group of journalists had asked the question the week before, and he had eluded them with a daring swirl of the cape.

"My heart tells me," he said, "that Diana and her colleagues have been delayed because of their work as reporters, but that it isn't a question of their being detained."

Their disillusionment was understandable after three months of fruitless efforts. This was Villamizar's interpretation, and instead of being infected by their pessimism, he brought a new spirit to their common struggle.

During this time a friend was asked what kind of man Villamizar was, and he defined him in a single stroke: "He's a great drinking companion." Villamizar had acknowledged this with good humor as an enviable and uncommon virtue. But on the day his wife was abducted, he realized it was also dangerous in his situation, and decided not to have another drink in public until she and his sister were free. Like any good social drinker, he knew that alcohol lowers your guard, loosens your tongue, and somehow alters your sense of reality. It is a hazard for someone who has to measure his actions and words in millimeters. And so the strict rule he imposed on himself was not a penitential act but a security measure. He attended no more gatherings, he said goodbye to his light-hearted bohemianism, his jovial drinking sessions with other politicians. On the nights when his emotional tension was at its height, Andrés listened as he vented his feelings, holding a glass of mineral water while his father found comfort in drinking alone.

In his meetings with Rafael Pardo, they studied alternative courses of action but always ran up against the government policy that left open the threat of extradition. They both knew this was the most powerful tool for pressuring the Extraditables into surrendering, and that the president used it with as much conviction as the Extraditables when they used it as a reason for not surrendering.

Villamizar had no military training, but he had grown up near military installations. For years his father, Dr. Alberto Villamizar Flórez, had been physician to the Presidential Guard and was very close to the lives of its officers. His grandfather, General Joaquín Villamizar, had been minister of war. One of his uncles, Jorge Villamizar Flórez, had been the general in command of the Armed Forces. From them Alberto had inherited his dual nature as a native of Santander and a soldier: He was cordial and domineering at the same time, a serious person who loved to drink, a man who never misses when he takes aim, who always says what he has to say in the most direct way, and who has never used the intimate *tú* with anyone in his life. The image of his father prevailed, however, and he completed his medical studies at Javieriana University but never graduated, swept away by the irresistible winds of politics. Not as a military man but as a Santanderean pure and simple, he always carries a Smith & Wesson .38 that he has never tried to use. In any case, armed or unarmed, his two greatest virtues are determination and patience. At first glance they may seem contradictory, but life has taught him they are not. With this kind of heritage, Villamizar had all the daring necessary to attempt an armed solution, but rejected it unless the situation became a matter of life or death.

Which meant that the only solution he could find in late November was to confront Escobar and negotiate, Santanderean to Antioquian, in a hard and equal contest. One night, tired of all the wheel-spinning, he presented his idea to Rafael Pardo. Pardo understood his anguish, but his reply was unhesitating.

"Listen to me, Alberto," he said in his solemn, direct way. "Take whatever steps you like, try anything you can, but if you want our cooperation to continue, you must know you can't overstep the bounds of the capitulation policy. Not one step, Alberto. That's all there is to it."

No other virtues could have served Villamizar as well as his determination and patience in sorting through the internal contradictions present in these conditions. In other words, he could do as he wished in his own way, using all his imagination, but he had to do it with his hands tied.

3

MARUJA OPENED HER eyes and thought of an old Spanish proverb: "God doesn't send anything we can't bear." It had been ten days since their abduction, and both she and Beatriz were growing accustomed to a routine that had seemed unthinkable on the first night. The kidnappers had repeated over and over again that this was a military operation, but the rules of their captivity were harsher than those of a prison. They could speak only if the matter was urgent, and never above a whisper. They could not get off the mattress that was their common bed, and they had to ask the two guards—who watched them all the time, even when they were sleeping—for everything they needed: permission to sit, to stretch their legs, to speak to Marina, to smoke. Maruja had to cover her mouth with a pillow to muffle the sound of her cough.

Marina had the only bed, lit day and night by a perpetual candle. On the floor beside the bed lay the mattress where Maruja and Beatriz slept, their heads facing opposite directions like the fish in the zodiac, with only one blanket for the two of them. The guards sat on the floor to watch them, leaning against the wall. The space was so narrow that if they straightened their legs, their feet were on the prisoners' mattress. They lived in semi-darkness because the one window was boarded over. Before they went to sleep, the cracks around the only door were stuffed with rags so that the light from Marina's candle would not be seen in the rest of the house. The only other light came from the television set, because Maruja had them turn off the blue lightbulb in the ceiling that gave them all a terrifying pallor. The closed, unventilated room was heavy with foul-smelling heat. The worst time was between six and nine in the morning, when the prisoners were awake, with no air, with nothing to drink or eat, waiting for the rags to be pulled away from the door so they could begin to breathe. The only consolation for Maruja and Marina was that they were given coffee and cigarettes whenever they asked for them. For Beatriz, a respiratory therapist, the smoke hanging in the little room was a calamity. She suffered it in silence, however, since it made the other two so happy. Marina, with her cigarette and her cup of coffee, once exclaimed: "How nice it will be when the three of us are in my house, smoking and drinking our coffee and laughing about this awful time." Instead of suffering, on that day Beatriz regretted not smoking.

The fact that the three women were in the same prison may have been an emergency measure: Their captors must have decided that the house where they had been taken first could not be used after the cab driver indicated the route they had taken. This was the only way to explain the last-minute change, the wretched fact that there was only one narrow bed, a single mattress for two people, and less than six square meters for the three hostages and the two guards on duty. Marina had also been brought there from another house—or another farm, as she called it—because the drinking and disorderliness of the guards at her first prison had endangered the entire organization. In any case, it was inconceivable that one of the largest transnational enterprises in the world did not have enough compassion to provide humane conditions for its kidnappers and their victims.

They had no idea where they were. They knew from the sound that they were very close to a highway with heavy truck traffic. There also seemed to be a sidewalk café with drinking and music that stayed open very late. Sometimes they heard a loudspeaker announcing either political or religious meetings, or broadcasting deafening concerts. On several occasions they heard campaign slogans for the Constituent Assembly that was to convene soon. More often they heard the whine of small planes taking off and landing just a short distance away, which led them to suppose they were somewhere near Guaymaral, a landing field for small aircraft about twenty kilometers to the north of Bogotá. Maruja, who had known savanna weather from the time she was a girl, felt that the cold in their room was not the chill of the countryside but of the city. And their captors' excessive precautions made sense only if they were in an urban center.

Most surprising of all was the occasional roar of a helicopter so close it seemed to be on the roof. Marina Montoya said it meant the arrival of an army officer who was responsible for the abductions. As the days passed, they would become accustomed to the sound, for during their captivity the helicopter landed at least once a month, and the hostages were sure it had something to do with them.

It was impossible to distinguish the line between truth and Marina's contagious fantasies. She said that Pacho Santos and Diana Turbay were in other rooms of the house, so that the officer in the helicopter could take care of all three cases during each visit. Once they heard alarming noises in the courtyard. The majordomo, the man who managed the house, was insulting his wife as he gave hurried orders to move it that way, bring it over here, a little higher, as if they were trying to force a corpse into a place that was too small. Marina, in her gloomy delirium, thought that perhaps they had cut up Francisco Santos and were burying the pieces under the tiles in the kitchen. "When the killings begin, they don't stop," she kept saying. "We're next." It was a terrifying night until they learned by chance that they had been moving an old wash tub that was too heavy for four men to carry.

At night the silence was total, interrupted only by a demented rooster with no sense of time who crowed whenever he felt like it. Barking dogs could be heard in the distance, and one very close by sounded to them like a trained guard dog. Maruja got off to a bad start. She curled up on the mattress, closed her eyes, and for several days did not open them again except when she had to, trying to think with more clarity. She was not sleeping for eight hours at a time but would doze off for half an hour and wake to find the same agony always lying in wait for her. She felt permanent dread: the constant physical sensation in her stomach of a hard knot about to explode into panic. Maruja ran the complete film of her life in an effort to hold on to good memories, but disagreeable ones always intervened. On one of three trips she had made to Colombia from Jakarta, Luis Carlos Galán had asked her, during a private lunch, to help him in his next presidential campaign. She had been his media adviser during an earlier campaign, traveling all over the country with her sister Gloria, celebrating victories, suffering defeats, averting mishaps, and so the offer was logical. Maruja felt appreciated and flattered. But when lunch was over, she noticed a vague look in Galán, a supernatural light: the instantaneous and certain vision that he would be killed. The revelation was so strong that she persuaded her husband to return to Colombia even though General Maza Márquez had warned him, with no further explanation, that they were risking death. A week before they left Jakarta, they heard the news that Galán had been murdered.

The experience left her with a depressive propensity that intensified during her captivity. She could find nothing to hold on to, no way to escape the thought that she too was pursued by mortal danger. She refused to speak or eat. She was irritated by Beatriz's indolence and the masked guards' brutishness, and she could not endure Marina's submissiveness or the way she identified with the regime of her kidnappers. She seemed like another jailer who admonished her if she snored or coughed in her sleep or moved more than she had to. Maruja would set down a glass, and Marina with a frightened "Careful!" would put it somewhere else. Maruja would respond with immense contempt. "Don't worry about it," she would say. "You're not the one in charge here." To make matters even worse, the guards were always uneasy because Beatriz spent the day writing down details of her imprisonment so she could tell her husband and children about them when she was set free. She had also made a long list of everything she hated in the room, and had to stop when she discovered there was nothing she did not hate. The guards had heard on the radio that Beatriz was a physical therapist, confused this with a psychotherapist, and would not allow her to write anymore because they were afraid she was developing a scientific method to make them lose their minds.

Marina's deterioration was understandable. After almost two months in the antechamber of death, the arrival of the other two hostages must have been an intolerable dislocation for her in a world she had made hers, and hers alone. Her relationship to the guards, which had become very close, changed on account of them, and in less than two weeks she was suffering again from the same terrible pain and intense solitude she had managed to overcome.

And yet, no night seemed as ghastly to Maruja as the first one. It was interminable and freezing cold. At one in the morning the temperature in Bogotá—according to the Meteorology Institute—had been between 55 and 59 degrees, and it had rained downtown and in the area around the airport. Maruja was overcome by exhaustion. She began to snore as soon as she fell asleep, but her persistent, uncontrollable smoker's cough, aggravated by the damp walls that released an icy moisture at dawn, kept waking her. Each time she coughed or snored, the guards would kick her in the head with their heels. Marina's fear was uncontrollable, and she backed them up, warning Maruja that they were going to tie her to the mattress so she wouldn't move around so much, or gag her to stop her from snoring.

Marina had Beatriz listen to the early morning news. It was a mistake. In his first interview with Yami Amat of Caracol Radio, Dr. Pedro Guerrero attacked the abductors with a string of defiant insults. He challenged them to behave like men and show their faces. Beatriz was prostrate with terror, certain that she and the others would be the ones to pay for his abuse.

Two days later, one of the bosses, his well-dressed bulk packed into six feet, two inches, kicked the door open and stormed into the room. His impeccable tropical wool suit, Italian loafers, and yellow silk tie were at variance with his churlish behavior. He cursed the guards with two or three obscenities, and raged at the most timid one, whom the others called Spots. "They tell me you're very nervous," he said. "Well let me warn you that around here nervous people get killed." And then he turned to Maruja and said in a rude, impatient voice:

"I heard you caused a lot of trouble last night, making noise and coughing."

Maruja replied with an exemplary calm that could have been mistaken for contempt.

"I snore when I'm asleep, and don't know I'm doing it," she said. "I can't control the cough because the room is freezing and the walls drip water in the middle of the night."

The man was in no mood for complaints.

"Do you think you can do whatever you want?" he shouted. "Let me tell you: If you snore again or cough at night, we can blow your head off."

Then he turned to Beatriz.

"And if not you, then your children and husbands. We know all of them, and we know exactly where they are."

"Do what you want," said Maruja. "There's nothing I can do to stop snoring. Kill me if you want to."

She was sincere, and in time would realize she had said the right thing. Harsh treatment beginning the first day is a method used by kidnappers to demoralize their captives. Beatriz, on the other hand, still shaken by her husband's rage on the radio, was less haughty.

"Why do you have to bring our children into it? What do they have to do with any of this?" she said, on the verge of tears. "Don't you have children?"

Perhaps he softened; he said he did. But Beatriz had lost the battle; her tears did not allow her to continue. Maruja had regained her composure and said that if they really wanted to settle things they should talk to her husband.

She thought the hooded man had followed her advice because on Sunday, when he came back, his manner had changed. He brought the day's papers with statements by Alberto Villamizar, which attempted to come to some agreement with the kidnappers. And they, it seems, began to change their behavior in response to that. The boss, at least, was so conciliatory that he asked the hostages to make a list of things they needed: soap, toothbrushes, toothpaste, cigarettes, skin cream, and books. Some of the things on the list arrived that same day, but they did not get certain books until four months later. As time passed they accumulated all kinds of pictures and mementos of the Holy Infant and Our Lady of Perpetual Help, which the various guards gave to them as gifts or souvenirs when they left or came back from their time off. After ten days a domestic routine had already been established. Their shoes were kept under the bed, and the room was so damp they had to be taken out to the courtyard from time to time to let them dry. The prisoners could walk around only in heavy wool men's socks, in a variety of colors, which had been given to them on the first day, and they had to put on two pairs at a time so that no one would hear their footsteps. The clothes they had been wearing on the night of the abduction had been confiscated, and they were given sweatsuits—one gray set and one pink for each of them—

which they lived and slept in, and two sets of underwear that they washed in the shower. At first they slept in their clothes. Later, when they had nightgowns, they wore them over their sweatsuits on very cold nights. They were also given bags to hold their few possessions: the spare sweatsuit and a clean pair of socks, their change of underwear, sanitary napkins, medicines, their grooming articles.

There was one bathroom for three prisoners and four guards. The women could close the bathroom door but not lock it, and were permitted no more than ten minutes in the shower even when they had to wash their clothes. They were allowed to smoke as much as they wanted, which for Maruja was over a pack a day, and even more for Marina. The room had a television set and a portable radio, so the captives could hear the news and the guards could listen to music. The morning news programs were played at very low volume, as if in secret, while the guards played their raucous music at a volume dictated only by their mood.

The television was turned on at nine, and they watched educational programs, then the soap operas and two or three other shows until the midday newscast. It played the longest from four in the afternoon until eleven at night. The television stayed on, as if it were in a child's room, but no one watched it. Yet the hostages scrutinized the newscasts with microscopic care, trying to discover coded messages from their families. They never knew, of course, how many they missed or how many innocent phrases were mistaken for messages of hope.

Alberto Villamizar appeared on various news shows eight times in the first two days, certain that the victims would hear his voice on at least one of them. And almost all of Maruja's children worked in the media. Some had regularly scheduled television programs and used them to maintain communication that they assumed was unilateral, and perhaps useless, but they persisted.

The first one the prisoners saw, on the following Wednesday, was the program aired by Alexandra on her return from La Guajira. Jaime Gaviria, a psychiatrist, a colleague of Beatriz's husband, and an old friend of the family, broadcast a series of instructions for maintaining one's spirit in confined spaces. Maruja and Beatriz knew Dr. Gaviria, understood the purpose of the program, and took careful note of his instructions.

This was the first in an eight-program series produced by Alexandra and based on a long conversation with Dr. Gaviria on the psychology of hostages. Her primary consideration was to select topics that Maruja and Beatriz would find interesting and to conceal personal messages that only they would understand. Then Alexandra decided that each week she would have a guest who was prepared to answer preselected questions that would stimulate immediate associations in the captives. The surprise was that many viewers who knew nothing about her plan could at least tell that something else was hidden behind the apparent innocence of the questions.

NOT FAR AWAY—in the same city—Francisco Santos lived in his captive's room under conditions as miserable as Maruja's and Beatriz's, but not as harsh. One explanation is that in addition to the political usefulness of their abduction, there may also have been a desire for revenge as far as the women were concerned. And it is almost certain that their guards and Pacho's belonged to two different crews. Though it may have been only for reasons of security, the crews acted on their own and did not communicate with each other. But even so, there were incomprehensible differences. Pacho's guards were more informal, more autonomous and accommodating, and less concerned with hiding their identities. The worst difficulty for Pacho was having to sleep shackled to the bars of the bed with a metal chain that was wrapped to prevent skin abrasions. The worst for Maruja and Beatriz was not even having a bed to be chained to.

From the very beginning of his captivity, Pacho was given

newspapers every day. In general, the press reports on his kidnapping were so inaccurate and fanciful they made his captors double
over with laughter. His schedule had already been established
when Maruja and Beatriz were abducted. He would stay awake all
night and go to sleep at about eleven in the morning. He watched
television, alone or with his guards, or chatted with them about
the news of the day, soccer games in particular. He read until he
got bored, yet still had enough nervous energy to play cards or
chess. His bed was comfortable, and he slept well from the first
night until he developed a painful rash and a burning in his eyes,
which cleared up when the cotton blankets were washed and the
room given a thorough cleaning. They never worried about anyone seeing the light from the outside because the windows were
boarded over.

In October an unexpected hope presented itself: Pacho was ordered to send proof to his family that he was alive. He had to make
a supreme effort to maintain his self-control. He asked for black
coffee and two packs of cigarettes, and began to compose a message straight from the heart, not changing a comma. He recorded
it onto a minicassette, which couriers preferred over full-size tapes
because they were easier to conceal. Pacho spoke as slowly as he
could and tried to keep his voice calm and to adopt an attitude that
would not reveal the dark shadows in his spirit. He concluded by
reading aloud the headlines in that day's *El Tiempo* as proof of the
date on which he taped the message. He felt satisfied, above all
with the first sentence: "Everyone who knows me knows how difficult this message is for me." Yet when the heat of the moment
had passed and he read it in published form, Pacho had the impression that with the last sentence he had put the noose around
his own neck: He asked the president to do everything he could to
free the journalists. "But," he warned, "what matters is not to ignore the laws and precepts of the Constitution, for these benefit
not only the nation but the freedom of the press, which is now
being held hostage." His depression deepened a few days later

when Maruja and Beatriz were abducted, because he interpreted their kidnapping as a sign that matters would be drawn out and complicated. This was the moment of conception for an escape plan that would become his irresistible obsession.

CONDITIONS FOR DIANA and her crew—five hundred kilometers north of Bogotá, and three months after their capture—were different from those of the other hostages, since holding two women and four men at the same time presented complex logistical and security problems. In Maruja's and Beatriz's prison, the surprising element was the total absence of leniency. In the case of Pacho Santos, it was the informal, easy behavior of the guards, who were all his age. In Diana's group, an improvisatory atmosphere kept captives and captors alike in a state of alarmed uncertainty; the instability infected everything and grated on everyone's nerves.

Diana's captivity was notable too for its migratory nature. During their long imprisonment the hostages were moved, with no explanation, at least twenty times, in Medellín and near it, to houses of differing styles and quality, and varying conditions. Perhaps this mobility was possible because their abductors, unlike those in Bogotá, were in their natural environment, over which they had complete control, and maintained direct contact with their superiors.

The hostages were not all together in the same house except on two occasions, and for only a few hours. At first they were divided into two groups: Richard, Orlando, and Hero Buss in one house, Diana, Azucena, and Juan Vitta in another not far away. Some of the moves came without warning—sudden, unplanned, no time to gather up their possessions because a police raid was imminent, almost always on foot down steep hillsides, slogging through mud in endless downpours. Diana was a strong, resilient woman, but those merciless, humiliating flights, in the physical and moral conditions of captivity, undermined her endurance. Other moves were heartstopping escapes through the streets of Medellín, in ordinary cabs, eluding checkpoints and street patrols. The hardest thing for all of them during the first few weeks was that they were prisoners and no one knew it. They watched television, listened to the radio, read the papers, but there was no report of their disappearance until September 14, when the news program "Criptón" announced, without citing sources, that they were not on assignment with the guerrillas but had been kidnapped by the Extraditables. And several more weeks had to go by before the Extraditables issued a formal acknowledgment of their abduction.

The person in charge of Diana's crew was an intelligent, easygoing Medellinese whom they all called don Pacho, with no last name or any other clue to his identity. He was about thirty but had the settled look of someone older. His mere presence had the immediate effect of solving the problems of daily living and sowing hope for the future. He brought the hostages gifts, books, candy, music cassettes, and kept them up-to-date on the war and other national news.

His appearances were infrequent, however, and he did not delegate authority well. The guards and couriers tended to be undisciplined, they were never masked and used nicknames taken from comic strips, and they carried oral or written messages—from one house to the other—that at least brought the hostages some comfort. During the first week the guards bought them the regulation sweatsuits, as well as toilet articles and local newspapers. Diana and Azucena played Parcheesi with them and often helped to prepare shopping lists. One of the guards made a remark that a stunned Azucena recorded in her notes: "Don't worry about money, that's one thing there's plenty of." At first the guards lived a chaotic life, playing music at top volume, not eating at regular hours, wandering through the house in their underwear. But Diana assumed a certain authority and imposed order. She obliged them to wear decent clothes, to lower the volume of the music that kept them awake, and even made one of them leave the room when he tried to sleep on a mattress next to her bed.

Azucena, at the age of twenty-eight, was a serene romantic who could not live without her husband after spending four years learning to live with him. She suffered attacks of imaginary jealousy and wrote him love letters knowing he would never receive them. During the first week of captivity she began to take daily notes that were very bold and quite useful in writing her book. She had worked on Diana's newscast for some years, and their relationship had never been more than professional, but they identified with each other in their misfortune. They read the papers together, talked all night, and tried to sleep until it was time for lunch. Diana was a compulsive conversationalist, and from her Azucena learned lessons about life that never would have been taught in school.

The members of her crew recall Diana as an intelligent, cheerful, animated companion, and an astute political analyst. When she felt discouraged, she confessed her sense of guilt for having involved them in this unforeseen adventure. "I don't care what happens to me," she said, "but if anything happens to you, I'll never have a moment's peace again." She was uneasy about Juan Vitta's health. An old friend, he had opposed the trip with great vehemence and even better arguments, and yet he had gone with her soon after his stay in the hospital because of a serious heart ailment. Diana could never forget it. On the first Sunday of their captivity, she came into his room in tears and asked if he didn't hate her for not having listened to him. Juan Vitta replied with absolute honesty. Yes, he had hated her with all his soul when they were told they were in the hands of the Extraditables, but he had come to accept captivity as a fate that could not be avoided. His initial rancor had also turned into guilt over his inability to talk her out of it.

For the moment, Hero Buss, Richard Becerra, and Orlando

Acevedo, who were in a nearby house, had fewer reasons for alarm. In the closets they had found an astonishing quantity of men's clothing still in the original packaging, with leading European designers' labels. The guards said that Pablo Escobar kept emergency wardrobes in various safe houses. "Go on, guys, ask for anything you want," they joked. "Transportation takes a little while, but in twelve hours we can satisfy any request." At first the amount of food and drink carried in by mule seemed the work of madmen. Hero Buss told them that no German could live without beer, and on the next trip they brought him three cases. "It was a carefree atmosphere," Hero Buss has said in his perfect Spanish. It was during this time that he persuaded a guard to take a picture of the three hostages peeling potatoes for lunch. Later, when photographs were forbidden in another house, he managed to hide an automatic camera on top of a closet and took a nice series of color slides of himself and Juan Vitta.

The guards played cards, dominoes, chess, but the hostages were no match for their irrational bets and sleight-of-hand cheating. They were all young. The youngest might have been fifteen and was proud of having won grand prize in a contest for the most police killed—two million pesos apiece. They were so contemptuous of money that Richard Becerra sold them sunglasses and his cameraman's jackets for a sum that would have purchased five new ones.

Sometimes, on cold nights, the guards smoked marijuana and played with their weapons. Twice they fired off shots by accident. One bullet went through the bathroom door and wounded a guard in the knee. When they heard on the radio that Pope John Paul II had called for the release of the hostages, one of the guards shouted:

"What the hell is that son of a bitch sticking his nose in for?"

Another guard jumped to his feet, offended by the insult, and the hostages had to intervene to keep them from pulling out their guns and shooting each other. Except for that incident, Hero Buss and Richard took everything as a joke to avoid bad feelings. Orlando, for his part, thought he was odd man out, that his name headed the list of those who would be executed.

At this time the captives had been divided into three groups in three different houses: Richard and Orlando in one, Hero Buss and Juan Vitta in another, and Diana and Azucena in a third. The first two groups were transported by taxi in plain view through snarled midtown traffic, while every security agency in Medellín was hunting for them. They were put in a house that was still under construction, into one two-by-two-meter room that was more like a cell, with a filthy unlit bathroom, and four men guarding them. They slept on two mattresses on the floor. In an adjoining room that was always locked, there was another hostage for whom—the guards said—they were demanding millions of pesos in ransom. A stout mulatto with a heavy gold chain around his neck, he was kept handcuffed and in total isolation.

The large, comfortable house where Diana and Azucena were taken and held for most of their captivity seemed to be the private residence of a high-ranking boss. They ate at the family table, took part in private conversations, listened to the latest CDs, Rocío Durcal and Juan Manuel Serrat among them, according to Azucena's notes. This was the house where Diana saw a television program filmed in her own apartment in Bogotá, which reminded her that she had hidden the keys to the armoire but could not recall if they were behind the cassettes or the television in the bedroom. She also realized she had forgotten to lock the safe in the rush to leave on her calamitous trip. "I hope nobody's rummaging around in there," she wrote in a letter to her mother. A few days later, on what seemed an ordinary television program, she received a reassuring reply.

Life in the house did not seem affected by the presence of the hostages. There were visits from women they did not know who treated them as if they were family and gave them medals and pictures of miracle-working saints in the hope they would help them go free. There were visits from entire families with their children and dogs who scampered through all the rooms. The worst thing was the bad weather. The few times the sun shone they could not go outside to enjoy it because there were always men working. Or, perhaps, they were guards dressed as bricklayers. Diana and Azucena took pictures of each other in bed, and there was no sign yet of any physical changes. In another taken of Diana three months later, she looked very thin and much older.

On September 19, when she learned of the abductions of Marina Montoya and Francisco Santos, Diana understood—with no access to information from the outside—that her kidnapping was not an isolated act, as she thought at first, but a long-term political operation to force the terms for Escobar's surrender. Don Pacho confirmed this: There was a select list of journalists and celebrities who would be abducted as necessary to further the interests of the abductors. It was then she decided to keep a diary, not so much to narrate her days as to record her states of mind and interpretations of events. She wrote down everything: anecdotes of her captivity, political analyses, human observations, one-sided dialogues with her family or with God, the Virgin, the Holy Infant. Several times she transcribed entire prayers—including the Our Father and Hail Mary—as an original, perhaps more profound way of saying prayers in writing.

It is obvious that Diana was not thinking about a text for publication but of a political and personal journal that the dynamic of events transformed into a poignant conversation with herself. She wrote in her large, rounded hand, clear-looking but difficult to decipher, that completely filled the spaces between the lines in her copybook. At first she wrote in secret, in the middle of the night, but when the guards discovered what she was doing they gave her enough paper and pencils to keep her busy while they slept.

She made the first entry on September 27, a week after the kidnapping of Marina and Pacho, and it read: "Since Wednesday the 19th, when the man in charge of this operation came here, so

many things have happened that I can hardly catch my breath."
She asked herself why their abduction had not been acknowledged by those responsible, and her reply to herself was so that
perhaps they could kill them with no public outcry in the event
the hostages did not serve their ends. "That's my understanding
of it and it fills me with horror," she wrote. She was more concerned with her companions' condition than with her own, and
was interested in news from any source that would allow her to
draw conclusions about their situation. She had always been a
practicing Catholic, like the rest of her family, her mother in particular, and as time passed her devotion would become more intense and profound until it reached mystical states. She prayed to
God and the Virgin for everyone who had anything to do with her
life, even Pablo Escobar. "He may have more need of your help,"
she wrote to God in her diary. "May it be your will that he see the
good and avoid more grief, and I ask you to help him understand
our situation."

THERE IS NO DOUBT that the most difficult thing for everyone
was learning to live with the guards. The four assigned to Maruja
and Beatriz were young, uneducated, brutal, and volatile boys who
worked in twos for twelve-hour shifts, sitting on the floor, their
submachine guns at the ready. All in T-shirts with advertisements
printed on them, sneakers, and shorts they had cut themselves
with shears. When the shift came in at six in the morning, one
could sleep until nine while the other stood guard, but both would
almost always fall asleep at the same time. Maruja and Beatriz
thought that if a police assault team raided the house early in the
morning, the guards would not have time to wake up.

The boys' common condition was absolute fatalism. They
knew they were going to die young, they accepted it, and cared
only about living for the moment. They made excuses to themselves for their reprehensible work: It meant helping the family,

buying nice clothes, having motorcycles, and ensuring the happiness of their mothers, whom they adored above all else in the world and for whose sakes they were willing to die. They venerated the same Holy Infant and Lady of Mercy worshipped by their captives, and prayed to them every day with perverse devotion, for they implored their protection and forgiveness and made vows and sacrifices so that their crimes would be successful. Second only to the saints, they worshipped Rohypnol, a tranquilizer that allowed them to commit movie exploits in real life. "You mix it with beer and get high right away," explained one guard. "Then somebody lends you a good knife and you steal a car and go for a ride. The fun is how scared they look when they hand you the keys." They despised everything else: politicians, the government, the state, the law, the police, all of society. Life, they said, was shit.

At first it was impossible to tell them apart because the only thing the women could see was their masks, and all the guards looked the same. In other words, like only one guard. In time they learned that masks can hide faces but not character. This was how they individualized them. Each mask had a different identity, its own personality, an unmistakable voice. Even more: It had a heart. Without wanting to, they came to share the loneliness of confinement with them. They played cards and dominoes and helped each other solve crosswords and puzzles in old magazines.

Marina was submissive to her jailers' rules, but she was not impartial. She was fond of some and despised others, gossiped to them about the others as if she were their mother, and sooner or later provoked internal discord that threatened peace in the room. But she obliged them to pray the rosary, and they all did.

Among the guards on duty during the first month, there was one who suffered from sudden and recurrent fits of rage. They called him Barrabás. He adored Marina and caressed and flirted with her. But from the first day he was Maruja's bitter enemy. With no warning he would go wild, kicking the television and banging his head against the wall.

The strangest guard was somber, silent, very thin, and almost six and a half feet tall. He wore a second dark-blue sweatshirt hood on top of his mask, like a demented monk. And that's what they called him: Monk. For long periods he would crouch down in a kind of trance. He must have been there a long time because Marina knew him very well and singled him out for special favors. He would bring her gifts when he came back from his time off, including a plastic crucifix that Marina hung around her neck on the ordinary string it had when she received it. She was the only hostage who had seen his face: Before Maruja and Beatriz arrived, none of the guards wore a mask or did anything to hide his identity. Marina had interpreted this as a sign she would not leave her prison alive. She said he was a good-looking teenager with the most beautiful eyes she had ever seen, and Beatriz believed it because his lashes were so long and curly they protruded from the holes in his mask. He was capable of the best and worst actions. It was he who discovered that Beatriz wore a chain with a medal of the Virgin of Miracles.

"No chains are allowed here," he said. "You have to give that to me."

Beatriz protested, distraught.

"You can't take it away," she said. "That would be a really bad omen, something awful will happen to me."

Her distress was contagious and affected him. He said medals were not allowed because they might have long-distance electronic trackers inside. But he found the solution:

"Here's what we can do," he proposed. "You keep the chain but give me the medal. I'm sorry, but those are my orders."

Spots, on the other hand, suffered panic attacks and was obsessed by the idea that he would be killed. He heard imaginary noises, and he pretended to have a huge scar on his face, perhaps to confuse anyone trying to identify him. He cleaned everything he touched with alcohol so he would leave no fingerprints. Marina made fun of him, but he could not control his manias. He would wake with a start in the middle of the night. "Listen!" he whispered in terror. "It's the cops!" One night he put out the candle and Maruja walked into the bathroom door, hitting her head so hard she almost passed out. To make matters worse, Spots shouted at her for not knowing how to walk in the dark.

"Cut it out," she stood up to him. "This isn't a gangster movie."

The guards seemed like hostages too. They were not allowed in the rest of the house, and when they were not on duty they slept in another room that was padlocked so they could not escape. They were all from the Antioquian countryside, they did not know Bogotá, and one said that when they had time off, every three or four weeks, they were blindfolded or put in the trunk of the car so they would not know where they were. Another was afraid he would be killed when he was no longer needed, a guarantee he would take his secrets to the grave. Bosses in hoods and better clothes would put in irregular appearances to receive reports and give instructions. Their decisions were unpredictable, and both the hostages and the guards were at their mercy.

The captives' breakfast—coffee and a corncake with sausage on top—would arrive at any hour. For lunch they had beans or lentils in grayish water, bits of meat in puddles of grease, a spoonful of rice, and a soda. They had to eat sitting on the mattress because there was no chair in the room, and they had to use only a spoon because knives and forks were not allowed for reasons of security. At supper they made do with reheated beans and other leftovers from lunch.

The guards said that the owner of the house, whom they called the majordomo, kept most of their allotment of money. He was a robust man in his forties, of medium height, whose satyr's face could be guessed at from his nasal voice and the tired, bloodshot eyes visible through the holes in his hood. He lived with a short, shrill woman who wore shabby clothes and had rotting teeth. Her name was Damaris, and she sang salsa, *vallenatos*, and *bambucos* all day at the top of her lungs and with the ear of an artilleryman but with so much enthusiasm it was impossible not to imagine her dancing alone to her own music in every room of the house.

The plates, glasses, and sheets were used over and over again without being washed until the hostages protested. The toilet could be flushed only four times a day, and the bathroom was locked on Sundays when the family went out so the neighbors would not hear the sound of running water. The guards urinated in the sink or the shower drain. Damaris attempted to conceal her negligence only when she heard the bosses' helicopter, and then she moved like lightning, using a fireman's technique to wash down floors and walls with a hose. She watched soap operas every morning until one, the hour when she tossed the food for lunch into a pressure cooker—meat, vegetables, potatoes, beans all mixed together—and heated it until the whistle blew.

Her frequent arguments with her husband displayed a capacity for rage and an originality in creating curses that sometimes reached inspired heights. She had two daughters, aged nine and seven, who attended a nearby school and on occasion invited other children to watch television or play in the courtyard. Their teacher dropped in from time to time on Saturdays, and other noisier friends came by any day of the week and had impromptu parties with music. Then the door of the room was padlocked and those inside had to turn off the radio, watch television without the sound, and not use the bathroom even in an emergency.

TOWARD THE END of October, Diana Turbay observed that Azucena was distracted and melancholy. She had not spoken the whole day, and was in no frame of mind to talk about anything. This was not unusual: Her powers of concentration were extraordinary, above all when she was reading, in particular if the book was the Bible. But this time her silence coincided with her alarming mood and exceptional pallor. After some urging, she revealed to Diana that for the past two weeks she had been afraid she was pregnant. Her calculations were exact. She had been a hostage for more than fifty days, and had missed two periods in a row. Diana was overjoyed at the good news—a typical reaction for her—but took responsibility for Azucena's distress.

On one of his early visits, don Pacho had promised them that they would be released on the first Thursday in October. They believed him because major changes occurred: better treatment, better food, greater freedom of movement. And yet there was always some pretext for shifting the date. After the Thursday had passed, they were told they would be freed on December 9 to celebrate the election of the Constituent Assembly. And so it continued—Christmas, New Year's Day, Epiphany, somebody's birthday—in a string of delays that seemed like little spoonfuls of consolation.

Don Pacho continued to visit them in November. He brought new books, current newspapers, back issues of magazines, and boxes of chocolates. He spoke about the other hostages. When Diana learned she was not the prisoner of Father Pérez, she was determined to have an interview with Pablo Escobar, not so much to publish it—if in fact it was true—as for the chance to discuss with him the terms of his surrender. At the end of October, don Pacho said her request had been approved. But the newscasts of November 7 struck the first mortal blow to her illusions: The broadcast of the soccer game between Medellín and El Nacional was interrupted by the announcement that Maruja Pachón and Beatriz Villamizar had been abducted.

Juan Vitta and Hero Buss heard the announcement in their prison and thought it the worst news possible. They too had reached the conclusion that they were no more than extras in a horror film. "Just filler," as Juan Vitta said. "Disposable," as the guards said. One of them, during a heated argument, had shouted at Hero Buss:

"You shut up! Nobody invited you here!"

Juan Vitta sank into a depression, stopped eating, slept badly, felt lost, and opted for the merciful solution of dying just once instead of a thousand times a day. He looked pale, one arm was numb, he found it difficult to breathe, his dreams were terrifying. His only conversations were with his dead relatives whom he saw standing around his bed. An alarmed Hero Buss created a Germanic uproar. "If Juan dies here, you're responsible," he told the guards. They heeded the warning.

The physician they brought in was Dr. Conrado Prisco Lopera, the brother of David Ricardo and Armando Alberto Prisco Lopera—of the famous Prisco gang—who had worked with Pablo Escobar since his early days as a trafficker, and were known as the creators of the crew of adolescent killers from the northeastern slums of Medellín. They were said to be the leaders of a gang of teenage assassins who took on the dirtiest jobs, among them guarding hostages. On the other hand, Conrado was deemed an honorable professional by the medical community, and the only mark against him was being, or having been, Pablo Escobar's principal physician. He wore no mask when he came in and surprised Hero Buss by greeting him in fluent German:

"Hallo Hero, wie geht's uns."

It was a providential visit for Juan Vitta, not because of the diagnosis—severe stress—but for the good it did him as a passionate reader. The only treatment the doctor prescribed was a dose of decent reading—just the opposite of the political news Dr. Prisco Lopera was in the habit of bringing, which for the captives was like a potion capable of killing the healthiest man.

Diana's malaise grew worse in November—severe headaches, attacks of colitis, intense depression—but there are no indications in her diary that the doctor visited her. She thought the depression might have been caused by the paralysis in her situation, which grew more uncertain as the year drew to a close. "Time passes here in a way we're not used to dealing with," she wrote. "There's no enthusiasm about anything." A note from this period spoke of the pessimism that was crushing her: "I've reexamined my life up to this point: so many love affairs, so much immaturity in making important decisions, so much time wasted on worthless things!" Her profession occupied a special place in this drastic stocktaking: "Though my convictions grow stronger about what the practice of journalism is and what it should be, I don't see it with any clarity or breadth." Her doubts did not spare even her own magazine, "which I see as so poor, not only financially but editorially." And she judged without flinching: "It lacks profundity and analysis."

The days of all the hostages, despite their separation, were spent waiting for don Pacho; his visits were always announced, rarely took place, and were their measure of time. They heard small planes and helicopters flying over the house and had the impression they were routine surveillance flights. But each one mobilized the guards, who assumed combat positions, weapons at the ready. The hostages knew, because it had been repeated so often, that in the event of an armed attack, the guards would begin by killing them.

In spite of everything, November ended with a certain amount of hope. Azucena Liévano's doubts melted away: Her symptoms were a false pregnancy, perhaps brought on by nervous tension. But she did not celebrate. On the contrary: After her initial fear, the idea of having a baby had become a desire, and she promised herself she would satisfy it as soon as she was released. Diana also saw signs of hope in statements by the Notables regarding the possibility of an agreement.

THE REST OF NOVEMBER had been a time of accommodation for Maruja and Beatriz. Each in her own way devised a survival strategy. Beatriz, who is brave and strong willed, took refuge in the consolation of minimizing reality. She dealt very well with the first ten days, but soon realized that the situation was more complex and hazardous than she had thought, and she faced adversity by looking away from it. Maruja, who is a coldly analytic woman despite her almost irrational optimism, had known from the start that she was facing an alien reality, and that her captivity would be long and difficult. She hid inside herself like a snail in its shell, hoarded her energy, and reflected deeply until she grew used to the inescapable idea that she might die. "We're not getting out of here alive," she thought, and was astonished that this fatalistic revelation had a contrary effect. From then on she felt in control of herself, able to endure everything and everybody, and, through persuasion, to make the discipline less rigid. By the third week of captivity, television had become unbearable; they had used up the crossword puzzles and the few readable articles in the entertainment magazines they had found in the room, the remains, perhaps, of some previous abduction. But even at her worst times, and as she always did in her real life, Maruja set aside two hours each day for absolute solitude.

In spite of everything, the news early in December indicated that there were reasons for them to be hopeful. As soon as Marina made her terrible predictions, Maruja began to invent optimistic games. Marina caught on right away: One of the guards had raised his thumb in a gesture of approval, and that meant things were going well. Once Damaris did not go to market, and this was interpreted as a sign she did not have to because they would be released soon. They played at visualizing how they would be freed, and they set the date and the method that would be used. Since they lived in gloom, they imagined they would be released on a sunny day and have a party on the terrace of Maruja's apartment. "What do you want to eat?" Beatriz asked. Marina, who was a skilled cook, recited a menu fit for a queen. They began it as a game, and it ended as a truth: They dressed to go out, they made each other up. On December 9, one of the dates that had been mentioned for their release because of the elections to the Constituent Assembly, they were ready, even for the press conference: They had prepared every answer. The day passed in nervous anticipation but ended without bitterness, because Maruja was certain, beyond the shadow of a doubt, that sooner or later her husband would free them.

4

THE ABDUCTION of the journalists was, in effect, a response to the idea that had preoccupied President César Gaviria since the time he was a minister in Virgilio Barco's government: how to create a judicial alternative to the war against terrorism. It had been a central theme in his campaign for the presidency. He had emphasized it in his acceptance speech, making the important distinction that terrorism by the drug traffickers was a national problem and might have a national solution, while the drug traffic was international and could only have international solutions. His first priority was narcoterrorism, for after the first bombs, public opinion demanded prison for the terrorists, after the next few bombings the demand was for extradition, but as the bombs continued to explode public opinion began to demand amnesty. For this reason, extradition had to be considered an emergency measure that would pressure the criminals into surrendering, and Gaviria was prepared to apply that pressure without hesitation.

In the first days after he took office, Gaviria barely had time to talk to anyone; he was exhausted by the job of organizing his government and convening a Constituent Assembly that would undertake the first major reform of the state in over a hundred years. Rafael Pardo had shared his concern with terrorism ever since the assassination of Luis Carlos Galán. But he too was caught up in endless organizational duties. He was in a peculiar position. His appointment as adviser on security and public order had been one of the first in a government palace shaken by the renovative drive of one of this century's youngest presidents, a Beatles fan and an avid reader of poetry, who had given his ideas for drastic changes a modest name: "The Shake-up," the *Revolcón*. Pardo walked through this windstorm carrying the briefcase he always had with him, working wherever he could find space. His daughter Laura thought he had lost his job because he did not leave for work or come home at regular hours. The truth is that the informality imposed by circumstances was well suited to Rafael Pardo, whose nature was more that of a lyric poet than a governmental bureaucrat. He was thirty-eight years old, with a solid academic background: a diploma from the Gimnasio Moderno in Bogotá, a degree in economics from the University of the Andes, where for nine years he had been a teacher and researcher in that same field, and a graduate degree in planning from the Institute for Social Sciences in The Hague. He was also a voracious reader of every book he could lay his hands on, in particular those dealing with two dissimilar subjects: poetry and security. He owned four ties, which he had received for Christmas over the past four years; he never chose to put them on but carried one in his pocket for emergencies. He never noticed if his trousers and jackets matched, was so absent-minded that his socks were often different colors, and whenever possible he was in shirtsleeves because he made no distinction between heat and cold. His greatest excesses were poker games with his daughter Laura until two in the morning, played in absolute silence and using beans instead of money. Claudia, his beautiful and patient wife, would become irritated because he wandered the house like a sleepwalker, not knowing where the water glasses were kept or how to close a door or take ice cubes from the freezer, and he had an almost magical faculty for ignoring the things he despised. And yet his most uncommon traits were a statue's impassivity that did not give the slightest clue as to what he was thinking, and a merciless talent for ending a conversation with two or three words, or a heated discussion with a single polished monosyllable.

His office and university colleagues, however, could not understand his lack of standing at home, for they knew him as an intelligent, organized worker who possessed an almost terrifying serenity, and whose befuddled air was no doubt intended to befuddle others. He became irritated with simple problems, displayed great patience with lost causes, and had a strong will tempered by an imperturbable, sardonic sense of humor. President Virgilio Barco must have recognized how useful his hermeticism and fondness for mysteries could be, for he put him in charge of negotiations with the guerrillas, and the rehabilitation programs in war zones, and in that capacity he achieved the peace accords with the M-19. President Gaviria, who was his equal in secretiveness and unfathomable silences, appointed him head of security and public order in one of the least secure and most disordered countries in the world. Pardo assumed the post carrying his entire office in his briefcase, and for two weeks had to ask permission to use the bathroom or the telephone in other people's offices. But the president often consulted with him on a variety of subjects, and listened with premonitory attention when he spoke at difficult meetings. One afternoon, when they were alone in the president's office, Gaviria asked him a question:

"Tell me something, Rafael, aren't you worried that one of these guys will suddenly turn himself in and we won't have any charge to arrest him with?"

It was the essence of the problem: The terrorists hunted by the police would not surrender because they had no guarantees for their own safety or the safety of their families. And the state had no evidence that would convict them if they were captured. The idea was to find a judicial formula by which they would confess their crimes in exchange for the state's guarantee of protection for them and their families. Rafael Pardo had worked on the problem for the previous government, and when Gaviria asked the question, he still had his notes among all the other papers in his briefcase. They were, in effect, the beginning of a solution: Whoever surrendered would have his sentence reduced if he confessed to a crime that would allow the government to prosecute, and a further sentence reduction if he turned goods and money over to the state. That was all, but the president could envision the entire plan because it was consonant with his own idea of a strategy focused not on war or peace but on law, one that would be responsive to the terrorists' arguments but not renounce the compelling threat of extradition.

President Gaviria proposed it to Jaime Giraldo Angel, his justice minister, who understood the concept immediately; he too had been thinking for some time about ways to move the problem of drug trafficking into a judicial framework. And both men favored the extradition of Colombian nationals as a means of forcing surrender.

Giraldo Angel, with his air of a distracted savant, his verbal precision, and his genius for organization, completed the formula, adding some of his own ideas combined with others already established in the penal code. Between Saturday and Sunday he composed a first draft on a laptop computer, and first thing Monday morning showed the president a copy that still had his handwritten deletions and corrections. The title, written in ink across the top of the first page, was a seed of historic importance: "Capitulation to the Law."

Gaviria is meticulous about his projects and would not present them to his Council of Ministers until he was certain they would be approved. He therefore reviewed the draft in detail with Giraldo Angel and with Rafael Pardo, who is not a lawyer but whose sparing comments tend to be accurate. Then he sent a revised version to the Council on Security, where Giraldo Angel found support from General Oscar Botero, the defense minister, and the head of Criminal Investigation, Carlos Eduardo Mejía Escobar, a young, effective jurist who would be responsible for implementing the decree in the real world. General Maza Márquez did not oppose the plan, though he believed that in the struggle against the Medellín cartel, any formula other than war would be useless. "This country won't be put right," he would say, "as long as Escobar is alive." For he was certain Escobar would only surrender in order to continue trafficking from prison under the government's protection.

The project was presented to the Council of Ministers with the specification that the plan did not propose negotiations with terrorism in order to conjure away a human tragedy for which the consuming nations bore primary responsibility. On the contrary: The aim was to make extradition a more useful judicial weapon in the fight against narcotraffic by making non-extradition the grand prize in a package of incentives and guarantees for those who surrendered to the law.

One of the crucial discussions concerned the time limits for the crimes that judges would have to consider. This meant that no crime committed after the issuing date of the decree would be protected. The secretary general of the presidency, Fabio Villegas, who was the most lucid opponent of time limits, based his position on a cogent argument: When the period of pardonable offenses ended, the government would have no policy. The majority, however, agreed with the president that for the moment they should not extend the time limits because of the certain risk that this would become a license for lawbreakers to continue breaking the law until they decided to turn themselves in.

To protect the government from any suspicion of illegal or unethical negotiations, Gaviria and Giraldo Angel agreed not to meet with any direct emissary from the Extraditables while the trials were in progress, and not to negotiate any question of law with them or with anyone else. In other words, they would not discuss principles but only procedural matters. The national head of Criminal Investigation—who is not dependent on or appointed by the chief executive—would be the official in charge of communicating with the Extraditables or their legal representatives. All exchanges would be written and, therefore, on record.

The proposed decree was discussed with an intensity and secrecy that are in no way usual in Colombia, and was approved on September 5, 1990. This was Decree 2047 under Martial Law: Those who surrendered and confessed to their crimes could receive the right not to be extradited; those who confessed and also cooperated with the authorities would have their sentences reduced, up to a third for surrender and confession, up to a sixth for providing information—in short, up to half of the sentence imposed for one or all the crimes for which extradition had been requested. It was law in its simplest, purest form: the gallows and the club. The same Council of Ministers that signed the decree rejected three extradition requests and approved three others, a kind of public announcement that the new government would view non-extradition only as a privilege granted under the decree.

In reality, rather than an isolated decree, this was part of a well-defined presidential policy for fighting terrorism in general, not only narcoterrorism but common criminal acts as well. General Maza Márquez did not express to the Council on Security what he really thought of the decree, but some years later, in his campaign for the presidency, he censured it without mercy as "a fallacy of the times." "With it the majesty of the law is demeaned," he wrote, "and traditional respect for the penal code is undermined."

The road was long and complex. The Extraditables—which everyone knew was a trade name for Pablo Escobar—rejected the decree out-of-hand while leaving doors open so they could continue to fight for much more. Their principal argument was that it did not state in an incontrovertible way that they would not be extradited. They also wanted to be considered as political offenders and therefore receive the same treatment as the M-19 guerrillas, who had been pardoned and recognized as a political party. One of the M-19's members was the minister of health, and all of them were participating in the campaign for the Constituent Assembly. Another concern of the Extraditables was the question of a secure prison where they would be safe from their enemies, and guarantees of protection for their families and followers.

It was said that the government had issued the decree as a concession to the traffickers under the pressure of the abductions. In fact, it had been in the planning stage before Diana's kidnapping, and had already been issued when the Extraditables tightened the vise with the almost simultaneous abductions of Francisco Santos and Marina Montoya. Later, when eight hostages were not enough to get them what they wanted, they took Maruja Pachón and Beatriz Villamizar. That was the magic number: nine journalists. Plus one—already condemned to death—who was the sister of a politician hunted by Escobar's private police force. In this sense, before the decree could prove its efficacy, President Gaviria began to be the victim of his own creation.

LIKE HER FATHER, Diana Turbay Quintero had an intense, passionate feeling for power, a capacity for leadership that shaped her life. She grew up surrounded by the great names in politics, and it was to be expected that she would have a political perspective on the world. "Diana was a stateswoman," a friend who understood and loved her has said. "And the central concern of her life was a stubborn desire to serve her country." But power—like love—is a double-edged sword: One wields it and is wounded by it. It generates a state of pure exaltation and, at the same time, its opposite: the search for an irresistible, fugitive joy, comparable only to the search for an idealized love that one longs for but fears, pursues but never attains. Diana experienced an insatiable hunger to know everything, be involved in everything, discover the why and how of things, the reason for her life. Some of those who were close to her perceived this in the uncertainties of her heart, and believed she was not happy very often.

It is impossible to know—without asking her the question directly—which of the two edges of power inflicted the more serious wounds. She must have felt them in her own flesh when she was her father's private secretary and right hand at the age of twenty-eight, and found herself trapped in the crosswinds of power. Her friends—and she had many—have said she was one of the most intelligent people they had ever known, with an unsuspected store of knowledge, an astonishing capacity for analysis, and a supernatural gift for sensing another person's most hidden agenda. Her enemies say straight out that she was a disruptive influence behind the throne. But others think she disregarded her own well-being in a single-minded desire to defend her father against everything and everybody, and could therefore be used by hypocrites and flatterers.

She was born on March 8, 1950, under the inclement sign of Pisces, at a time when her father was already in line for the presidency. She was an innate leader wherever she happened to be: the Colegio Andino in Bogotá, the Academy of the Sacred Heart in New York, or Saint Thomas Aquinas University of Bogotá, where she completed her law studies but did not wait to receive her degree.

Her belated career in journalism—which is, fortunately, power without the throne—must have been a reencounter with the best in herself. She founded the magazine *Hoy x Hoy* and the television news journal "Criptón" as a more direct way to work for peace. "I'm not ready to fight anymore, or give anybody any arguments," she said at the time. "I've become totally conciliatory." To the point where she sat down to talk about peace with Carlos Pizarro, the commander of the M-19, who had fired the rocket that just missed the room where President Turbay had been sitting. The friend who told this story says, with a laugh: "Diana understood that in this business she had to be a chess player, not a boxer punching at the world."

And therefore it was only natural that her abduction—above and beyond its emotional impact—would have a political weight that was difficult to control. Former President Turbay said, in public and in private, that he had heard nothing from the Extraditables, because this seemed the most prudent course until it was known what they wanted, but in fact he had received a message from them soon after the kidnapping of Francisco Santos. He had told Hernando Santos about it as soon as Santos returned from Italy, when Turbay invited him to his house to devise a common strategy. Santos found Turbay in the semi-darkness of his immense library, devastated by the certainty that Diana and Francisco would be executed. What struck him—and everyone else who saw Turbay during this time—was the dignity with which he bore his misfortune.

The letter addressed to both men consisted of three handwritten pages printed in block letters, with no signature, and an unexpected salutation: "A respectful greeting from the Extraditables." What did not permit any doubt regarding its authenticity was the concise, direct, unequivocal style typical of Pablo Escobar. It began by taking responsibility for the abduction of the two journalists who, the letter said, were "in good health and in good conditions of captivity that can be considered normal in such cases." The rest was a brief against abuses committed by the police. Then it stated three nonnegotiable conditions for the release of the hostages: total suspension of military operations against them in Medellín and Bogotá; withdrawal of the Elite Corps, the special police unit dedicated to the fight against drug trafficking; dismissal of its commander and twenty other officers accused of responsibility for the torture and murder of some four hundred young men from the northeastern slums of Medellín. If these conditions were not met, the Extraditables would undertake a war of extermination, including bombings in major cities and the assassinations of judges, politicians, and journalists. The conclusion was simple: "If there is a coup, then welcome to it. We don't have much to lose."

Their written response, with no preliminary discussions, was to be delivered within three days to the Hotel Intercontinental in Medellín, where a room would be reserved in Hernando Santos's name. The Extraditables would choose the intermediaries for any further communications. Santos agreed with Turbay's decision not to say anything about this message, or any that might follow, until they had more substantive information. "We cannot allow ourselves to be anybody's messengers to the president," Turbay concluded, "or to behave in an improper way."

Turbay suggested to Santos that each of them write a separate response, which they would then combine into a single letter. This was done. The result, in essence, was a formal statement to the effect that they had no power to interfere in governmental matters but were prepared to make public any violation of the law or of human rights for which the Extraditables had conclusive evidence. As for the police raids, they reminded the Extraditables that they had no means to stop them, could not seek to have the twenty accused men removed from office without proof, or write editorials against a situation they knew nothing about.

Aldo Buenaventura, a public notary and solicitor, a fervent aficionado of the bullfights since his student days at the Liceo Nacional in Zipaquirá, and an old and trusted friend of Hernando Santos's, agreed to carry the letter. No sooner had he walked into room 308 at the Hotel Intercontinental, than the phone rang.

"Are you Señor Santos?"

"No," Aldo replied, "but I am here as his representative."

"Did you bring the package?"

The voice sounded so proprietary that Aldo wondered if it was Pablo Escobar himself, and he said he had. Two young men who dressed and behaved like executives came to the room. Aldo gave them the letter. They shook his hand with well-bred bows and left.

In less than a week, Turbay and Santos were visited by Guido Parra Montoya, an Antioquian lawyer, who had another letter from the Extraditables. Parra was not unknown to political circles in Bogotá, but he always seemed to live in the shadows. He was forty-eight years old, had served twice in the Chamber of Deputies as a replacement for two Liberal representatives, and once as a principal for the National Popular Alliance (ANAPO), which gave rise to the M-19. He had been an adviser to the judicial office of the presidency in the government of Carlos Lleras Restrepo. In Medellín, where he had practiced law since his youth, he was arrested on May 10, 1990, on suspicion of abetting terrorism, and released two weeks later because the case lacked merit. Despite these and other lapses, he was considered an expert lawyer and a good negotiator.

However, as a confidential representative of the Extraditables, it was hard to imagine anyone less likely to be self-effacing. He was one of those men who take ceremony seriously. He wore silver-gray suits, which were the executive uniform of the time, with bright-colored shirts and youthful ties with wide Italian-style knots. His manners were punctilious, his rhetoric high-flown, and he was more obsequious than affable—suicidal circumstances if one wishes to serve two masters at the same time. In the presence of a former Liberal president and the publisher of the most important newspaper in the country, his eloquence knew no bounds. "My illustrious Dr. Turbay, my distinguished Dr. Santos, I am completely at your service," he said, and then made the kind of slip that can cost a man his life:

"I am Pablo Escobar's attorney."

Hernando caught the error in midflight.

"Then the letter you've brought is from him?"

"No," Guido Parra corrected the mistake without batting an eye, "it is from the Extraditables, but you should direct your response to Escobar because he will be able to influence the negotiation."

The distinction was important, because Escobar left no clues for the police. Compromising letters, such as those dealing with the abductions, were printed in block letters and signed by the Extraditables or a simple first name: Manuel, Gabriel, Antonio. When he played the part of accuser, however, he wrote in his own, rather childish hand, and not only signed the letters with his name and rubric but drove the point home with his thumbprint. At the time the journalists were abducted, it would have been reasonable to doubt his very existence. The Extraditables may have been no more than his pseudonym, but the opposite was also possible: Perhaps Pablo Escobar's identity was nothing more than a front for the Extraditables.

Guido Parra always seemed prepared to go beyond what the Extraditables stated in writing. But everything had to be examined with a magnifying glass. What he really wanted for his clients was the kind of political treatment the guerrillas had received. He brought up the question of internationalizing the narcotics problem by proposing the participation of the United Nations. Yet in the face of Santos's and Turbay's categorical refusal, he was ready with a variety of alternative suggestions. This was the beginning of a long, fruitless process that would go in circles until it reached a dead end.

After the second letter, Santos and Turbay communicated in person with the president. Gaviria saw them at eight-thirty in the evening in the small room off his private library. He was calmer than usual, and anxious to have news about the hostages. Turbay and Santos brought him up-to-date regarding the two exchanges of letters and the mediation of Guido Parra.

"A bad emissary," said the president. "Very smart, a good lawyer, but extremely dangerous. Of course, he does have Escobar's complete backing."

He read the letters with the power of concentration that always impressed everyone: as if he had become invisible. His complete comments were ready when he finished, and his conjectures on the subject were laconic. He said that none of the intelligence agencies had the slightest idea where the hostages were being held. The important news for the president was confirmation that they were in the hands of Pablo Escobar.

That night Gaviria demonstrated his skill at questioning everything before reaching a final decision. He thought it possible that the letters were not genuine, that Guido Parra was working for somebody else, even that it was all a clever ploy by someone who had nothing to do with Escobar. Santos and Turbay left more discouraged than when they came in, for the president seemed to view the case as a serious problem of state that left very little room for his own feelings.

A major obstacle to an agreement was that Escobar continued to change the terms as his own situation evolved, delaying the release of the hostages in order to obtain additional, unforeseen advantages while waiting for the Constituent Assembly to pass judgment on extradition, and perhaps on a pardon. This was never made clear in the astute correspondence that Escobar maintained with the families of the hostages. But it was very clear in the secret correspondence he maintained with Guido Parra to instruct him in strategy and the long-term view of the negotiation. "It's a good idea for you to convey all concerns to Santos so we don't get further entangled in this," he said in one letter. "Because it must be in writing, in a decree, that under no circumstances will we be extradited, not for any crime, not to any country." He also asked for specific details regarding the confession required for surrender. Two other essential points were security at the special prison, and protection for families and followers.

HERNANDO SANTOS's friendship with former President Turbay, which had always had its foundation in politics, now became personal and very close. They could spend hours sitting across from each other in absolute silence. Not a day went by that they did not speak on the phone, exchanging their intimate thoughts, secret assumptions, new information. They even devised a code for handling confidential matters.

It could not have been easy. Hernando Santos is a man with extraordinary responsibilities: With a single word he could save or destroy a life. He is emotional and raw-nerved, and has a tribal sense of family that weighs heavily in his decisions. Those who accompanied him during his son's captivity were afraid he would not survive the blow. He did not eat, or sleep through the night, he always kept a telephone within reach and grabbed at it on the first ring. During those months of grief, he socialized very little, received psychiatric counseling to help him endure his son's death, which he viewed as inevitable, and lived in seclusion, in his office or rooms, looking at his brilliant collection of stamps, and letters scorched in airplane accidents. Elena Calderón, his wife and the mother of his seven children, had died seven years earlier, and he was truly alone. His heart and vision problems grew worse, and he made no effort to hold back his tears. His exemplary virtue in these dramatic circumstances was keeping the newspaper separate from his personal tragedy.

One of his essential supports in that bitter period was the strength of his daughter-in-law María Victoria. Her memory of the days following the abduction was of her house invaded by relatives and her husband's friends who stretched out on the carpets and drank whiskey and coffee until the small hours of the morning. They always said the same thing, while the impact of the abduction, the very image of the victim, grew fainter. When Hernando came back from Italy, he went straight to María Victoria's house and greeted her with so much emotion that she broke down, but when he had anything confidential to say about the kidnapping, he asked her to leave him alone with the men. María Victoria, who has a strong character and mature intelligence, realized she had always been a marginal figure in a male-dominated family. She cried for an entire day, but in the end she was fortified by the determination to have her own identity and place in her own house. Hernando not only understood her reasoning but reproached himself for his own thoughtlessness, and he found in her the greatest support in his sorrow. From then on they maintained an invincible intimacy, whether face-to-face, or on the telephone, or in writing, or through an intermediary, and even by telepathy: In the most intricate family meetings they only needed to exchange glances to know what the other was thinking, and what they should say. She had some very good ideas, among them to publish editorial notes in the paper—making no effort to conceal their purpose—to let Pacho know about events in the life of the family.

THE LEAST-REMEMBERED victims were Liliana Rojas Arias, the wife of the cameraman Orlando Acevedo, and Martha Lupe Rojas, Richard Becerra's mother. Though they were not close friends, or relatives—despite their last names—the abduction made them inseparable. "Not so much because of our pain," Liliana has said, "but to keep each other company."

Liliana was nursing Erick Yesid, her eighteen-month-old son, when "Criptón" called to tell her that Diana Turbay's entire crew had been abducted. She was twenty-four years old, had been married for three, and lived on the second floor of her in-laws' house in the San Andrés district in southern Bogotá. "She's such a happy girl," a friend has said, "she didn't deserve such ugly news." And imaginative as well as happy, because when she recovered from the initial blow she sat the child in front of the television set during the news programs so that he could see his daddy, and continued to do this without fail until his release.

Both she and Martha Lupe were informed by the people at the news program that they would continue to provide them with money, and when Liliana's son became sick, they took care of the expenses. Nydia Quintero, Diana's mother, also called the two women to try to imbue them with a serenity she herself never had.

She promised that all the efforts she made with the government would be not only for her daughter but also for the entire crew, and that she would pass on any information she received about the hostages. And she did.

Martha Lupe lived with her two daughters, who were then fourteen and eleven years old, and was supported by Richard. When he left with Diana's team, he said it would be a three-day trip, so that after the first week she began to feel uneasy. She does not believe it was a premonition, she has said, but the fact is that she called the news program over and over again until they told her that something strange had happened. A little while later it was announced that the crew had been abducted. From then on she played the radio all day, waiting for them to be returned, and called the show whenever her heart told her to. She was troubled by the thought that her son was the most vulnerable of the hostages. "But all I could do was cry and pray," she says. Nydia Quintero convinced her there were many other things she could do for their release. She invited her to civic and religious meetings and filled her with her own fighting spirit. Liliana had a similar feeling about Orlando, and this caught her in a dilemma: He might be the last one executed because he was the least valuable, or the first because his death would provoke the same public outcry but with fewer serious consequences for the kidnappers. This idea made her burst into uncontrollable weeping, and continued to do so throughout his entire captivity. "Every night after I put the baby to bed, I would sit on the terrace and cry, watching the door so I would see him come in," she has said. "And that is what I did, night after night, until I saw him again."

IN MID-OCTOBER Dr. Turbay called Hernando Santos with a message worded in their personal code. "I have some very good newspapers if you're interested in bullfighting. I'll send them to you if you like." Hernando understood this to mean an important development concerning the hostages. In fact, it was a cassette sent to Dr. Turbay's house and postmarked Montería, the evidence that Diana and her companions were still alive, which the family had asked for over and over again during the past few weeks. The voice was unmistakable: "Daddy, it's difficult to send you a message under these conditions, but after our many requests they've allowed us to do it." Only one sentence gave any clues to possible future actions: "We watch and listen to the news constantly."

Dr. Turbay decided to show the message to the president, and find out at the same time if there were new developments. Gaviria received Turbay and Santos as his workday was ending, as always in his private library, and he was relaxed and more talkative than usual. He closed the door, poured the whiskey, and allowed himself a few political confidences. The capitulation process seemed to have run aground because of the Extraditables' obstinacy, and the president was prepared to get it back in the water by appending certain legal clarifications to the original decree. He had worked on this all afternoon and was confident it would be resolved that same night. Tomorrow, he promised, he would have good news for them.

They returned the next day, as arranged, and found him transformed into a wary, morose man whose first words set the tone for a conversation without hope. "This is a very difficult moment," Gaviria said. "I've wanted to help you, and I have been helping within the limits of the possible, but pretty soon I won't be able to do anything at all." It was obvious that something fundamental in his spirit had changed. Turbay sensed it right away, and before ten minutes had passed he rose from his chair with solemn composure. "Mr. President," he said without a trace of resentment, "you are proceeding as you must, and we must act as the fathers of our children. I understand, and ask you not do anything that might create a problem for you as head of state." As he concluded he pointed at the presidential chair.

"If I were sitting there, I would do the same."

Gaviria stood, pale as death, and walked with them to the elevator. An aide rode down with them and opened the door of the car waiting for them in the courtyard of the private residence. Neither of them spoke until they had driven out into the melancholy rain of an October evening. The noisy traffic on the avenue sounded muffled through bulletproof windows.

"We shouldn't expect anything else from him," Turbay said with a sigh after a long, thoughtful silence. "Something happened between last night and today, and he can't say what it is."

This dramatic meeting with the president was the reason doña Nydia Quintero moved to the foreground. She had been married to former president Turbay Ayala, her uncle, and the father of her four children, the eldest of whom was Diana. Seven years before the abduction, her marriage to Turbay had been annulled by the Holy See; her second husband was Gustavo Balcázar Monzón, a Liberal parliamentarian. She had been first lady and knew the limits protocol placed on a former president, above all in his dealings with a successor. "The only thing he could have done," Nydia had said, "was try to make President Gaviria see his obligation and his responsibilities." And that was what she attempted, though she had few illusions.

Her public activity, even before the official announcement of the abduction, reached staggering proportions. She had planned the appearance of groups of children on radio and television newscasts all over the country to read a plea for the release of the hostages. On October 19, the "Day of National Reconciliation," she had arranged for simultaneous noon masses in various cities and towns to pray for goodwill among Colombians. In Bogotá, while crowds waving white handkerchiefs gathered in many neighborhoods to demonstrate for peace, the ceremony took place on the Plaza de Bolívar, where a torch was lit, the flame to burn until the safe return of the captives. Through her efforts, television newscasts began each program with photographs of all the hostages, kept a tally of the days they had been held captive, and removed the corresponding picture as each prisoner was freed. It was also on her initiative that soccer matches throughout the country opened with a call for the release of the hostages. Maribel Gutiérrez, Colombia's beauty queen for 1990, began her acceptance speech with a plea for their freedom.

Nydia attended the meetings held by the families of the other hostages, listened to the lawyers, made efforts in secret through the Colombian Solidarity Foundation, which she has presided over for twenty years, and almost always felt as if she were running in circles around nothing. It was too much for her resolute, impassioned nature, her almost clairvoyant sensitivity. She waited for results of other people's efforts until she realized they had reached an impasse. Not even men as influential as Turbay and Hernando Santos could pressure the president into negotiating with the kidnappers. This certainty seemed absolute when Dr. Turbay told her about the failure of his last meeting with the president. Then Nydia decided to act on her own and opened a freewheeling second front to try to obtain her daughter's freedom by the most straightforward route.

It was during this time that the Colombian Solidarity Foundation received an anonymous phone call in its Medellín offices from someone who said he had firsthand information about Diana. He stated that an old friend of his on a farm near Medellín had slipped a note into his basket of vegetables, claiming that Diana was there, that the guards watched soccer games and swilled beer until they passed out, and that there was no chance they could react to a rescue attempt. To make a raid even more secure, he offered to send a sketch of the farm. The message was so convincing that Nydia traveled to Medellín to give him her answer. "I asked the informant," she has said, "not to discuss his information with anybody, and I made him see the danger to my daughter, and even to her guards, if anyone attempted a rescue."

The news that Diana was in Medellín suggested the idea of paying a visit to Martha Nieves and Angelita Ochoa, the sisters of

Jorge Luis, Fabio, and Juan David Ochoa, who had been accused of drug trafficking and racketeering and were known to be personal friends of Pablo Escobar. "I went with a fervent hope that they would help me contact Escobar," Nydia reported years later, recalling those bitter days. The Ochoa sisters told her of the abuse their families had suffered at the hands of the police, listened to her with interest, expressed sympathy for her situation, but also said there was nothing they could do as far as Pablo Escobar was concerned.

Martha Nieves knew what an abduction meant. In 1981 she had been kidnapped by the M-19, who demanded an exorbitant ransom from her family. Escobar responded by creating a brutal gang called the MAS, or Death to Kidnappers, which obtained her release after three months of bloody war with the M-19. Her sister Angelita also considered herself a victim of police violence, and both women recounted devastating stories of police abuses, raids on their homes, and countless violations of human rights.

Nydia did not lose heart. If nothing else, she wanted them to deliver a letter for her to Escobar. She had sent one earlier through Guido Parra but had received no reply. The Ochoa sisters refused to deliver another for fear Escobar would accuse them later of creating problems for him. By the end of the visit, however, they were more responsive to Nydia's fervent pleas, and she returned to Bogotá certain that a door had been opened that could lead in two different directions: one toward the release of her daughter, the other toward the peaceful surrender of the three Ochoa brothers. This made it seem appropriate to tell the president in person about her visit.

He saw her without delay. Nydia came right to the point, recounting the Ochoa sisters' complaints about the actions of the police. The president let her speak, asking only a few pertinent questions. His obvious intention was to give less weight to the accusations than she did. As for her own situation, Nydia wanted three things: the release of the hostages, the assertion of presidential authority to prevent a rescue attempt that could have calamitous results, and the extension of the time limit for the surrender of the Extraditables. The only assurance the president gave her was that no rescue of Diana or any other hostage would be attempted without authorization from their families.

"That's our policy," he said.

Even so, Nydia wondered if the president had taken sufficient precautions against someone making the attempt without authorization.

In less than a month, Nydia returned for more talks with the Ochoa sisters at the home of a mutual friend. She also visited one of Pablo Escobar's sisters-in-law, who spoke to her at length of the brutality she and her family had suffered at the hands of the police. Nydia brought her a letter for Escobar: two and a half full-size sheets covered almost completely by her ornate hand and written with an expressive precision achieved after many drafts. Her purpose was to touch Escobar's heart. She began by saying that she was not writing to the fighter capable of doing anything to achieve his ends, but to Pablo the man, "a feeling man who loves his mother and would give his life for her, who has a wife and young, innocent, defenseless children whom he wishes to protect." She understood that Escobar had abducted the journalists as a means of calling public attention to his cause, but in her opinion he had already succeeded. And so—the letter concluded— "show the world the human being you are, and in a great, humanitarian act that everyone will understand, return the hostages to us."

Escobar's sister-in-law seemed truly moved as she read it. "You can be absolutely sure this letter will touch him," she said as if to herself. "Everything you're doing touches him, and that can only work in your daughter's favor." Then she refolded the letter, put it in the envelope, and sealed it herself.

"Don't worry," she told Nydia with evident sincerity. "Pablo will have the letter today."

Nydia returned to Bogotá that night, hopeful about the effect the letter would have and determined to ask the president for what Dr. Turbay had not dared to request: a halt in police operations while the release of the hostages was being negotiated. She did so, and Gaviria told her straight out he could not give that order. "It was one thing for us to offer an alternative judicial policy," he said later. "But suspending operations would not have meant freedom for the hostages but only that we had stopped hunting down Escobar."

Nydia felt she was in the presence of a man of stone who cared nothing for her daughter's life. She had to control her rage as the president explained that law enforcement was not a negotiable subject, that the police did not have to ask permission to act, that he could not order them not to act within the limits of the law. The visit was a disaster.

After their failed efforts with the president, Turbay and Santos decided to try other avenues, and they could think of none better than the Notables. The group was composed of two former presidents, Alfonso López Michelsen and Misael Pastrana; the parliamentarian Diego Montaña Cuéllar; and Cardinal Mario Revollo Bravo, archbishop of Bogotá. In October the families of the hostages met with them at the home of Hernando Santos. They began by recounting their conversations with President Gaviria. The only part that interested López Michelsen was the possibility of amending the decree with judicial specifications, which might create new openings for the capitulation policy. "We have to get a foot in the door," he said. Pastrana favored formulas that would pressure the drug dealers into surrender. But using what weapons? Hernando Santos reminded Montaña Cuéllar that he could mobilize the guerrilla forces.

After a long, informed discussion, López Michelsen reached the first conclusion. "Let's play the Extraditables' game," he said. And he proposed writing a public letter announcing that the Notables were now spokesmen for the families of the hostages.

The unanimous decision was that López Michelsen would write the letter.

Two days later the first draft was read to a second gathering attended by Guido Parra and another of Escobar's lawyers. This document articulated for the first time the thesis that drug trafficking could be considered a collective, sui generis crime, which meant that the negotiation could move in unprecedented directions. Guido Parra was startled.

"A sui generis crime," he exclaimed in astonishment. "That's brilliant!"

With that as a starting point, Guido Parra elaborated the concept in his own way, as a God-given right on the murky border between ordinary and political crimes, making possible the dream that the Extraditables, like the guerrillas, would be treated as political offenders. Each man spoke. Then, one of Escobar's lawyers asked the Notables to obtain a letter from Gaviria that would guarantee Escobar's life in an explicit, unequivocal way.

"I'm very sorry," said Hernando Santos, shocked at the request, "but I won't get involved in that."

"And I certainly won't," said Turbay.

López Michelsen's refusal was vehement. Then the lawyer asked them to arrange a meeting between him and the president so that Gaviria could give him an oral guarantee for Escobar. "We won't deal with that subject here," López Michelsen replied.

Before the Notables met to revise the draft of their statement, Pablo Escobar had already been informed of their most confidential intentions. This is the only way to explain his extraordinary instructions in an urgent letter to Guido Parra. "You are free to find some way to have the Notables invite you to their discussion," he wrote. And then he listed a series of decisions the Extraditables had already made in anticipation of any fresh initiative.

The Notables' letter was ready in twenty-four hours, and contained an important departure with regard to their previous efforts: "Our good offices have acquired a new dimension, not limited to an occasional rescue but concerned with how to achieve peace for all Colombians." It was a new definition of their function that could only increase hope. President Gaviria approved but thought it prudent to establish a certain distance to avoid any misinterpretation of the official attitude, and he instructed the justice minister to issue a statement affirming that the capitulation policy was the government's sole position with respect to the surrender of the terrorists.

Escobar did not like a word of the Notables' letter. As soon as he read it in the papers on October 11, he sent Guido Parra a furious response, which he wanted him to circulate in the salons of Bogotá. "The letter from the Notables is almost cynical," it said. "We are supposed to release the hostages quickly because the government is dragging its feet as it studies our situation. Can they really believe we will let ourselves be deceived again?" The position of the Extraditables, it continued, was the same one indicated in their first letter. "There was no reason to change it, since we have not received positive replies to the requests made in our first communication. This is a negotiation, not a game to find out who is clever and who is stupid."

The truth was that by this time Escobar had traveled light-years ahead of the Notables. His aim was for the government to give him his own secure territory—a prison camp, as he called it—like the one granted the M-19 while the terms of their surrender were being negotiated. More than a week earlier he had sent Guido Parra a detailed letter regarding the special prison he wanted for himself. The perfect location, he said, twelve kilometers outside Medellín, was a property he owned, though an agent of his was listed as owner, which the municipality of Envigado could lease and convert into a prison. "Since this requires money, the Extraditables would assume the costs," the letter continued. It ended with an astounding disclosure: "I'm telling you all this because I want you to talk to the mayor of Envigado and tell him you represent me and explain the idea to him. But the reason I want you to talk to him is to get him to write a public letter to the justice minister saying he thinks the Extraditables have not accepted Decree 2047 because they fear for their safety, and that the municipality of Envigado, as its contribution to peace for the Colombian people, is prepared to build a special prison that will offer protection and security to those who surrender. Talk to him in a direct, clear way so he'll talk to Gaviria and propose the camp." The stated goal was to force a public response from the justice minister. "I know that will have the impact of a bomb," said Escobar's letter. And it ended with stunning arrogance: "This way we'll have them where we want them."

The minister, however, turned down the terms of the offer as presented to him, and Escobar found himself obliged to soften his tone with another letter in which, for the first time, he offered more than he demanded. In exchange for the prison camp, he promised to resolve the conflicts among the various cartels, crews, and gangs, to guarantee the surrender of more than a hundred repentant traffickers, and to at last open an avenue to peace. "We are not asking for amnesty, or dialogue, or any of the things they say they cannot give," he said. This was a simple offer to surrender, "while everybody in this country is calling for dialogue and for treating us as politicals." He even downplayed what he held most dear: "I have no problem with extradition, since I know that if they take me alive they'll kill me, like they've done with everybody else."

His strategy at this time was to demand huge favors in exchange for mail from the hostages. "Tell Señor Santos," he said in another letter, "that if he wants proof that Francisco is alive, he should first publish the report from Americas Watch, an interview with Juan Méndez, its director, and a report on the massacres, tortures, and disappearances in Medellín." But by this time Hernando Santos had learned how to cope with the situation. He knew that the constant flow back and forth of proposals and counterproposals was a strain not only on him but on his adversaries as well. Guido Parra, for one, was in a state of nervous exhaustion by the end of October. Santos's reply to Escobar was that he would not publish a line of anything or see his emissary again until he had conclusive proof that his son was alive. Alfonso López Michelsen backed him up by threatening to withdraw from the Notables.

It worked. In two weeks Guido Parra called Hernando Santos from a truck stop. "I'm in the car with my wife, and I'll be at your house by eleven," he said. "I'm bringing you the most delicious dessert, and you can't imagine how much I've enjoyed it, and how much you're going to enjoy it." Hernando was elated, thinking he was bringing Francisco home. But it was only his voice recorded on a minicassette. They could not listen to it for over two hours because they did not have the right equipment, and then someone discovered they could play it on the answering machine.

Pacho Santos could have been successful in many professions, but not as a diction teacher. He tries to speak at the speed of his thoughts, and his ideas come in a simultaneous rush. The surprise that night was his slow speech, modulated voice, and perfectly constructed sentences. In reality there were two messages—one for his family and the other for the president—which he had recorded the week before.

The guards' idea that Pacho should read the day's headlines to prove the date of the recording was a mistake that Escobar probably never forgave them for. It did, however, give Luis Cañón, the legal editor of *El Tiempo*, the opportunity to display a piece of brilliant journalism.

"They're holding him in Bogotá," he said.

The paper Pacho had read from had a late headline that appeared only in the local edition, whose circulation is limited to the northern part of the city. This fact was worth its weight in gold and would have been decisive if Hernando Santos had not been opposed to an armed rescue attempt.

The moment restored him, above all because the content of the message convinced him that his captive son approved of how he was handling matters. Besides, the family had always thought of Pacho as the most vulnerable of the children because of his impulsive temperament and volatile spirit, and no one could have imagined that he would be so rational and self-possessed after sixty days of captivity.

Hernando called the entire family to his house, and they listened to the message till dawn. Only Guido Parra gave in to his emotions. He wept. Hernando came over to comfort him, and in the perspiration that soaked his shirt he recognized the smell of panic.

"Remember, I won't be killed by the police," Guido Parra said through his tears. "I'll be killed by Pablo Escobar because I know too much."

María Victoria was not moved. She thought Parra was toying with Hernando's feelings, exploiting his weakness, giving a little so he could get back more. At some point during the evening, Guido Parra must have sensed this because he said to Hernando: "That woman's an iceberg."

Matters had reached this stage on November 7, when Maruja and Beatriz were abducted. The Notables had no firm ground to stand on. On November 22—following his prior announcement—Diego Montaña Cuéllar made the formal proposal to his fellow members that the group disband, and they, in a solemn meeting, presented the president with their conclusions regarding the Extraditables' principal demands.

If President Gaviria was hoping that the capitulation decree would elicit an immediate mass surrender by the drug traffickers, he must have been disappointed. It did not. Reactions in the press, in political circles, among distinguished jurists, and even some of the valid objections raised by the Extraditables' lawyers, made it clear that Decree 2047 had to be revised. To begin with, it left the possibility wide open for any judge to interpret the extradition process in his own way. Another weakness was that although conclusive evidence against the drug dealers lay outside the country, the entire question of cooperation with the United States had reached a critical stage, and the time limits for obtaining evidence were too short. The solution—not contained in the decree—was to extend the time limits and transfer to the presidency the responsibility for negotiating the return of evidence to Colombia.

Alberto Villamizar had also not found in the decree the decisive support he was hoping for. Until now his exchanges with Santos and Turbay, and his initial meetings with Pablo Escobar's lawyers, had allowed him to form a broad view of the situation. His first impression was that the capitulation decree, a flawed move in the right direction, left him very little maneuvering room to obtain the release of his wife and sister. In the meanwhile, time was passing without any news of them, without the slightest proof they were still alive. His only opportunity to communicate with them had been a letter sent through Guido Parra, in which he gave them his optimistic assurance that he would do nothing else but work for their release. "I know your situation is terrible but stay calm," he wrote to Maruja.

The truth was that Villamizar had no idea what to do. He had exhausted every avenue, and the only thing he could hold on to during that long November was Rafael Pardo's assurance that the president was considering another decree to complement and clarify 2047. "It's just about ready," he said. Rafael Pardo stopped by his house almost every evening and kept him up-to-date on his efforts, but not even he was very certain how to proceed. Villamizar concluded from his long, slow conversations with Santos and Turbay that negotiations had reached an impasse. He had no faith in Guido Parra. He had known him since the days when he stalked the halls of congress, and he thought him an opportunist and a crook. But for better or worse, Parra was the only card, and Villamizar decided to gamble everything on him. He had no other choice, and time was pressing.

At his request, former president Turbay and Hernando Santos made an appointment to see Guido Parra, on the condition that

Dr. Santiago Uribe, another of Escobar's attorneys, with a good reputation as a serious man, also be present. Guido Parra began the conversation with his usual high-flown rhetoric, but Villamizar brought him back down to earth with the brutal directness of a man from Santander.

"Don't fuck with me," he said. "Let's get to the point. You've stalled everything because your demands are moronic, and there's only one damn thing at issue here: Your boys have to turn themselves in and confess to some crime that they can serve a twelve-year sentence for. That's what the law says, period. And in exchange for that, they'll get a reduced sentence and a guarantee of protection. All the rest is bullshit."

Guido Parra had no choice but to change his tone.

"Look, Doctor," he said, "the thing is that the government says they won't be extradited, everybody says so, but where does the decree say it specifically?"

Villamizar agreed. If the government was saying there would be no extraditions, since that was the sense of the law, then their job was to persuade the government to eliminate the ambiguities. All the rest—clever interpretations of a sui generis crime, or refusing to confess, or the immorality of implicating others— amounted to nothing more than Guido Parra's rhetorical distractions. It was obvious that for the Extraditables—as their very name indicated—the only real and urgent requirement was not to be extradited. And it did not seem impossible to have this spelled out in the decree. But first Villamizar demanded from Guido Parra the same frankness and determination demanded by the Extraditables. First, he wanted to know how far Parra was authorized to negotiate, and second, how soon after the decree was amended would the hostages be released. Guido Parra was solemn.

"They'll be free in twenty-four hours," he said.

"All of them, of course," said Villamizar.

"All of them."

5

A MONTH AFTER the abduction of Maruja and Beatriz, the absurd rules of their captivity had been relaxed. They no longer had to ask permission to stand, and they could pour their own coffee or change television channels. Inside the room they still spoke in whispers, but their movements had become more spontaneous. Maruja did not have to bury her face in the pillow when she coughed, though she did take minimal precautions not to be heard outside the room. Lunch and dinner were still the same, the same beans, the same lentils, the same bits of dry meat and ordinary packaged soup.

The guards talked a good deal among themselves, taking no precaution except to speak in whispers. They exchanged blood-soaked news about how much they had earned hunting down the police at night in Medellín, about their sexual prowess and their melodramatic love affairs. Maruja had succeeded in convincing them that in the case of an armed rescue attempt, it would be more realistic to protect the captives so that they at least would be sure of receiving decent treatment and a compassionate trial. At first they seemed indifferent, for they were absolute fatalists, but her strategy of mollification meant they no longer pointed their guns at the prisoners while they slept, and their weapons, wrapped in cloths, were kept out of sight behind the television. Little by little, their mutual dependence and shared suffering brought a thin veneer of humanity to their relations.

It was in Maruja's nature not to keep bitter feelings to herself. She gave vent to her emotions with the guards, who were always ready for violence, and faced them down with a chilling determination: "Go on, kill me." Sometimes she turned on Marina, whose eagerness to please the guards infuriated her, and whose apocalyptic fantasies drove her to distraction. Sometimes, for no apparent reason, Marina would look up and make a disheartening remark or sinister prophecy.

"On the other side of that courtyard is a repair shop for the killers' cars," she once said. "They're all there, day and night, armed with rifles, ready to come and shoot us."

Their most serious quarrel, however, occurred one afternoon when Marina began her habitual cursing of journalists because her name had not been mentioned on a television program about the hostages.

"They're all sons of bitches," she said.

Maruja confronted her.

"You're out of line," she replied in a rage. "You can show a little respect."

Marina did not answer and later, in a calmer moment, apologized. In reality, she lived in a world apart. She was sixty-four years old and had been a famous beauty, with wonderful large black eyes and silver hair that still gleamed even in misfortune. She had become nothing but skin and bones. When Beatriz and Maruja arrived, she had spent almost two months with no one to talk to but her guards, and time and effort were needed for her to assimilate their presence. Fear had wreaked havoc on her: She had lost forty-five pounds, and her morale was very low. She was a phantom.

When she was very young, she had married a chiropractor who

was well respected in the athletic world, a stout, good-hearted man who loved her without reservation and with whom she had four daughters and three sons. She managed everything, in her own house and in several others, for she felt obliged to solve the problems of her large family in Antioquia. Marina was like a second mother to them all, as much for her authority as her solicitude, but she also concerned herself with any outsider who touched her heart.

Because of her indomitable independence rather than any financial need, she sold cars and life insurance, and seemed able to sell anything simply because she wanted to spend her own money. But those closest to her lamented the fact that a woman with so many natural talents was also hounded by misfortune. For almost twenty years her husband had been incapacitated by mental illness, two brothers had been killed in a terrible car accident, one died of a heart attack, another was crushed by a traffic light in a freak mishap, and still another, who loved to wander, had disappeared forever.

Her situation as a hostage had no solution. Even she accepted the widespread idea that she had been abducted only because her captors wanted a significant hostage whom they could kill without thwarting the negotiations for their surrender. But the fact that she had spent sixty days in prison may have allowed her to think that they saw a chance to obtain some advantage in exchange for her life.

It was noteworthy that even at her worst moments she spent long hours absorbed in the meticulous care of her fingernails and toenails. She filed and buffed them, and brightened them with natural polish, so that they looked like the nails of a younger woman. She devoted the same attention to tweezing her eyebrows and shaving her legs. Once they were past their initial problems, Maruja and Beatriz helped her. They learned to deal with her. She held interminable conversations with Beatriz about people she loved and people she hated, speaking in an endless whisper that irritated even the guards. Maruja tried to comfort her. Both felt distress at being the only people, apart from her jailers, who knew she was alive, yet could not let anyone else know.

One of the few diversions during this time was the unexpected return of the masked boss who had visited them on the first day. Cheerful and optimistic, he brought the news that they might be released before December 9, the date of the election for the Constituent Assembly. This had special significance for Maruja because December 9 was her birthday, and the thought of spending it with her family filled her with anticipatory joy. But it was an ephemeral hope: A week later, the same boss said that not only would they not be released on December 9, but their captivity would be a long one and they would not be free by Christmas or the New Year. It was a harsh blow. Maruja suffered the onset of phlebitis that caused severe pains in her legs. Beatriz had an attack of asphyxia, and her gastric ulcer began to bleed. One night, maddened by pain, she pleaded with Spots to make an exception to the prison rules and let her have an unscheduled visit to the bathroom. He agreed, after thinking it over for a long time, and told her he was taking a great risk. But it did not help. Beatriz continued to whimper in pain like a wounded dog, and thought she was dying until Spots took pity on her and got some Buscapina from the majordomo.

In spite of their efforts, the hostages had no reliable clues as to where they were. The guards' fear that neighbors might hear them, and the sounds and voices coming from outside, led them to think they were in the city. A confirmation seemed to be the deranged rooster that crowed at any hour of the day or night, since roosters kept on high floors tend to lose their sense of time. Nearby they often heard different voices calling the same name: Rafael. Small, low-flying planes passed overhead, and when the helicopter arrived it sounded as if it were right on top of the house. Marina insisted on the unproven theory that a high-ranking army officer was supervising their imprisonment. For Maruja and Bea-

triz it was just another fantasy, but whenever they heard the helicopter, strict military rules were reimposed: the house as orderly
as a barracks, the door latched on the inside and padlocked on the
outside, conversation in whispers, weapons always at the ready,
and a slight improvement in the vile food.

The four guards who had been with them since the first day
were replaced by another four early in December. One was dis-
tinctive and strange and looked like a character in a horror movie.
They called him Gorilla, and in fact he resembled one: enormous
and strong as a gladiator, with dark black skin covered in thick,
curly hair. His voice was so loud he had difficulty whispering, and
no one dared to ask him to lower his voice. The sense of inferior-
ity felt by the other guards was obvious. Instead of the cutoffs
worn by everyone else, he wore gymnast's shorts, a ski mask, and
a tight undershirt that displayed his perfect torso. He had a Holy
Infant medal around his neck, handsome arms, and a Brazilian
wristband that he wore for good luck. His hands were enormous,
and the fate lines seemed etched into his pale palms. He barely fit
into the room, and every time he moved he left chaos in his wake.
For the hostages, who had learned how to deal with the previous
guards, this was a disturbing turn of events—above all for Beatriz,
whom he hated on sight.

The condition shared by both guards and hostages was absolute boredom. As a prelude to their celebration of Christmas,
the owners of the house held a novena with a priest of their acquaintance, perhaps innocent, perhaps not. They prayed, sang
carols, gave candy to the children, and toasted one another with
the apple wine that was the family's official drink. At the end the
house was exorcised with sprinklings of holy water. They needed
so much that it was brought in gallon oil cans. When the priest
left, Damaris came into the room and sprinkled the television, the
mattresses, the walls. The three captives, taken by surprise, did not
know what to do. "It's holy water," she said as she sprinkled everything with her hand. "It'll help to make sure nothing happens to

us." The guards crossed themselves, fell to their knees, and received the purifying shower with angelic devotion.

That love of parties and prayer, so typical of Antioquians, did not let up for a moment during the month of December. Maruja, in fact, had been careful not to let her captors know that December 9 was her fifty-third birthday. Beatriz agreed to keep the secret, but the guards found out while they were watching a special television program that Maruja's children dedicated to her on the evening of December 8.

The guards could not hide their emotion at feeling themselves somehow involved in the intimacy of the program. "Doña Maruja," said one, "how young Dr. Villamizar looks, how nice he looks, how he loves you." They hoped Maruja would introduce them to her daughters so they could take them out. In any case, watching that program in captivity was like being dead and watching life from the next world without taking part, and without the living knowing you were there. At eleven the next morning, the majordomo and his wife burst into the room with a bottle of local champagne, enough glasses for everyone, and a cake that looked as if it were covered in toothpaste. They congratulated Maruja with great displays of affection, and they and the guards sang "Happy Birthday." They all ate and drank, and left Maruja struggling with contrary emotions.

JUAN VITTA WOKE on November 26 to learn that he was being released because of ill health. He froze in terror, for in recent days he had been feeling better than ever, and he thought the announcement was simply a subterfuge that would give the public its first corpse. As a consequence, when the guard told him a few hours later to get ready for his release, he had an attack of panic. "I would have preferred to die on my own," he has said, "but if this was my fate, I had to accept it." He was told to shave and put on clean clothes, and he did, certain he was dressing for his own funeral. He was given instructions on what he must do once he was free, and above all, on what he must say during press interviews to avoid giving clues the police might use in a rescue operation. A little after twelve, they drove him through some labyrinthine districts in Medellín and then, without ceremony, dropped him off on a street corner.

After Vitta's release they moved Hero Buss again, this time to a good neighborhood, across the street from an aerobics school for women. The owner of the house was a free-spending, high-living mulatto. His wife, about thirty-five years old and in her seventh month of pregnancy, spent the day from breakfast on covering herself in expensive jewelry that was far too noticeable. They had a young son who was staying in another house with his grandmother, and it was his room, filled with every kind of mechanical toy, that was occupied by Hero Buss. And he, considering how they made him part of the family, prepared himself for a long captivity.

The owners must have enjoyed this German like the ones in Marlene Dietrich's movies: more than six feet tall and a yard wide, a fifty-year-old adolescent with a sense of humor that protected him from creditors, and who spoke a Spanish spiced with the Caribbean slang of his wife, Carmen Santiago. He had faced real dangers as a correspondent for German newspapers and radio in Latin America, including the night he had spent, under the military regime in Chile, expecting to be shot at dawn. So he already had a tough hide, and could enjoy the folkloric aspects of his captivity.

And it was just as well in a house where a courier made regular visits bringing bags full of money for expenses, and still there was never enough. The owners would spend it as soon as they could on parties and trinkets, and in a few days they had nothing left for food. On weekends they gave parties and huge dinners for their brothers and sisters, cousins and close friends. Children took over the house. On the first day they were overwhelmed with emotion when they recognized the German giant, whom they treated as if he were a soap opera star because they had seen him so often on television. No fewer than thirty people who had nothing to do with the abduction asked to take his picture, requested autographs, ate with him, and even danced with him, all without masks in that madhouse where he lived until his captivity ended.

Their accumulated debts drove the owners to distraction, and they had to pawn the television, the VCR, the stereo, whatever, to feed the hostage. The wife's jewelry began to disappear from her throat, wrists, and ears, until there was nothing left. Once, in the middle of the night, the owner woke Hero Buss to ask for a loan because his wife had gone into labor and he did not have a penny to pay the hospital. Hero Buss lent him his last fifty thousand pesos.

They freed him on December 11, two weeks after Juan Vitta. For the occasion they bought him a pair of shoes that he could not use because he wore size 46 and the largest they could find, after much searching, was a 44. They bought him a shirt and trousers two sizes smaller because he had lost thirty-five pounds. They returned his camera equipment and the bag with his notebooks hidden in the lining, and they paid him back the fifty thousand pesos for the birth and another fifteen thousand he had lent them earlier to replace money that had been stolen from them at the market. They offered him a great deal more, but the only thing he asked them for was an interview with Pablo Escobar. They never replied.

The crew that had been with him in recent days drove him away in a private car. After taking a circuitous route through the best neighborhoods in Medellín, they dropped him half a block from the newspaper *El Colombiano*, with his bags on his back and a message from the Extraditables; it recognized his struggle in defense of human rights in Colombia and other Latin American countries, and reiterated the determination of the Extraditables to accept the capitulation policy with no conditions other than judicial guarantees of safety for themselves and their families. A journalist to the end, Hero Buss handed his camera to the first passerby and asked him to take a picture of his release.

Diana and Azucena heard the news on the radio, and their guards said they would be next. But they had been told the same thing so often, they did not believe it. In the event only one was freed, each woman wrote a letter for the other to give to her family. And then nothing happened, nothing else was said, until two days later—at dawn on December 13—when Diana was awakened by whispers and unusual movements in the house. The feeling that they would be released made her jump out of bed. She alerted Azucena, and before anyone announced anything to them they began to pack.

Both Diana and Azucena recounted that dramatic moment in their journals. Diana was in the shower when one of the guards, without any ceremony, told Azucena to get ready to go. Only Azucena. In the book she would publish a short while later, she narrated this with admirable simplicity:

I went to the room and put on the clothes I had laid out on the chair while doña Diana was still in the bathroom. When she came out and saw me she stopped, looked at me, and said:

"Are we going, Azu?"

Her eyes shone, waiting for the answer she longed to hear. And I could not tell her anything. I lowered my head, took a deep breath, and said:

"No. I'm going alone."

"I'm so happy for you," Diana said. "I knew it would be this way."

In her diary, Diana wrote: "I felt as if I had been stabbed in the heart, but I said I was happy for her, and not to worry." She gave

Azucena the letter to Nydia she had written earlier, in the event she was not released. In the letter she asked Nydia to celebrate Christmas with Diana's children. Azucena was crying, and Diana put her arms around her to comfort her. Then she walked with Azucena to the car, and they embraced again. Azucena turned to watch her through the car window, and Diana waved goodbye.

An hour later, in the car that was taking her to the Medellín airport where she would catch a plane to Bogotá, Azucena heard a reporter on the radio asking her husband what he had been doing when he heard the news of her release. He replied with the truth:

"I was writing a poem for Azucena."

And so their wish was granted, and they were together on December 16 to celebrate their fourth wedding anniversary.

RICARDO AND ORLANDO, tired of sleeping on the floor of their foul-smelling cell, persuaded the guards to put them in another room. They moved the hostages to the bedroom where they had seen the handcuffed mulatto, whom they never saw again. To their horror, they discovered that the mattress on the bed had large, recent bloodstains that might have come either from slow tortures or sudden slashes with a knife.

They had learned of the release of other hostages on television and radio. Their guards had said they would be next. Very early on December 17 a boss they knew as the Old Man—and who in fact was the same don Pacho in charge of Diana—walked into Orlando's room without knocking.

"Put on some clothes because you're leaving now," he said.

He barely had time to shave and dress, and no time to tell Richard, who was in the same house. They gave him a communiqué for the press, put a pair of strong glasses over his eyes, and the Old Man, on his own, drove him with the ritual twists and turns through various neighborhoods in Medellín, gave him five thousand pesos for a cab, and left him at a traffic circle he could not identify because he does not know the city. It was nine in the morning on a cool, clear Monday. Orlando could not believe it: Until that moment, while he signaled in vain for cabs that were all occupied, he had been sure it would be cheaper for his captors to kill him than run the risk of freeing him while he was alive. He called his wife from the first telephone he saw.

Liliana was bathing the baby, and ran to answer the phone with soapy hands. She heard a stranger's calm voice:

"Slim, it's me."

She thought it was a joke and was about to hang up when she recognized his voice. "Oh my God," she cried. Orlando was in such a hurry he only managed to tell her he was still in Medellín and would be in Bogotá that afternoon. Liliana was tormented the rest of the day because she had not recognized her husband's voice. Juan Vitta had told her when he was released that Orlando had changed so much in captivity that it was hard to recognize him, but she never thought the change would affect even his voice. That afternoon at the airport it was even worse when she made her way through the crowd of reporters and did not recognize the man who kissed her. But it was Orlando after four months of captivity, fat and pale, with a dark, rough mustache. Each of them had decided on their own to have a second child as soon as they were together again. "But there were so many people around we couldn't that night," Liliana has said, weak with laughter. "Or the next day either, because of the shock." But at last they made up for lost time: Nine months after the third day they had another boy, and twins the following year.

THE SERIES OF RELEASES—a breath of hope for the other captives and their families—were a convincing sign to Pacho Santos that no reasonable progress had been made in his favor. He thought Pablo Escobar had simply gotten rid of the low cards to increase the pressure for amnesty and non-extradition in the Constituent Assembly, and was holding on to his three aces: the daughter of a former president, the son of the publisher of the most important paper in the country, and the sister-in-law of Luis Carlos Galán. Beatriz and Marina, on the other hand, felt renewed hope, though Maruja preferred not to deceive herself with overly optimistic interpretations. Her spirits were low, and the approach of Christmas was devastating. She despised obligatory holidays. She never put up crèches or Christmas trees, did not send cards or give gifts, and found nothing more depressing than dreary Christmas Eve celebrations when people sing because they're sad or cry because they're happy. The majordomo and his wife prepared a ghastly dinner. Beatriz and Marina made an effort to join in, but Maruja took two strong sleeping pills and woke with no regrets.

On the following Wednesday, Alexandra's weekly program was devoted to Christmas night at Nydia's house with the entire Turbay family around the former president, along with the families of Beatriz, and of Maruja and Alberto Villamizar. The children were in the foreground: Diana's two boys, and Maruja's grandson—Alexandra's son. Maruja wept with emotion: The last time she had seen him he barely babbled a few words, and now he could talk. At the end, Villamizar spoke, slowly and in great detail, about the progress of his efforts. Maruja summed up the program with absolute precision: "It was very nice, and really awful."

Villamizar's message raised Marina Montoya's spirits. She became human again and revealed the greatness of her heart. With a political acumen they had not known she possessed, she began to show interest in listening to the news and interpreting its significance. Her analysis of the decrees led her to conclude that their chances for freedom were greater than ever. Her health improved so much that she ignored the rules and spoke in her natural voice, which was beautiful and well modulated.

December 31 was their big night. When Damaris brought breakfast she said they would celebrate with a real party, complete with champagne and a pork roast. Maruja thought it would be the saddest night of her life, the first New Year's Eve away from her family, and she sank into depression. Beatriz was in a state of total collapse. The last thing they wanted was a party. Marina, however, was overjoyed by the news and used all her persuasive powers to cheer them up, even the guards.

"We have to be fair," she told Maruja and Beatriz. "They're away from their families too, and our job is to make their New Year's Eve as pleasant as it can be."

She had been given three nightgowns on the night of her abduction, but she had used only one and kept the other two in her bag. Later, when Maruja and Beatriz were captured, the three women used sweatsuits as their prison uniform, washing them every two weeks.

No one thought about the nightgowns again until the afternoon of December 31, when Marina carried her enthusiasm one step further. "I have an idea," she said. "I have three nightgowns here, and we'll wear them for good luck in the new year." And she asked Maruja:

"All right, darling, which color do you want?"

Maruja said it was all the same to her. Marina decided that green suited her best. She gave the pink gown to Beatriz, and kept the white one for herself. Then she took a cosmetics case out of her bag, and suggested they make each other up. "So we'll look pretty tonight," she said. Maruja, who'd had all she could bear with the idea of dressing up in nightgowns, turned her down with sour humor.

"I'll go so far as to put on the nightgown," she said. "But paint myself up like a madwoman, under these circumstances? No, Marina, that's something I won't do."

Marina shrugged.

"Well, I will."

Because they had no mirror, she handed the case to Beatriz and sat down on the bed to be made up. Beatriz did a complete and tasteful job in the light of the bedside candle, some blush to hide the deathly pallor of her skin, bright lipstick, eye shadow. They were both surprised at how attractive this woman, who had been famous for her grace and beauty, could still look. Beatriz settled for her ponytail and schoolgirl appearance.

That night Marina displayed all her irresistible Antioquian charm. The guards followed suit, and they all said what they had to say in their God-given voices, except the majordomo, who even on the high seas of intoxication still spoke in whispers. Spots, emboldened by drink, found the courage to give Beatriz a bottle of aftershave. "So you can all smell nice when you get a million hugs on the day you're released," he said to the women. The boorish majordomo could not let it pass and said it was the gift of a secret admirer. A new terror was added to the many that plagued Beatriz.

The party consisted of the hostages, the majordomo and his wife, and the four guards. Beatriz had an unbearable lump in her throat. Maruja felt nostalgic and embarrassed, but even so she could not hide her admiration for Marina who looked splendid, rejuvenated by makeup, with her white gown and snowy hair, her delicious voice. It was inconceivable that Marina could be happy, but she made everyone think she was.

She joked with the guards who lifted their masks to drink. Sometimes, when the heat got to be too much for them, they asked the hostages to turn their backs so they could take a free breath. At midnight, when the fire engine sirens wailed and the church bells rang, they were all crowded into the room, sitting on the bed, on the mattress, sweating in the infernal heat. The national anthem began to play on television. Then Maruja stood and told them all to get to their feet and sing with her. When it was over she raised her glass of apple wine and made a toast to peace in Colombia. The party ended half an hour later when the bottles were empty and nothing was left on the platter but bones and the remains of some potato salad.

The hostages greeted the replacement crew of guards with a

sigh of relief, for they were the same ones who had been waiting for them on the night of the abduction and the prisoners knew how to deal with them. Maruja in particular felt a sense of deliverance, for her poor health had kept her in low spirits. At first her terror had taken the form of erratic pains all over her body, which forced her into uncomfortable postures. But then the pain became concrete as a result of the inhuman regime imposed by the guards. Early in December, to punish her rebelliousness, they would not allow her to use the bathroom for an entire day, and when at last they gave permission, nothing happened. This was the beginning of a chronic cystitis, and then bleeding, which lasted until the end of her captivity.

Marina, who had learned sports massage from her husband, committed her meager strength to healing her. She still had high spirits left over from New Year's Eve. She remained optimistic, told stories: She was alive. The inclusion of her name and photograph in a television campaign in support of the hostages restored her sense of hope and joy. She was her old self again: She existed again, she was there. Her picture was always shown in the first segment of the campaign, and then one day, with no explanation, it did not appear. Maruja and Beatriz did not have the heart to tell her that perhaps she had been removed from the list because no one thought she was still alive.

December 31 was important to Beatriz because that was the latest date she had fixed for her release. She was so devastated by disappointment that her cellmates did not know what to do for her. At one point Maruja could not look at her because when she did, Beatriz broke down and burst into tears, and they began to ignore each other in a space not much larger than a bathroom. The situation became untenable.

The most reliable distraction for the three hostages, in the endless hours following their bathroom privileges, was to massage their legs with the moisturizing cream their jailers supplied in sufficient quantities to keep them from going mad. One day Beatriz realized it was running out.

"What are we going to do when there's no more cream?" she asked Maruja.

"Well, we can always ask for more," Maruja replied in a caustic tone. And she added with an emphasis that was even more caustic: "Or else we'll just have to make a decision when the time comes. Okay?"

"Don't you dare talk to me like that!" Beatriz shouted in a sudden explosion of rage. "Not when it's your damn fault I'm here!"

The explosion was inevitable. In an instant she said everything she had kept to herself during so many days of repressed tensions, so many nights of horror. The surprise was that it had not happened earlier or been more rancorous. Beatriz had kept to the sidelines, holding back, swallowing her rancor whole without tasting it. The inconsequential effect, of course, was that sooner or later a simple, thoughtless phrase would release the fury that terror had suppressed. But the guard on duty did not think that way, and fearing a major blowup, threatened to lock Beatriz and Maruja into separate rooms.

They were dismayed. The dread of sexual assault was still very much alive. Certain that being together made it difficult for the guards to attempt a rape, they were alarmed by the thought of being separated. On the other hand, the guards, who were always in pairs, did not get along and seemed to keep a cautious eye on one another as a way of maintaining internal discipline and avoiding serious incidents with the hostages.

But the repression of the guards created an unhealthy atmosphere in the room. Those on duty in December had brought in a VCR and watched violent films with strong erotic elements, and some pornographic movies. At times the room became saturated with unbearable tension. Furthermore, when the prisoners went to the bathroom, they had to leave the door partially opened, and on more than one occasion they had caught a guard watching them. One of the guards, who insisted on holding the door with his hand so it would not close all the way while the women were using the bathroom, almost lost his fingers when Beatriz slammed it shut. Another unsettling sight was a pair of homosexual guards who worked the second shift and kept each other in a perpetual state of arousal with all kinds of perverse games. Spots's excessive vigilance at Beatriz's slightest gesture, his gift of aftershave, and the majordomo's insolent remark were all unsettling. The stories the guards told each other about their rapes of strangers, their erotic perversions, their sadistic pleasures, rarefied the atmosphere even further.

At the request of Maruja and Marina, the majordomo had a doctor come to see Beatriz on January 12, sometime before midnight. He was a young, well-dressed man with beautiful manners, wearing a yellow silk mask that complemented his outfit. It is difficult to believe in the seriousness of a hooded physician, but this one demonstrated his skill as soon as he came in. His self-assurance was comforting. He carried a fine leather bag as big as a suitcase, with a phonendoscope, a tensiometer, a battery-operated electrocardiograph, a laboratory kit for home-analysis, and other emergency equipment. He gave each hostage a thorough examination, and analyzed their blood and urine in the portable laboratory.

As he was examining Maruja, the doctor whispered in her ear: "I am the most embarrassed person in the world at having to see you in this situation. I want to tell you that I am not here voluntarily. I was a great friend and supporter of Dr. Luis Carlos Galán, and I voted for him. You don't deserve to suffer like this, but try to endure. Serenity is good for your health." Maruja appreciated his explanations but could not overcome her astonishment at his moral flexibility. He made identical comments to Beatriz.

The diagnosis for both women was severe stress and incipient malnutrition, for which he ordered an enriched, more balanced diet. He discovered circulatory problems and a serious bladder infection in Maruja, and prescribed a course of treatment based on Vasotón, diuretics, and tranquilizers. He prescribed a sedative for Beatriz's gastric ulcer. As for Marina—whom he had seen before—he only advised that she take better care of her health but did not find her very receptive. He ordered all three to walk at a brisk pace for at least an hour every day.

After this, each woman was given a box with twenty tranquilizers. They were to take one pill in the morning, another at noon, and the third before they went to sleep. In an emergency they could exchange the tranquilizer for a powerful barbiturate that allowed them to escape many of the horrors of their captivity. Just a quarter of a pill was enough to make them lose consciousness before the count of four.

At one o'clock that morning, they began their walks in the dark courtyard with the nervous guards, who kept their submachine guns, safeties off, trained on them. The women felt dizzy their first time out, in particular Maruja, who had to lean against the walls to keep from falling. With the help of the guards, and sometimes Damaris, they grew accustomed to the exercise. At the end of two weeks, Maruja was able to circle the yard up to a thousand times—two kilometers—at a quick pace. Their spirits rose, and this in turn improved domestic tranquillity.

The courtyard was the only part of the house they saw except for their room. They took their walks in the dark, but on moonlit nights they could make out a large laundry area half in ruins, clothes hung out to dry on lines, and a great jumble of broken packing cases and worn-out household articles. Above the canopy over the laundry, there was a second story with a sealed window, its streaked panes curtained by sheets of newspaper. The hostages thought it must be where the guards slept when they were not on duty. There was a door to the kitchen, another to the room where the prisoners were kept, and a gate made of old boards that did not reach all the way to the ground. It was the gate out to the world.

Later they would learn that it led to a quiet pen where Easter lambs and a few hens were kept. It seemed very simple to open it and get away, but it was guarded by a German shepherd that looked incorruptible. Still, Maruja became his friend, and at a certain point he stopped barking when she came close to pet him.

AFTER AZUCENA'S RELEASE, Diana was alone. She watched television, listened to the radio, at times she read the papers with more interest than ever, but knowing the news and not having anyone to discuss it with was almost worse than not knowing anything at all. She thought the guards treated her with decency, and she recognized their efforts to accommodate her. "I don't want, and it isn't easy, to describe what I feel at each moment: the pain, the anguish, the terrifying days I've experienced," she wrote in her diary. She feared for her life, in fact, in particular because she dreaded an armed rescue attempt. The possibility of her release was reduced to a single, insidious phrase: "Pretty soon, now." She was terrified at the idea that this was a delaying tactic, a way of waiting for the Constituent Assembly to convene and reach concrete decisions on extradition and amnesty. Don Pacho, who used to spend long hours with her discussing various matters and keeping her well informed, grew more and more distant. With no explanation, they stopped bringing her the papers. The news, even the soap operas on television, acquired the slow pace of a country brought to a standstill by the New Year's holiday exodus.

For over a month they had distracted her with the promise that she would meet Pablo Escobar in person. She rehearsed her attitude, her arguments, her tone, sure she would be able to open a negotiation with him. But the eternal delay had brought her to inconceivable depths of pessimism.

In this horror, her tutelary image was that of her mother, from whom she inherited, perhaps, her passionate nature, unshakable faith, and elusive dream of happiness. They had a gift for communicating with each other that appeared, like a clairvoyant miracle, during the dark months of captivity. Each word uttered by Nydia on radio or television, each of her gestures, the most casual emphasis, conveyed volumes to Diana's imagination in the dark days of her confinement. "I have always felt she was my guardian angel," she wrote. She was sure that in the midst of so many frustrations the final victory would belong to her mother's devotion and strength. Encouraged by this certainty, she conceived the illusion of a Christmas night release.

That illusion kept her in a state of anticipation during the party that the owners of the house had for her on Christmas Eve, complete with barbecued meat, salsa records, liquor, fireworks, and colored lights. Diana interpreted this as a going-away party. Even more: she had her bag—prepared in November so as not to lose any time when they came for her—ready on the bed. The night was freezing and the wind howled through the trees like a pack of wolves, but she interpreted this as an omen of better times. While they gave gifts to the children, she thought about her own, and consoled herself with the hope that she would be with them the following night. The dream became less improbable when her jailers presented her with a lined leather jacket, chosen perhaps to keep her warm in this foul weather. She was certain her mother had supper waiting for her, as she did every year, and had hung the wreath of mistletoe on the door with a message for her: *Welcome*. Diana was so sure of her release that she waited until the final holiday lights were turned off in the distance, and another morning dawned, full of uncertainties.

The following Wednesday she was sitting alone in front of the television, changing channels, and all at once she saw Alexandra's little boy on the screen. It was a Christmas show put on by "Enfoque." Her surprise increased when she realized it was the Christmas Eve she had requested of her mother in the letter delivered by Azucena. Maruja's and Beatriz's family were there, and all of the Turbays: Diana's two children, her brothers and sisters, and her tall, morose father in the center. "We were in no frame of mind for celebrations," Nydia has said. "Still, I decided to give Diana her wish, and in one hour I set up the Christmas tree and the crèche by the fireplace." In spite of everyone's best intentions not to leave the hostages with a sad impression, it was more a mourning rite than a celebration. But Nydia was so sure Diana would be released that night that she hung the Christmas decoration on the door with the sign in gold letters: *Welcome.* "I confess my sorrow at not being there, not sharing the day with all of them," Diana wrote in her journal. "But it cheered me so, I felt very close to everyone, it made me happy to see them all together." She was delighted by how María Carolina had grown, concerned about Miguelito's shyness, and recalled with alarm that he was not yet baptized; her father's sadness made her sad, and she was moved by her mother, who had put a gift for her in the crèche and hung a welcome on the door.

Instead of feeling demoralized by the disillusionment of Christmas, Diana's reaction was to turn against the government. At one time she had shown a certain enthusiasm for Decree 2047, the basis for the illusions of November. She was encouraged by the efforts of Guido Parra, the diligence of the Notables, the expectations for the Constituent Assembly, the possibilities for amendments to the capitulation policy. But her frustration at Christmas overflowed the dikes of her understanding. She was appalled when she asked herself why the government could not even conceive of a dialogue that was not determined by the absurd pressure of the abductions. She made it clear that she was well aware of how difficult it was to act under threat of blackmail. "I'm pure Turbay as far as that's concerned," she wrote, "but I believe that as time has passed, things have moved backwards." She could not understand the government's passivity in the face of what she considered deception by the abductors. She could not understand why the government was not more energetic in pursuing their surrender if it had established a policy and satisfied some of their reasonable requests. "As long as that is not demanded of them," she wrote in her journal, "they will feel more comfortable about taking their time, knowing they have in their power the most important weapon for exerting pressure on the government." It seemed to her that good offices and mediation had turned into a chess game in which the players moved their men around until somebody declared a checkmate. "But which piece am I?" she asked herself. And answered the question without any evasions: "I can't help thinking we're all dispensable." As for the Notables—now extinct—she gave the group her coup de grâce: "They started out with an eminently humanitarian mission and ended up doing a favor for the Extraditables."

ONE OF THE GUARDS finishing his tour of duty in January burst into Pacho Santos's room.

"It's all fucked up," he said. "They're going to kill hostages."

According to him, this was in retaliation for the death of the Priscos, Escobar's close associates. The communiqué was ready and would be released in the next few hours. First they would kill Marina Montoya, and then one hostage every three days in this order: Richard Becerra, Beatriz, Maruja, and Diana.

"You'll be the last," the guard concluded by way of consolation. "But don't worry, this government can't stomach more than two dead bodies."

Pacho made his terrified calculations based on the guard's information: He had eighteen more days to live. Then he decided to write to his wife and children, and with no rough draft he composed a letter that filled six full-size sheets of notebook paper, printing the words in lowercase letters as he always did, but these were more legible than usual, and his hand was steady though he knew this was not only a letter of farewell, but also his will and testament.

"My only wish is for this drama to end as soon as possible, regardless of the outcome, so that we may all have some peace at last," it began. He was profoundly grateful, he said, to María Victoria, with whom he had grown as a man, as a citizen, and as a father, and his only regret was having given greater importance to his work as a journalist than to his life at home. "I take this remorse with me to the grave," he wrote. As for his children, who were still babies, he was reassured by the certainty that he was leaving them in the best hands. "Tell them about me when they can understand what happened and accept with some equanimity the needless pain of my death." He thanked his father for all that he had done for him in his life, and asked him only "to take care of everything before you come to join me so my children can receive their inheritance without major difficulties." In this way he led into a subject that he considered "boring but fundamental" for the future: financial security for his children and family unity within *El Tiempo*. The first depended in large part on the life insurance the paper had purchased for his wife and children. "I ask you to demand what they promised," he said, "because it would not be fair if my sacrifices for the paper proved to be completely useless." As for the professional, commercial, or political future of the paper, his only concerns were its internal rivalries and disagreements, though he knew that in great families discord is never trivial. "It would be very sad, after this sacrifice, if *El Tiempo* were broken up or sold to outsiders." The letter closed with final words of gratitude to Mariavé for the memory of the good times they had shared.

The guard was moved when Pacho handed it to him.

"Don't you worry, man," he said, "I'll make sure it gets there."

The truth was that Pacho Santos did not have the eighteen days he had calculated but just a few hours. He was first on the list, and the killing had been ordered the day before. Fortunately, Martha Nieves Ochoa happened to hear about it—from third parties—at the eleventh hour and sent Escobar a plea for a reprieve, convinced that this killing would leave the country in ruins. She never knew if he received it, but the fact was that the order to kill Pacho Santos was not carried out, and in its place a second, irrevocable order was issued against Marina Montoya.

Marina seemed to have foreseen this early in January. For reasons she never explained, she decided to take her exercise in the company of her old friend the Monk, who had returned with the year's first change of guard. They would walk for an hour after the television programs went off the air, and then Maruja and Beatriz would go out with their guards. One night Marina came in very frightened because she had seen a man dressed in black, wearing a black mask, watching her in the dark from the laundry area. Maruja and Beatriz thought it had to be another of her recurrent hallucinations, and they paid no attention to it. Their impression was confirmed that same night, because there was not enough light to see a man in black standing in the darkness of the laundry. And if by some chance it were true, he had to be someone well known in the house because the German shepherd did not raise the alarm, and the dog barked at its own shadow. The Monk said it must have been a ghost that only she could see.

Two or three nights later, however, she came back from her walk in a real state of panic. The man had returned, still dressed all in black, and with frightening attention had watched her for a long time, not caring that she was looking at him too. On this night, in contrast to the previous occasions, there was a full moon illuminating the courtyard with an eerie green light. Marina told her story in front of the Monk, and he denied it, but with such tangled reasoning that Maruja and Beatriz did not know what to believe. Marina stopped going out for walks. The doubts regarding her fantasies and reality made so strong an impression that Maruja experienced a real hallucination when she opened her eyes one night and saw the Monk in the light of the bedside candle, squatting as always, his mask turned into a skull. The effect on Maruja was even greater because she connected the vision to the anniversary of her mother's death on January 23.

Marina spent the weekend in bed, suffering from an old back pain that she thought had been cured long ago. Her dark mood returned. Because she could do nothing for herself, Maruja and Beatriz did everything for her. They almost had to carry her to the bathroom. They fed her and held the glass for her, and arranged a pillow behind her back so she could watch television from bed. They pampered her, and felt real affection for her, but never had they felt so despised.

"Look how sick I am and you two won't even help me," Marina would say. "And I've done so much for you."

Often she only succeeded in deepening the sense of abandonment that tormented her. Marina's only real solace during that final crisis were the furious prayers she murmured without letup for hours on end, and the care of her nails. After several days, weary of everything, she lay prostrate on her bed and whispered with a sigh:

"All right, it's in God's hands now."

On the afternoon of January 22, they were visited by the "Doctor" who had been there during the first few days of captivity. He spoke in secret to the guards and listened with great attention to Maruja's and Beatriz's comments on Marina's health. At last he sat down on the edge of the bed to talk to her. The topic must have been serious and confidential because their whispers were so faint no one could make out a word. The "Doctor" left the room in a better humor than when he came in, and promised to return soon.

Marina remained in bed in a state of utter dejection. She cried from time to time. Maruja attempted to comfort her, and Marina thanked her with gestures so as not to interrupt her prayers, and almost always responded with affection, squeezing Maruja's hand with her stiff, ice-cold one. She treated Beatriz, with whom she had a warmer relationship, with the same affection. The only habit that kept her alive was filing her nails.

At ten-thirty on the night of Wednesday, January 23, they began to watch "Enfoque," eager for any unusual word, familiar joke, casual gesture, or subtle changes in the lyrics of a song that might contain a coded message. But there was no time. Just as the theme music began, the door opened at this unusual hour and the Monk came in, though he was not on duty that night.

"We came to take Granny to another house," he said.

He said it as if it were a Sunday outing. In her bed, Marina looked like a marble carving, with her hair disheveled and a pallor so intense that even her lips were white. Then the Monk spoke to her in the affectionate tones of a grandson.

"Get your things together, Granny," he said. "You have five minutes."

He tried to help her up. Marina opened her mouth to say something, but no sound came out. She stood without help, picked up the bag that held her personal effects, and went to the bathroom with the light step of a sleepwalker who does not seem to touch the ground. Maruja confronted the Monk, her voice steady.

"Are you going to kill her?"

The Monk bristled.

"You can't ask a thing like that!" he said. But he regained his composure right away and said: "I told you she's going to a better house. I swear."

Maruja tried everything to stop them from taking her away. Because no boss was there, which was very unusual in so important a decision, she told them to call one for her so that they could discuss it. But the dispute was interrupted when another guard came in to take away the radio and television. He disconnected them with no further explanation, and the last traces of the New Year's Eve party vanished from the room. Maruja asked them to at least let them see the end of the program. Beatriz's response was even more aggressive, but it did no good. They took the radio and television and said they would be back for Marina in five minutes. Maruja and Beatriz, alone in the room, did not know what to believe, or whom, or to what extent this inscrutable decision played a part in their own destinies.

Marina spent much more than five minutes in the bathroom. She came back wearing the pink sweatsuit, the maroon men's socks, and the shoes she had worn on the day of her abduction. The sweatsuit was clean and freshly ironed. The shoes were mildewed and seemed too big, because her feet had shrunk two sizes in four months of suffering. Marina looked ashen and gleaming with icy perspiration, but she still held on to a shred of hope.

"Who knows, maybe they're going to release me!" she said.

Without arranging it ahead of time, Maruja and Beatriz each decided that, regardless of Marina's fate, the most Christian thing was to deceive her.

"Of course they are," said Beatriz.

"That's right," said Maruja with her first radiant smile. "How wonderful!"

Marina's reaction was surprising. In a half-joking, half-serious way she asked what messages they wanted to send to their families. They did their best to improvise something. Marina, laughing at herself a little, asked Beatriz to lend her some of the aftershave that Spots had given her on New Year's Eve. Beatriz did, and Marina dabbed it behind her ears with innate elegance, arranged her beautiful snow-white hair without a mirror, touching it lightly with her fingertips, and when she was finished seemed ready to be free and happy.

In reality she was on the verge of fainting. She asked Maruja for a cigarette and sat on the bed to smoke it until they came for her. She smoked slowly, in great, anguished mouthfuls, while she looked over every millimeter of that hole where she had not found a moment's pity, and where at the end they did not even grant her the dignity of dying in her bed.

Beatriz, to keep from crying, repeated with absolute gravity the message for her family: "If you have a chance to see my husband and children, tell them I'm well and love them very much." But Marina was no longer of this world.

"Don't ask me to do that," she replied, not even looking at her. "I know I'll never have the chance."

Maruja brought her a glass of water with two of the barbiturates that could have put her to sleep for three days. She had to hold the glass for her while she drank because Marina's hands were trembling so much she could not raise it to her lips. That was when Maruja looked deep into her brilliant eyes and realized that Marina was deceiving no one, not even herself. She knew very well who she was, how much she was worth to her captors, and where they were taking her, and if she had followed the lead of the last friends left to her in life, it had been out of compassion.

They brought her a new hood of pink wool that matched her sweatsuit. Before they put it over her head, she said goodbye to Maruja with a hug and a kiss. Maruja blessed her and said, "Don't worry." She said goodbye to Beatriz with another hug and kiss and said: "God bless you." Beatriz, true to herself to the end, kept up the illusion.

"How marvelous, you'll be seeing your family," she said.

Marina turned to the guards without a tear. They turned the hood around, with the openings for the eyes and mouth at the back of her head so she could not see anything. The Monk took both her hands and led her out of the house, walking backward. Marina followed with unfaltering steps. The other guard locked the door from the outside.

Maruja and Beatriz stood motionless in front of the closed door, not knowing how to take up their lives again, until they heard the engines in the garage and then the sound fading away in the distance. Only then did they realize that the television and radio had been taken away to keep them from knowing how the night would end.

6

AT DAWN THE NEXT DAY, Thursday, January 24, the body of Marina Montoya was found in an empty lot north of Bogotá. Almost sitting upright in grass still damp from an early rain, she was leaning against the barbed-wire fence, her arms extended. Criminal Investigation magistrate 78, who examined the body, described her as a woman of about sixty with abundant white hair, dressed in a pink sweatsuit and a pair of maroon men's socks. Beneath the sweatsuit she wore a scapular with a plastic cross. Someone who had arrived on the scene before the police had stolen her shoes.

The head of the corpse was covered by a hood, stiff with dried blood, that had been put on with the openings for the mouth and eyes at the back of the head, and it was almost in tatters because of the entrance and exit holes of six bullets fired from a distance of more than fifty centimeters, since they had left no powder burns on the cloth and skin. The bullet holes were distributed over the skull and the left side of the face, and there was one very clean hole, like a coup de grâce, in the forehead. However, only five 9mm shells were found near the body soaked by wet grasses, and the technical unit of the investigative police had already taken five sets of fingerprints.

Some students from the San Carlos secondary school across the street from the lot had gathered there with other curious on-lookers. Among those who watched the examination of the body was a flower-seller at the Northern Cemetery who had gotten up early to enroll her daughter in a nearby school. The body made a strong impression on her because of the fine quality of the dead woman's underwear, her beautiful, well-tended hands, and her obvious distinction despite her bullet-riddled face. That after-noon, the wholesaler who supplied the flower-seller at her stand in the Northern Cemetery—some five kilometers away—found her suffering from a severe headache and in an alarming state of depression.

"You can't imagine how sad it was to see that poor lady just thrown onto the grass," the flower-seller told her. "You should have seen her underwear, she looked like a great lady with her white hair, her fine hands, her beautiful nails."

The wholesaler was concerned about her and gave her an anal-gesic for her headache, advised her not to think sad thoughts, and above all not to take other people's problems to heart. Neither of them realized until a week later that they had been involved in an unbelievable event: The wholesaler was Marta de Pérez, the wife of Marina's son, Luis Guillermo Pérez.

The Institute of Forensic Medicine received the corpse at five-thirty on Thursday afternoon and left it in storage until the next day because bodies with more than one bullet hole are not autop-sied at night. Two other corpses, males picked up on the streets that morning, were also awaiting identification and a postmortem. During the night two more adult males, also discovered outdoors, were brought in, as well as the body of a five-year-old boy.

Dr. Patricia Alvarez, who began the autopsy of Marina Mon-toya at seven-thirty Friday morning, found the remains of recog-nizable food in her stomach and concluded that death had occurred very late Thursday night. She too was impressed by the quality of the underwear and the buffed and polished nails. She called to her supervisor, Dr. Pedro Morales, who was performing another autopsy two tables away, and he helped her find other un-equivocal signs of the dead woman's social position. They took a dental impression, photographs, X rays, and three more sets of fingerprints. Finally they did an atomic absorption test and dis-covered no trace of psychopharmacologicals despite the two barbiturates that Maruja Pachón had given Marina a few hours be-fore her death.

When they had completed the essential procedures, they sent the body to the Southern Cemetery, where three weeks earlier a mass grave had been dug for two hundred corpses. She was buried there along with the four unidentified males and the boy.

IT WAS EVIDENT during that savage January that Colombia had reached the worst circumstances imaginable. Since 1984, when Minister Rodrigo Lara Bonilla had been assassinated, we had experienced all kinds of abominable acts, but it was not over yet, and the worst was not behind us. All the elements of violence had been unleashed and exacerbated.

Among the many atrocities that had convulsed the country, narcoterrorism stood out as the most virulent and cruel. Four presidential candidates had been assassinated before the 1990 campaign. Carlos Pizarro, the M-19 candidate, was killed by a lone assassin on a commercial plane, even though his flight reser-vations had been changed four times, in absolute secrecy and with every kind of misleading subterfuge. Ernesto Samper, a pre-candidate, survived eleven bullets and reached the presidency five years later with four of them still in his body; they set off airport security alarms. A car bomb made with 350 kilos of dynamite ex-ploded in the path of General Maza Márquez, and he had escaped from his lightly armored automobile, pulling out one of his wounded bodyguards. "All at once I felt as if I had been tossed into the air by the surf," the general commented. The upheaval was so great that he needed psychiatric help to regain his emotional equilibrium. He was still in treatment seven months later, when a truck carrying two tons of dynamite destroyed the huge Administrative Department for Security building in an apocalyptic explosion that left 70 dead, 620 wounded, and incalculable physical destruction. The terrorists had waited for the precise moment when the general walked into his office, but in the midst of the cataclysm he was not even scratched. That same year, a bomb exploded aboard a passenger plane five minutes after takeoff, causing 107 deaths, among them Andrés Escabí—Pacho Santos's brother-in-law—and Gerardo Arellano, the Colombian tenor. The accepted version of events was that the intended victim had been the candidate César Gaviria—a sinister mistake, since Gaviria never intended to take that flight. His campaign security services had forbidden him to use commercial planes, and on one occasion when he made the attempt he had to stop because the other passengers panicked and tried to get off to avoid the danger of flying with him.

The truth was that the country was trapped in a vicious circle. On one hand, the Extraditables refused to surrender or temper the violence because the police gave them no quarter. Escobar had denounced in all the media the fact that the police would go into the Medellín slums at any hour of the day or night, pick up ten boys at random, ask no questions, and shoot them in basements or empty lots. Their blanket assumption was that most of the boys were working for Pablo Escobar, or supported him, or soon would do one or the other, either by choice or through coercion. On the other hand, the terrorists were relentless in their murder of ambushed police, their assaults and abductions. And for their part, the two oldest and strongest guerrilla movements, the Army of National Liberation (ELN) and the Revolutionary Armed Forces

(FARC), had just responded with all kinds of terrorist acts to the first peace proposal offered by the government of César Gaviria.

One of the groups most affected by the blind warfare were journalists, the victims of assassinations and abductions, and also of desertions because of threats and corruption. Between September 1983 and January 1991, twenty-six journalists working in various Colombian media were murdered by the drug cartels. Guillermo Cano, director of *El Espectador*, and the gentlest of men, was killed on December 17, 1986, by two gunmen who followed him to the door of his newspaper. He drove his own van, and although he was one of the most threatened men in the country because of his suicidal editorials attacking the drug trade, he refused to use a bulletproof car or travel with a bodyguard. His enemies even tried to go on killing him after his death. A bust erected in his memory was dynamited in Medellín. Months later, a truck carrying three hundred kilos of dynamite exploded, reducing the paper's presses to rubble.

Easy money, a narcotic more harmful than the ill-named "heroic drugs," was injected into the national culture. The idea prospered: The law is the greatest obstacle to happiness; it is a waste of time learning to read and write; you can live a better, more secure life as a criminal than as a law-abiding citizen—in short, this was the social breakdown typical of all undeclared wars.

Abduction was not a new element in recent Colombian history. None of the four preceding presidents had escaped the destabilizing trials of an abduction. And certainly, as far as anyone knows, none had given in to the demands of the kidnappers. In February 1976, during the government of Alfonso López Michelsen, the M-19 had kidnapped José Raquel Mercado, the president of the Federation of Colombian Workers. He was tried and condemned to death by his captors as a traitor to the working class, and executed with two bullets in the back of the head when the government refused to comply with a series of political demands.

Sixteen elite members of the same armed movement took over the embassy of the Dominican Republic in Bogotá as they were celebrating their national holiday on February 27, 1980, during the presidency of Julio César Turbay. For sixty-one days almost the entire accredited diplomatic corps in Colombia, including the ambassadors of the United States, Israel, and the Vatican, were held hostage. The M-19 demanded a fifty-million-dollar ransom and the release of 311 of their members who were in prison. President Turbay refused to negotiate, but the hostages were freed on April 28 with no expressed conditions, and their abductors left the country under the protection of the Cuban government, which had responded to a request by the Colombian government. The guerrillas stated in private that they had received a ransom of five million dollars in cash collected by the Jewish community in Colombia with the help of other Jews throughout the world.

On November 6, 1985, a commando unit of the M-19 took over the crowded Supreme Court building at the busiest time of day and demanded that the highest court in the nation put President Belisario Betancur on trial for not having kept his promise to establish peace. The president did not negotiate, and the army stormed the building and recaptured it after ten hours of bloody fighting that cost an unknown number of missing and ninety-five civilian deaths, including nine magistrates of the Supreme Court and its president, Alfonso Reyes Echandía.

President Virgilio Barco, who was almost at the end of his term, did not resolve the abduction of Alvaro Diego Montoya, the son of his secretary general. Seven months later, Pablo Escobar's rage blew up in the face of Barco's successor, César Gaviria, who began his presidency facing the grave crisis of ten well-known hostages.

In his first five months, however, Gaviria had created a less turbulent atmosphere for weathering the storm. He had achieved a political agreement to convene a Constituent Assembly, invested by the Supreme Court with unlimited power to decide any issue—including, of course, the hottest ones: the extradition of Colombian nationals, and amnesty. But the underlying problem, for the government as well as the drug traffickers and the guerrillas, was that as long as Colombia did not have an effective judicial system, it was almost impossible to articulate a policy for peace that would position the state on the side of good, and criminals of any stripe on the side of evil. But nothing was simple in those days, least of all obtaining objective information from any quarter, or teaching children the difference between good and evil.

The government's credibility was not at the high level of its notable political successes but at the abysmal level of its security forces, which were censured in the world press and by international human rights organizations. Pablo Escobar, however, had achieved a credibility that the guerrillas never enjoyed in their best times. People tended to believe the lies of the Extraditables more than the truths told by the government.

DECREE 3030 was issued on December 14, 1990, modifying 2047 and nullifying all previous decrees. Among other innovations, it introduced the judicial accumulation of sentences; that is, a person tried for several crimes, whether in the same trial or in subsequent ones, would not serve the total time of the various sentences, but only the longest one. It also established a series of procedures and time limits relating to the use of evidence from other countries in trials held in Colombia. But the two great obstacles to surrender were still firmly in place: the somewhat uncertain conditions for non-extradition, and the fixed time limit on pardonable crimes. In other words, capitulation and confession remained the indispensable requirements for non-extradition and reduced sentences, as long as the crimes had been committed before September 5, 1990. Pablo Escobar objected in an angry message. His reaction this time had another motivation he was careful not to reveal in public: the accelerated exchange of evidence with the United States that facilitated extradition hearings.

Alberto Villamizar was the most surprised of men. His daily contacts with Rafael Pardo had led him to expect a more lenient decree, but this one seemed harsher than the first. And he was not alone in his response. Criticism was so widespread that on the same day the second degree was issued, a third one began to be considered.

An easy conjecture as to the reasons for the greater severity of Decree 3030 was that the more radical sector of the government—in reaction to a campaign of conciliatory communiqués and the gratuitous release of four journalists—had convinced the president that Escobar was cornered. In fact, he had never been stronger than he was then, with the tremendous pressure of the abductions and the possibility that the Constituent Assembly would abolish extradition and proclaim an amnesty.

The three Ochoa brothers, on the other hand, took immediate refuge in the capitulation option. This was interpreted as a rupture at the top of the cartel. In reality, however, the process of their surrender had begun in September, at the time of the first decree, when a well-known senator from Antioquia asked Rafael Pardo to see a person he would not identify ahead of time. It was Martha Nieves Ochoa, who with this bold step initiated negotiations for the surrender of each of her three brothers, at one-month intervals. And that is how it happened. Fabio, the youngest, turned himself in on December 18; on January 15, when it seemed least feasible, Jorge Luis surrendered, as did Juan David on February 16. Five years later, a group of reporters from the United States put the question to Jorge Luis in prison, and his reply was categorical: "We surrendered to save our skins." He acknowledged that behind it lay irresistible pressure from the women in his family, who would not rest until their brothers were safe inside the fortified prison in Itagüí, an industrial suburb of Medellín. It was an act of familial confidence in the government, which at the time could still have extradited them to serve life sentences in the United States.

DOÑA NYDIA QUINTERO, always mindful of her premonitions, did not discount the importance of the Ochoas' surrender. Less than three days after Fabio turned himself in, she went to see him in prison, accompanied by her daughter María Victoria, and María Carolina, Diana's daughter. Faithful to the tribal protocol of Medellín, five members of the Ochoa family had come for her at the house where she was staying: the mother, Martha Nieves and one of her sisters, and two young men. They took her to Itagüí prison, a forbidding structure at the top of a narrow, hilly street decorated with colored-paper wreaths for Christmas.

Waiting for them in the prison cell, in addition to the younger Fabio, was the father, don Fabio Ochoa, a patriarch weighing 330 pounds with the face of a boy, who at the age of seventy bred fine-gaited Colombian horses and was the spiritual head of a vast family of intrepid men and powerful women. He liked to preside over family visits sitting in a thronelike chair and wearing his perpetual horseman's hat with a ceremonious air that suited his slow, determined speech and folk wisdom. Beside him was his son, who is lively and talkative but barely uttered a word that day while his father was speaking.

Don Fabio began by praising the courage with which Nydia had moved heaven and earth to rescue Diana. He formulated the possibility of his intervening with Pablo Escobar on her behalf with masterful rhetoric: He would, with the greatest pleasure, do whatever he could, but he did not believe he could do anything. At the end of the visit, the younger Fabio asked Nydia to please explain to the president the importance of extending the time limit for surrender in the capitulation decree. Nydia said she could not do it but they could, with a letter to the appropriate authorities. It was her way of not permitting them to use her as their messenger to the president. The younger Fabio understood this, and said goodbye with the comforting phrase: "Where there's life, there's hope."

When Nydia returned to Bogotá, Azucena gave her the letter in which Diana asked that she celebrate Christmas with her children, and Hero Buss telephoned, urging her to come to Cartagena so that they could talk in person. She found him in good physical and emotional condition after three months of captivity, and that helped to reassure Nydia somewhat about her daughter's health. Hero Buss had not seen Diana after the first week, but there had been a constant exchange of news among the guards and the people who ran the houses, which filtered down to the hostages, and he knew that Diana was well. The only serious and ongoing danger was an armed rescue. "You cannot imagine the constant threat that they'll kill you," said Hero Buss. "Not only because the law, as they call it, is there, but because they're always so edgy they think the tiniest noise is a rescue operation." His only advice to her was to prevent an armed rescue at any cost, and to persuade the government to change the time limit on surrender in the decree.

On the same day she returned to Bogotá, Nydia expressed her forebodings to the justice minister. She visited the defense minister, General Oscar Botero, accompanied by her son, the parliamentarian Julio César Turbay Quintero, and her anguished plea, on behalf of all the hostages, was that they use intelligence agencies rather than rescue teams. Her disquiet was accelerating, the premonition of tragedy becoming more and more acute. Her heart was breaking. She wept constantly. Nydia made a supreme effort to regain her self-control, but bad news gave her no peace. On the radio she heard a message from the Extraditables, threatening to dump the captives' bodies, in sacks, outside the presidential palace if the terms of the second decree were not modified. In mortal despair, Nydia called the president. He was at a meeting of the Council on Security, and she spoke to Rafael Pardo.

"I implore you to ask the president and the members of the Council on Security if they need to find bags of dead hostages at their door before they change the decree."

She was in the same agitated state hours later, when she asked the president in person to change the time limit in the decree. He had already heard that Nydia was complaining about his insensitivity to other people's grief, and he made an effort to be more patient and forthcoming. He said that Decree 3030 had just been issued, and the least they could do was give it enough time to work. But Nydia thought the president's arguments were no more than rationalizations for not doing what he should have done at the opportune moment.

"A change in the deadline is necessary not only to save the lives of the hostages," Nydia replied, tired of so much talk, "but it's the one thing that will make the terrorists surrender. Change it, and they'll let Diana go."

Gaviria did not yield. Convinced that the time limit was the greatest obstacle to the capitulation policy, he resisted changing it in order to keep the Extraditables from getting what they were after when they took the hostages. The Constituent Assembly, shrouded in uncertainties, would meet in the next few days, and he could not allow weakness on the part of the government to result in an amnesty for the drug traffickers. "Democracy was never endangered by the assassinations of four presidential candidates, or because of any abduction," Gaviria would later comment. "The real threat came at those moments when we faced the temptation, or risk, or even the rumor of a possibility of an amnesty"—in short, the unthinkable danger that the conscience of the Constituent Assembly would also be taken hostage. Gaviria already knew what he would do: If that happened, his calm, irrevocable decision was to dissolve the Assembly.

For some time Nydia had been thinking that Dr. Turbay should do something for the captives that would shake the entire country: a mass demonstration outside the presidential palace, a general strike, a formal protest to the United Nations. But Dr. Turbay tried to mollify her. "He was always that way, because he was responsible and moderate," Nydia has said. "But you knew that inside he was dying of grief." That certainty, rather than soothing her, only intensified her anguish. This was when she decided to write a private letter to the president "that would move him to take the action he knew was necessary."

Dr. Gustavo Balcázar, Nydia's husband, was worried about her, and on January 24 he persuaded his wife to spend a few days with him in their house in Tabio—an hour's drive from the city, on the Bogotá savanna—to try to alleviate her despair. She had not been there since her daughter had been abducted, and so she brought her statue of the Virgin, and two large fifteen-day candles, and everything she needed to stay connected to reality. In the icy solitude of the savanna, she spent an interminable night on her knees, praying to the Virgin to protect Diana with an invulnerable bell jar that would shield her from abuse and fear, and not let bullets touch her. At five in the morning, after a brief, troubled sleep, she sat at the dining-room table and began to write the letter from her soul to the president of the republic. Dawn found her scrawling random ideas, crying, tearing up drafts as she wept, making clean copies in a sea of tears.

In contrast to her own expectations, she was writing the most judicious and forceful letter of her life. "I don't pretend to be composing a public document," it began. "I want to communicate with the president of my country and, with all due respect, convey to him my most considered thoughts, and a justifiably anguished plea." Despite the president's repeated promise that no armed effort to rescue Diana would ever be attempted, Nydia left written evidence of a prescient appeal: "The country knows, and all of you know, that if they happen to find the kidnappers during one of those searches, a terrible tragedy might ensue." Convinced that the obstacles present in the second decree had interrupted the process of releasing hostages begun by the Extraditables before Christmas, Nydia alerted the president to a new, self-evident danger: If the government did not take some immediate action to remove those obstacles, the hostages risked having the issue left in the hands of the Constituent Assembly. "This would mean that the distress and anguish suffered not only by the families but by the entire nation would be prolonged for endless months," she wrote. Nydia ended with an elegant closing: "Because of my convictions, because of the respect I have for you as First Magistrate of the Nation, I would be incapable of suggesting any initiative of my own devising, but I do feel inclined to entreat you, for the sake of innocent lives, not to underestimate the danger that time represents." When it was finished and copied out in a fair hand, it came to two and a quarter full-size sheets. Nydia called the president's private secretary to find out exactly where it should be sent.

That same morning the storm broke with the news that the leaders of the Prisco gang had been killed: David Ricardo and Armando Alberto Prisco Lopera, the brothers accused of the seven assassinations of public figures during this time, and of being the brains behind the abductions, including the capture of Diana Turbay and her crew. One had died carrying false papers that identified him as Francisco Muñoz Serna, but when Azucena Liévano saw the photograph in the papers she recognized don Pacho, the man responsible for her and Diana in their captivity. His death and his brother's, at that turbulent moment, were an irreparable loss for Escobar, and he would not wait long to make that known by actions.

In a threatening communiqué, the Extraditables said that David Ricardo had not been killed in combat but cut down by the police in front of his young children and pregnant wife. As for his brother Armando, the communiqué insisted he had not been killed in a gunfight, as the police claimed, but murdered on a farm in Rionegro even though he was paralyzed as the result of an earlier attempt on his life. His wheelchair, the message said, could be seen clearly on the regional newscast.

This was the communiqué that had been mentioned to Pacho Santos. It was made public on January 25 with the announcement that two captives would be executed within a week's time, and that the first order had already been issued against Marina Montoya— a stunning piece of news, since it was assumed that Marina had been murdered at the time of her abduction in September.

"That's what I was referring to when I sent the president the message about the bodies in sacks," Nydia has said, recalling that ghastly day. "It's not that I was impulsive, or temperamental, or in need of psychiatric care. But they were going to kill my daughter because I might not be able to move the people who could stop it."

Alberto Villamizar was no less desperate. "That was the most horrible day of my life," he said at the time, convinced that the executions would not be long in coming. Who would be first: Diana, Pacho, Maruja, Beatriz, Richard? It was a deadly lottery he did not even want to imagine. He called President Gaviria in a rage.

"You have to stop these raids," he said.

"No, Alberto," Gaviria responded with his blood-chilling calm. "That isn't why I was elected."

Villamizar slammed down the phone, astonished at his own vehemence. "Now what do I do?" he asked himself. To begin with, he requested help from former presidents Alfonso López Michelsen and Misael Pastrana, and Monsignor Darío Castrillón, the bishop of Pereira. They all made public statements repudiating the methods used by the Extraditables and pleading for the lives of the captives. On the National Radio Network López Michelsen called for the government and Escobar to stop the war and search for a political solution.

AT THAT MOMENT the tragedy had already occurred. Minutes before dawn on January 21, Diana had written the last page of her diary. "It's close to five months, and only we know what this means," she wrote. "I don't want to lose the faith or the hope that I'll go home safe and sound."

She was no longer alone. Following the release of Azucena and Orlando, she had asked to be with Richard, and her request was granted after Christmas. It was good for both of them. They talked until they were exhausted, listened to the radio until dawn, and in this way acquired the habit of sleeping by day and living at night. They had learned about the death of the Priscos from the guards' conversation. One guard was crying. The other, certain this meant the end and no doubt referring to the hostages, asked: "And what do we do now with the merchandise?" The one who was crying did not have to give it a second thought.

"We'll get rid of it," he said.

Diana and Richard could not sleep after breakfast. Days earlier they had been told they would be changing houses. They had not paid much attention, since in the brief month they had been together they had been moved twice to nearby safe houses in anticipation of real or imaginary police raids. A little before eleven on the morning of January 25, they were in Diana's room discussing the guards' conversation in whispers, when they heard the sound of helicopters coming from Medellín.

In recent days police intelligence agencies had received numerous anonymous phone calls reporting the movement of armed people along the Sabaneta road—municipality of Copacabana—in particular around the farms of Alto de la Cruz, Villa del Rosario, and La Bola. Perhaps their captors planned to transfer Diana and Richard to Alto de la Cruz, the most secure of the properties because it was located at the top of a high, wooded hill and had a commanding view of the entire valley all the way to Medellín. As a result of the calls, and other leads of their own, the police were about to raid the house. It was a major military operation involving two captains, nine officers, seven noncommissioned officers, and ninety-nine agents, half of them traveling overland and half in four combat helicopters. The guards, however, no longer paid attention to helicopters because they flew over so often and nothing ever happened. Suddenly one of them was at the door and shouted at them in fright:

"The law's all over us!"

Diana and Richard took as long as they could because this was the right time for a police assault: The four guards on duty were not the toughest ones, and seemed too panicked to defend themselves. Diana brushed her teeth and put on a white shirt she had washed the day before; she put on her sneakers and the jeans she had been wearing the day she was kidnapped, too big for her now because she had lost weight. Richard changed his shirt and gathered up the camera equipment that had been returned to him in the past few days. The guards seemed crazed by the growing noise of the helicopters that flew over the house, went back toward the valley, and returned almost grazing the treetops. The guards shouted for them to hurry and pushed the hostages toward the outside door. They gave them white hats so they would look like campesinos from the air. They threw a black shawl over Diana, and Richard put on his leather jacket. The guards ordered them to run for the mountain, while they spread out and ran too, their weapons ready to fire when the helicopters were within range. Diana and Richard began to climb a narrow, rocky path. The slope was very steep, and the hot sun burned straight down from the middle of the sky. Diana was exhausted after only a few meters, when the helicopters were already in view. At the first burst of gunfire, Richard threw himself to the ground. "Don't move," Diana shouted. "Play dead." And then she fell facedown beside him.

"They killed me," she screamed. "I can't move my legs."

She could not, in fact, but she felt no pain either, and she asked

Richard to look at her back because before she dropped she had felt something like an electric shock at her waist. Richard raised her shirt and just above the left hip bone saw a clean tiny hole, with no blood.

The shooting continued, coming closer and closer, and a desperate Diana insisted that Richard leave her there and get away, but he stayed, hoping for help that would save her too. While they waited, he placed in her hand a Virgin that he always carried in his pocket, and he prayed with her. The gunfire came to an abrupt end, and two members of the Elite Corps appeared on the trail, their weapons at the ready.

Richard, who was kneeling beside Diana, raised his arms and said, "Don't shoot!" One of the agents stared at him with a look of astonishment and asked:

"Where's Pablo?"

"I don't know," Richard said. "I'm Richard Becerra, I'm a journalist. This is Diana Turbay, and she's wounded."

"Prove it," said an agent.

Richard showed him his identity card. With the help of some campesinos who emerged from the underbrush, they made an improvised litter from a sheet and carried her to the helicopter. The pain had become unbearable, but she was calm and lucid, and knew she was going to die.

HALF AN HOUR LATER, former president Turbay received a call from a military source informing him that his daughter Diana and Francisco Santos had been rescued in Medellín in an operation carried out by the Elite Corps. He immediately called Hernando Santos, who let out a victory whoop and ordered the telephone operators at his newspaper to relay the news to the entire family. Then he called Alberto Villamizar's apartment and repeated the news word for word. "How wonderful," shouted Villamizar. His joy was sincere, but he realized right away that with Pacho and Diana free, the only killable hostages still in Escobar's hands were Maruja and Beatriz.

As he made urgent phone calls, he turned on the radio and discovered that the news was not yet on the air. He was about to dial Rafael Pardo's number when the phone rang again. It was a disheartened Hernando Santos, calling to tell him that Turbay had amended his first information. It was not Francisco Santos who had been freed but the cameraman Richard Becerra, and Diana was seriously wounded. Hernando Santos, however, was not as disturbed by the error as he was by Turbay's consternation at having caused him a counterfeit happiness.

MARTHA LUPE ROJAS was not home when someone from the news program called to tell her that her son Richard was free. She had gone to her brother's house, and was so anxious for news that she carried a portable radio with her wherever she went, but that day, for the first time since the abduction, the radio was not working.

Someone told her that her son was safe, and in the cab on the way to the television station, she heard the familiar voice of the radio journalist Juan Gossaín bringing her back to reality: The reports from Medellín were still very confused. It had been confirmed that Diana Turbay was dead, but there was nothing definite about Richard Becerra. Martha Lupe began to pray in a quiet voice: "Dear God, send the bullets to the side, don't let them touch him." At that moment, Richard called his house from Medellín to tell her he was safe, and no one was home. But an emotional shout from Gossaín returned Martha Lupe's soul to her body:

"Extra! Extra! The cameraman Richard Becerra is alive!"

Martha Lupe burst into tears and could not stop crying until late that night, when she welcomed her son in the editorial offices of the newscast "Criptón." Today she recalls: "He was nothing but skin and bone, pale and bearded, but he was alive."

RAFAEL PARDO HAD received the news in his office just a few minutes earlier, when a reporter who was a friend of his called to confirm a version of the rescue. He telephoned General Maza Márquez and then the head of the National Police, General Gómez Padilla, and neither one knew anything about any rescue operations. A little while later, Gómez Padilla called to inform him that it had been a chance encounter with the Elite Corps during a search for Escobar. The units involved, Gómez Padilla said, had no prior information regarding hostages in that location.

Since receiving the report from Medellín, Dr. Turbay had been trying to reach Nydia at the house in Tabio, but her telephone was out of order. He sent his chief bodyguard in a van to tell her that Diana was safe and in a Medellín hospital for a routine examination. Nydia heard the news at two in the afternoon, but instead of shouting with joy, as the rest of the family had, she looked stunned by grief, and exclaimed:

"They've killed Diana!"

On the drive back to Bogotá, as they were listening to the news on the radio, her uncertainty intensified. "I was still crying," she would later say. "Not shrieking and moaning, as I had before, just shedding tears." She stopped at her house to change clothes before going on to the airport, where the presidential plane—a decrepit Fokker that flew only by the grace of God after almost thirty years of forced labor—was waiting for the family. The latest report said that Diana was in intensive care, but Nydia did not believe anyone or anything except her own instincts. She went straight to the telephone and asked to speak to the president.

"They killed Diana, Mr. President," she said. "And it's your doing, it's your fault, it's what comes of having a soul of stone."

The president was glad he could contradict her with a piece of good news.

"No, Señora," he said in his calmest voice. "It seems there was a raid, and nothing is confirmed yet. But Diana is alive."

"No," Nydia replied. "They killed her."

The president, who was in direct communication with Medellín, had no doubts.

"How do you know that?"

Nydia answered with absolute conviction:

"Because I'm her mother and my heart tells me so."

Her heart was correct. An hour later, María Emma Mejía, the presidential adviser for Medellín, came aboard the plane that was carrying the Turbay family and gave them the bad news. Diana had bled to death despite several hours of medical intervention, which would have been hopeless in any case. She had lost consciousness in the helicopter that transported her to Medellín, and had never regained it. Her spinal column had been shattered at the waist by a high-velocity, medium-caliber explosive bullet that splintered inside her body and caused a general paralysis from which she never would have recovered.

Nydia suffered a major shock when she saw her in the hospital, lying naked on the operating table under a blood-soaked sheet, her face without expression and her skin without color because of the loss of blood. There was an enormous incision in her chest where the doctors had inserted their hands to massage her heart.

As soon as she left the operating room, when she was beyond grief and despair, Nydia held a ferocious press conference right in the hospital. "This is the story of a death foretold," she began. Convinced that Diana had been the victim of an assault ordered from Bogotá—according to information she had received since her arrival in Medellín—she gave a detailed account of the appeals she and the family had made to the president that the police not attempt a rescue. She said that the stupidity and criminality of the Extraditables were responsible for her daughter's death, but the guilt was shared equally by the government and the president, above all by the president, "who with lack of feeling, almost with coldness and indifference, turned a deaf ear to the appeals that there be no rescues and that the lives of the hostages not be placed in danger."

This categorical statement, quoted verbatim in all the media, generated solidarity in public opinion, and indignation in the government. The president held a meeting with Fabio Villegas, his secretary general; Miguel Silva, his private secretary; Rafael Pardo, his security adviser; and Mauricio Vargas, his press adviser. The purpose was to devise a resounding denial of Nydia's statement. But more careful reflection led them to the conclusion that one cannot argue with a mother's grief. Gaviria understood this, rescinded the purpose of the meeting, and gave an order:

"We'll go to the funeral."

Not only he but the entire government.

Nydia's rancor gave her no peace. With someone whose name she could not remember, she had sent Gaviria Diana's letter—after she knew she was dead—perhaps so that he would always carry with him the burden of its premonition. "Obviously I didn't expect him to answer," she said.

At the end of the funeral mass in the cathedral—it had rarely been more crowded—the president rose from his seat and walked the empty central nave alone, followed by everyone's eyes, and photographers' flashbulbs and television cameras, and held out his hand to Nydia, certain she would leave him with his hand outstretched. Nydia took it with icy distaste. In reality, she felt relieved, for what she feared was that the president would embrace her. However, she appreciated the condolence kiss from his wife, Ana Milena.

It was not over yet. As soon as the obligations of mourning had eased somewhat, Nydia requested another meeting with the president to give him important information that he ought to know before delivering his speech that day on Diana's death. Silva conveyed the precise message he had received, and then the president gave the smile that Nydia would never see.

"She's coming to cut out my heart," he said. "But have her come, of course."

He greeted her as he always did. Nydia, however, dressed in black, walked into the office with a different air: simple, and grieving. She came straight to the point, which she revealed to the president with her opening words:

"I've come to do you a favor."

The surprise was that she began by begging his pardon for believing that he had ordered the raid in which Diana died. She knew now that he had not been aware of it. And she also wanted to tell him that at present he was being deceived again, because it was not true that the purpose of the mission had been to find Pablo Escobar, but to free the hostages, whose whereabouts had been revealed under torture by a gang member who had been captured by the police. And who, Nydia explained, had later shown up as one of those killed in the shooting.

She spoke with energy and precision, and with the hope of arousing the interest of the president, but she could not detect even the slightest sign of compassion. "He was like a block of ice," she would say later when recalling that day. Not knowing why, or at what point it happened, and unable to stop herself, she began to cry. Then the temperament she had kept under control rebelled, and her manner and the subject underwent a complete transformation. She berated the president for his indifference and coldness in not fulfilling his constitutional obligation to save the lives of the hostages.

"Just think about it," she concluded. "What if your daughter had been in this situation. What would you have done then?"

She looked straight into his eyes but was so agitated by this time that the president could not interrupt her. Later he would say: "She asked me questions but gave me no chance to answer them." Nydia, in fact, stopped him cold with another question: "Don't you think, Mr. President, that you were mistaken in your handling of this problem?" For the first time the president revealed a shred of doubt. "I've never suffered so much," he would say years later. But he only blinked and said in his natural voice:

"It's possible."

Nydia stood, extended her hand in silence, and left the office before he could open the door for her. Then Miguel Silva came into the office and found the president very affected by the story of the dead gunman. Gaviria lost no time in writing a personal letter to the prosecutor general telling him to investigate the case and bring it to trial.

MOST PEOPLE AGREED that the purpose of the raid had been to capture Escobar or one of the important capos, but that even with this rationale it was stupid and doomed to failure. According to the immediate police version, Diana had died in the course of a search mission carried out with the support of helicopters and ground personnel. Without intending to, they had encountered the armed unit guarding Diana Turbay and the cameraman Richard Becerra. As they were fleeing, one of the kidnappers shot Diana in the back and shattered her spine. The cameraman was not hurt. Diana was taken to the Medellín General Hospital in a police helicopter, and died there at 4:35 in the afternoon.

Pablo Escobar's version was quite different and agreed in its essential points with the story Nydia told to the president. According to him, the police had carried out the raid knowing that the hostages were in that location. They had obtained the information under torture from two of his men whom he identified with their real names and the numbers on their identity cards. His communiqué claimed they had been arrested and tortured by the police, and that one of them had guided the officers there from a helicopter. He said that Diana was killed by the police when she was running away from the fighting and had already been released by her captors. He concluded by stating that three innocent campesinos had also been killed in the skirmish, but the police described them to the press as criminals who had been shot during the fighting. This report must have given Escobar the satisfaction he had hoped for when he denounced police violations of human rights.

ON THE NIGHT of the tragedy, Richard Becerra, the only available witness, was besieged by reporters in a room at General Police Headquarters in Bogotá. He was still wearing the black leather jacket he had on when he had been kidnapped, and the straw hat his captors had given him so he would be mistaken for a campesino. He was not in any state of mind to provide illuminating details.

The impression he made on his more understanding colleagues was that the confusion of events had not allowed him to form an opinion about the incident. His statement that the bullet that killed Diana was fired intentionally by one of the kidnappers was not supported by any evidence. The widespread belief, over and above all the conjectures, was that Diana died by accident in the cross fire. But the definitive investigation would be handled by the prosecutor general, in accordance with the letter sent to him by President Gaviria following the revelations of Nydia Quintero.

The drama had not ended. In response to public uncertainty regarding the fate of Marina Montoya, the Extraditables issued another communiqué on January 30, acknowledging that they had given the order to execute her on January 23. But, "because we are in hiding and communications are poor, we have no information—at present—as to whether she was executed or released. If she was executed, we do not understand why the police have not yet reported finding her body. If she was released, it is now up to her family." Only then, seven days after the order to kill her was given, did the search for her body begin.

Pedro Morales, one of the pathologists who had performed the autopsy, read the bulletin in the paper and believed the corpse of the lady with the fine clothes and impeccable nails was in fact Marina Montoya. He was correct. As soon as her identity was established, however, someone claiming to be from the Justice Ministry called the Institute of Forensic Medicine, urging them not to reveal that the body was in a mass grave.

Luis Guillermo Pérez Montoya, Marina's son, was leaving for lunch when he heard the preliminary report on the radio. At the Institute, they showed him the photograph of the woman disfigured by bullets, and he had difficulty recognizing her. A special deployment of police was required at the Southern Cemetery, because the news had already been announced and they had to clear a path to the grave site for Luis Guillermo Pérez through a mass of curious onlookers.

According to regulations at the Institute, an anonymous corpse has to be buried with a serial number stamped on the torso, arms, and legs so that it can be identified even in case of dismemberment. It has to be enclosed in black plastic, the kind used for trash bags, and tied at the ankles and wrists with strong cord. The body of Marina Montoya—according to her son—was naked and covered in mud, and had been tossed into the common grave without the identifying tattoos required by law. Beside her was the body of the boy who had been buried at the same time, wrapped in the pink sweatsuit.

Back in the amphitheater, after she had been washed down with a high-pressure hose, her son examined her teeth and hesitated for a moment. He seemed to remember that Marina was missing her left premolar, and this corpse had all its teeth. But when he looked at the hands, and placed them over his own, all his doubts vanished: They were the same. Another suspicion would persist, perhaps forever: Luis Guillermo Pérez was convinced that his mother's corpse had been identified at the time of the on-site examination, and had been sent straight to the common grave to get rid of evidence that might upset the public or embarrass the government.

DIANA'S DEATH—even before the discovery of Marina's body—had a powerful impact on the country. When Gaviria had refused to modify the second decree, he had not given in to Villamizar's harshness or Nydia's entreaties. His argument, in brief, was that the decrees could not be judged in terms of the abductions but with a view to the public interest, since Escobar was not taking hostages to put pressure on the capitulation policy but to force non-extradition and obtain an amnesty. These thoughts led him to a final modification of the decree. It was difficult, after having resisted Nydia's pleas and the grief of so many other people, to change the date, but he resolved to do it.

Villamizar received the news through Rafael Pardo. The wait seemed infinite to him. He had not had a minute's peace. His life revolved around the radio and telephone, and his relief was immense when he heard no bad news. He called Pardo at all hours. "Any news?" he would ask. "How long can this go on?" Pardo calmed him down with doses of rationality. Every night he came home in the same state. "That decree has to be issued or they'll kill everybody in sight," he would say. Pardo calmed him down. At last, on January 28, it was Pardo who made the call to say that the final version of the decree was ready for the president's signature. The delay had been due to the fact that all the ministers had to sign it, and they had not been able to locate Alberto Casas Santamaría, the communications minister, until Rafael Pardo reached him by phone and threatened him, as amiable as an old friend.

"Mr. Minister," he told him. "Either you're here in half an hour to sign the decree, or you're not a minister anymore."

On January 29, Decree 303 was issued, clearing away all the obstacles that had interfered so far with the surrender of the drug traffickers. Just as many in the government expected, they were never able to dispel the widespread belief that the decree was an act of contrition for Diana's death. This, as usual, generated still other objections: those who thought it was a concession to the traffickers, the result of a stunned public opinion, and those who saw it as a step the president could not avoid taking, though it came too late for Diana Turbay. In any case, President Gaviria signed it out of conviction, knowing that the delay could be interpreted as proof of his hard heart, and the belated decision proclaimed as an act of weakness.

The next day, at seven in the morning, the president returned a call he had received from Villamizar the night before to thank him for the decree. Gaviria listened to his reasons in absolute silence, and shared with him his anguish of January 25.

"It was a terrible day for everyone," he said.

Then Villamizar called Guido Parra with a clear conscience. "You're not going to start all that shit now about how this decree is no good," he said. Guido Parra had already studied it with care.

"Right," he said, "no problem on this end. Just think how much grief it could have saved us if it had come out earlier."

Villamizar wanted to know what the next step would be.

"Nothing," said Guido Parra. "It's a matter of forty-eight hours."

The Extraditables immediately let it be known in a communiqué that they would cancel the announced executions in light of appeals from several well-known persons. They may have been referring to the radio messages addressed to them by former presidents López Michelsen and Pastrana, and Monsignor Castrillón. But in essence it could also be interpreted as their acceptance of the decree. "We will respect the lives of the remaining hostages," said the communiqué. As a special concession, they also announced that early that same day they would release a hostage. Villamizar, who was with Guido Parra, gave a start of surprise.

"What do they mean just one!" he shouted. "You said they'd let them all go!"

Guido Parra did not turn a hair.

"Take it easy, Alberto," he said. "It's a matter of a week."

7

MARUJA AND BEATRIZ had not heard about the deaths. With no television or radio, and the enemy their only source of information, it was impossible to guess the truth. The guards' contradictions undermined the story that they had taken Marina to a farm, and any other conjecture led to the same impasse: She was free, or she was dead. In other words, they had once been the only people who knew she was alive, and now they were the only people not to know she was dead.

Uncertainty about what they had done with Marina turned the empty bed into a phantom. The Monk had returned half an hour after she was taken away. He came in like a ghost and huddled in a corner. Beatriz asked him point-blank:

"What did you do with Marina?"

The Monk said that when he walked outside with her, two new bosses who had not come to the room were waiting for him in the garage. That he asked where they were taking her, and one of them answered in a rage: "You don't ask questions here, you son of a bitch." And that then they told him to get back in the house and leave Marina with Barrabás, the other guard on duty.

At first hearing the story seemed credible. It would not have been easy for the Monk to go away and come back so soon if he had taken part in the crime, or for him to have the heart to kill a ruin of a woman, whom he seemed to love as if she were his grand-mother, and who doted on him as if he were her grandson. Barrabás, however, had a reputation as a heartless killer who even bragged about his crimes. The uncertainty became even more dis-quieting in the middle of the night, when Maruja and Beatriz were awakened by the moans of a wounded animal, and it was the Monk sobbing. He did not want breakfast, and they heard him sigh sev-eral times and say: "How sad that they took Granny away!" But he never said outright that she was dead. Even the majordomo's stub-born refusal to return the television and the radio increased their suspicion that she had been killed.

Damaris, after several days away from the house, returned in a frame of mind that only added to the confusion. During one of their night walks, Maruja asked her where she had gone, and Damaris answered in the same voice she would have used to tell the truth: "I'm taking care of doña Marina." And without giving Maruja time to think about it, she added: "She always thinks of you and sends you both her best." And then, in an even more ca-sual tone, she said that Barrabás had not come back because he was in charge of her security. From then on, every time Damaris went out, she came back with news that grew less believable the more enthusiastic she became. She always ended with a ritual phrase:

"Doña Marina is just marvelous."

Maruja had no reason to believe Damaris more than she be-lieved the Monk or any of the other guards, but she also had no reason not to believe them in circumstances where everything seemed possible. If Marina really was alive, they had no motive for depriving the hostages of news and distractions, unless it was to hide the worst from them.

To Maruja's overheated imagination, nothing seemed absurd. So far she had hidden her worry from Beatriz, afraid she could not tolerate the truth. But Beatriz was safe from all infection. From the very first she had rejected any thought that Marina might be dead. Her dreams helped her. She dreamed that her brother Alberto, as real as he was in life, told her in detail about his efforts, about how well things were going, about how little time they had to wait to be free. She dreamed that her father reassured her with the news that the credit cards she had left in her bag were safe. The images were so vivid that when she recalled them later they were indistinguishable from reality.

At this time, a seventeen-year-old they called Jonás was finishing up his guard duty with Maruja and Beatriz. Beginning at seven in the morning, he would listen to music on a tinny cassette player. He played his favorite songs over and over, at a deafening volume, until they were sick of them. And in the meantime, as part of the chorus, he would shout: "What a fucking life, I don't know why I ever got into this!" In his calmer moments he would talk to Beatriz about his family. But this only brought him to the edge of the abyss, and with a measureless sigh he would say: "If you only knew who my father was!" He never told, but this and many other of the guards' enigmas made the atmosphere in the room even more rarefied.

The majordomo, caretaker of their domestic welfare, must have informed his bosses about the prevailing restiveness, because two showed up in a conciliatory mood. Again they refused to return the radio and television, but they did make an effort to improve the hostages' daily lives. They promised books but brought very few, and one was a novel by Corín Tellado. They gave them entertainment publications but no news magazines. A large light-bulb replaced the blue one, and orders were given to turn it on for an hour at seven in the morning, and an hour at seven in the evening, so they could read, but Beatriz and Maruja were so accustomed to semi-darkness they could not tolerate a bright light. Besides, the bulb heated the air in the room and made it unbreathable.

Maruja allowed herself to succumb to the inertia of the desperate. She spent days and nights lying on the mattress, pretending to be asleep, her face turned to the wall so she would not have to speak. She ate almost nothing. Beatriz occupied the empty bed and took refuge in the crossword puzzles and games in the magazines. The fact was brutal and painful, but it was the fact: There was more room with four people instead of five, fewer tensions, more air to breathe.

Jonás finished his tour of duty at the end of January and said goodbye to the hostages with a demonstration of his trust. "I'll tell you something if you promise not to say who told you." And then he revealed the news that had been gnawing at him inside:

"They killed doña Diana Turbay."

The blow woke them. For Maruja it was the most terrible moment of her captivity. Beatriz tried not to think about what seemed irremediable to her: "If they killed Diana, I'll be next." After all, since the first of January, when the old year had ended and they were still not free, she had been telling herself: "Either they let me go or I let myself die."

One day, when Maruja was playing a game of dominoes with another guard, the Gorilla touched various places on his chest with his index finger and said: "I feel something funny here. What do you think it is?" Maruja stopped playing, looked at him with all the contempt she could summon, and said: "It's either gas or a heart attack." He dropped his submachine gun to the floor, stood up in terror, spread his hand over his chest, and with a colossal shout he roared:

"My heart hurts, damn it!"

He collapsed onto the remains of breakfast and lay there, facedown. Beatriz, who knew he hated her, felt a professional impulse to help him, but just then the majordomo and his wife came in, frightened by the shouting and the noise of his fall. The other guard, who was small and thin, had tried to help him but his submachine gun got in the way, and he handed it to Beatriz.

"You're responsible for doña Maruja," he told her.

He, the majordomo, and Damaris together could not lift the Gorilla. They took hold of him and dragged him to the living room. Beatriz, weapon in hand, and a dumbfounded Maruja saw the submachine gun on the floor, and both were shaken by the same temptation. Maruja knew how to fire a revolver, and she had once been shown how to use a submachine gun, but a providential lucidity kept her from picking it up. For her part, Beatriz was familiar with military procedures. For five years she had trained with the reserves twice a week, and had been promoted from second lieutenant to lieutenant to the rank of captain as a civilian affiliated with the Military Hospital. She had taken a special artillery course. But she too realized that they had everything to lose. The two women consoled themselves with the thought that the Gorilla would never return. And, in fact, he never did.

WHEN PACHO SANTOS watched Diana's funeral and the exhumation of Marina Montoya on television, he knew his only alternative was escape. By this time he had a rough idea of where he was. From the guards' conversations and things they had let slip, and through other reporter's arts, Pacho had established that he was in a corner house in some sprawling, crowded neighborhood in western Bogotá. He was in the main room on the second floor, and the window faced the street but was boarded over. He knew the house was rented, perhaps without a lease, because the woman who owned it arrived at the beginning of each month to collect the rent. She was the only outsider who came in and went out, and before they opened the street door for her they would chain Pacho to the bed, warning him with threats to keep absolutely quiet, and turning off the radio and television.

He had established that the boarded window in his room overlooked the garden, and that there was a door to the outside at the end of the narrow hall where the bathroom was located. He could

use it whenever he chose, with no one guarding him, just by walking across the hall, but first he had to ask to be unchained. The
only ventilation in the bathroom was a window where he could see
the sky. The window was very high and would not be easy to reach,
but it was wide enough to get through. He had no idea where it
led. In the adjoining room were the red metal bunk beds where the
off-duty guards slept. There were four of them, and two-man
teams worked six-hour shifts. In the ordinary course of events,
they never displayed their weapons, though they always carried
them. Only one slept on the floor next to the double bed.

He had established that they were close to a factory, whose
whistle could be heard several times a day, and because of daily
choral singing and the noise at recess, he knew he was near a
school. On one occasion he had asked for a pizza, and it was still
hot when they brought it back in less than five minutes, and so he
knew it could have been made and sold on the same block. There
was no doubt about their buying newspapers right across the
street, in a shop large enough to carry *Time* and *Newsweek*. The
smell of fresh-baked bread would wake him at night. With shrewd
questions he managed to find out from the guards that within a
hundred meters there was a pharmacy, an automobile mechanic,
two bars, a restaurant, a shoemaker, and two bus stops. With these
and many other scraps of information gathered piecemeal, he tried
to solve the puzzle of his escape routes.

One of the guards had told him that in case the law came they
had orders to go straight to his room and shoot him three times
point-blank: one bullet in the head, another in the heart, the third
in the liver. After he heard this, he managed to hide a liter soda
bottle and kept it within reach to use as a club. It was the only
weapon he had.

Chess—a guard taught him to play with outstanding skill—had
given him a new way to measure time. Another guard on the October shift was an expert in television soap operas and introduced
him to the vice of following them regardless of whether they were

good or bad. The secret was not to worry too much about today's episode, and learn to imagine the surprises that tomorrow would bring. Together they watched Alexandra's programs, and listened to the news on radio and television.

Another guard had taken the twenty thousand pesos Pacho had in his pocket on the day of the kidnapping, but as compensation he promised to bring him anything he asked for, books in particular: several by Milan Kundera, *Crime and Punishment*, the biography of General Santander de Pilar Moreno de Angel. Pacho may have been the only Colombian of his generation who had heard of José María Vargas Vila, the world's most popular Colombian writer at the turn of the century, and he was moved to tears by his books. He read almost all of them, lifted for him by one of the guards from his grandfather's library. With the mother of another guard, he maintained a pleasant correspondence for several months until the men in charge of security made them stop. His reading ration was completed with the daily newspapers, which were given to him, still folded, in the afternoon. The guard whose job it was to bring them in had a visceral hatred for journalists. For a well-known television newscaster in particular, and when he appeared on the screen, the guard would aim his submachine gun at him.

"I'd do him for nothing," he would say.

Pacho never saw the bosses. He knew they visited from time to time, though they never came up to his bedroom, and held security meetings at a café in Chapinero. But with the guards he managed to establish a kind of emergency friendship. They had the power of life and death over him, but they always recognized his right to negotiate certain living conditions. Almost every day he would win some arguments and lose others. He always lost the one about sleeping with the chain, but he won their confidence playing *remis*, a childish, undemanding game that consists of making three- and four-card melds with ten cards. Every two weeks an invisible boss would send them a loan of 100,000 pesos that was divided among them so they could gamble. Pacho always lost. At the end of six months, they confessed that they had all cheated, and if they happened to let him win from time to time, it was only to keep him from losing his enthusiasm. They used sleight of hand with the mastery of professional magicians.

This had been his life until the New Year. From the first he had guessed it would be a long captivity, and his relationship with the guards had made him think he could get through it. But the deaths of Diana and Marina shattered his optimism. The same guards who used to cheer him up now came back to the house in low spirits. Everything seemed to be on hold until the Constituent Assembly made its decision on extradition and an amnesty. At this time he had no doubt that the escape option was possible. On one condition: He would attempt it only when he saw every other alternative closed to him.

FOR MARUJA AND BEATRIZ, prospects had also been dimmed after the hopes of December, but they began to brighten again toward the end of January with rumors that two hostages would be freed. They had no idea at the time how many were left or if there were any new ones. Maruja took it for granted that Beatriz would be the one released. On the night of February 2, during the walk in the courtyard, Damaris confirmed the rumors. She was so sure, she had purchased lipstick, blush, eyeshadow, and other cosmetics for the day they left. Beatriz shaved her legs on the assumption that there would be no time when the moment came.

But two bosses who visited them the next day gave no precise details about who would be released, or if in fact either one would go free. Their high rank was obvious. They were different from the others, and much more communicative. They confirmed that a communiqué from the Extraditables had announced the release of two hostages, but there might be some unforeseen obstacles. This reminded the captives of the earlier broken promise that they would be released on December 9.

The new bosses began creating an optimistic atmosphere. They came in at odd hours, jubilant for no reason. "Things are really moving along," they would say. They commented on the news with the enthusiasm of children, but refused to return the television and radio so that the hostages could hear it for themselves. One, through malice or stupidity, said goodbye one night with words whose double meaning almost scared them to death: "Don't worry, ladies, it'll be very quick."

The tension lasted for four days, while they were given discrete pieces of news, one item at a time. On the third day they said only one hostage would be released, and that it might be Beatriz because they were saving Francisco Santos and Maruja for higher things. What distressed the women most was not being able to compare this information with news from outside—above all, with news from Alberto, who may have known better than the bosses themselves the real cause for all the uncertainty.

At last, on February 7, the men arrived earlier than usual and laid their cards on the table: Beatriz was going. Maruja would have to wait another week. "Just a few minor details left to settle," said one of the men in hoods. Beatriz suffered an attack of loquacity that exhausted first the bosses, then the majordomo and his wife, and finally the guards. Maruja ignored her, for she was wounded by a wordless rancor toward her husband when it occurred to her that he had chosen to free his sister rather than his wife. She burned with festering rage the entire afternoon, and the embers remained warm for several days afterward.

She spent that night instructing Beatriz on what she should tell Alberto Villamizar about their captivity, how to handle the details to protect everyone's safety. Any mistake, no matter how innocent it might seem, could cost a life. So Beatriz had to provide her brother with a simple, truthful description of the situation without minimizing or exaggerating anything that would make him suffer less or worry more: just the bare truth. What she must not tell him was anything that could identify the house. Beatriz resented it.

"Don't you trust my brother?"

"More than anybody in this world," said Maruja, "but this is between you and me, and no one else. You have to promise me that nobody will find out."

Her fear was well founded. She knew her husband's impulsive nature, and for all their sakes she wanted to avoid an armed rescue attempt. She had another message for Alberto: Could he find out if the medicine she was taking for her circulation had any side effects? She spent the rest of the night devising a more efficient code for messages on radio and television, and for written correspondence in the event it was allowed in the future. Deep in her soul, however, she was dictating her will: what should be done with the children, with her antiques, with ordinary things that deserved special attention. She was so impassioned that one of the guards overheard her and said:

"Take it easy. Nothing's going to happen to you."

The next day they waited, even more uneasy, but nothing occurred. They talked through the afternoon. At last, at seven o'clock, the door burst open and the two bosses, and one they did not know, came in and walked over to Beatriz.

"We've come for you. Get ready."

Beatriz was terror-stricken at the dreadful repetition of the night they took away Marina: the same door opening, the same words that might mean either freedom or death, the same mystery regarding her fate. She did not understand why on both occasions they said: "We've come for you," instead of what she longed to hear: "We're letting you go." Trying to trick them into an answer, she asked:

"Are you going to release Marina too?"

The two bosses started.

"No questions!" one of them answered with a harsh growl. "How am I supposed to know that?"

Another, more conciliatory, ended the conversation:

"One thing has nothing to do with the other. This is political."

The word Beatriz longed to hear—freedom—was left unspoken. But the atmosphere was encouraging. The bosses were not in a hurry. Damaris, wearing a schoolgirl's miniskirt, brought in drinks and a cake for a farewell party. They discussed the big news of the day, news that the captives knew nothing about: In two separate operations the industrialists Lorenzo King Mazuera and Eduardo Puyana had been abducted in Bogotá, apparently by the Extraditables. But they also said that Pablo Escobar really wanted to turn himself in after living so long on the run. Even hiding in sewers, it was said. They promised to bring back the television and radio that same night so Maruja could see Beatriz with her family.

Maruja's analysis seemed reasonable. Until now she had suspected that Marina had been executed, but that night she had no doubts at all because of the difference in procedure. In Marina's case, bosses had not prepared them several days in advance. They had not come for her themselves but had sent two low-level killers with no authority and only five minutes to carry out their orders. The farewell cake and wine for Beatriz would have been a truly macabre celebration if they were going to murder her. In Marina's case the television and radio had been taken away so they would not find out about her execution, and now they were offering to give them back so that good news would soften the devastating effects of bad. This was when Maruja concluded, with no further hesitations, that Marina had been killed, and Beatriz was going free.

The bosses gave her ten minutes to get ready while they went to drink some coffee. Beatriz could not rid herself of the idea that she was reliving Marina's final night. She requested a mirror to put on her makeup, and Damaris brought her a large one with a gilt-leaf frame. Maruja and Beatriz, after three months without a mirror, rushed to look at themselves. It was one of the most shaking experiences of their captivity. Maruja had the impression she would not have recognized herself on the street. "I almost died of panic," she has said. "I looked skinny, unfamiliar, as if I had makeup on for a part in a play." Beatriz saw herself—ashen, weighing twenty-two pounds less, her hair long and limp—and exclaimed in horror: "That's not me!" She had often felt a half-serious embarrassment at the thought that one day she would be released and look awful, but she never dreamed the reality would be so bad. And then it became worse: One of the bosses turned on the overhead light, and the atmosphere in the room turned even more sinister.

One of the guards held the mirror for Beatriz while she combed her hair. She wanted to put on some makeup, but Maruja stopped her. "What's gotten into you?" she said in a shocked voice. "As pale as you are, you'll look awful if you put that on!" Beatriz listened. She dabbed on the aftershave that Spots had given her. Then, without water, she swallowed a tranquilizer.

The clothes she had been wearing on the night of her kidnapping were in the bag, along with her other things, but she preferred the least-worn pink sweatsuit. She hesitated about putting on her flat-heeled shoes, which had mildewed under the bed and did not really go with the sweatsuit. Damaris offered to give her a pair of sneakers she used when she exercised. They were her size but looked so shabby that Beatriz turned them down, saying they were too tight. And so she wore her own shoes, and used a rubber band to pull her hair back into a ponytail. In the end, making do with odds and ends, she looked like a schoolgirl.

They did not put a hood over her head, as they had with Marina, but tried to cover her eyes with adhesive tape so she would not see the route or their faces. She objected, knowing that when it was taken off it would tear away her eyebrows and lashes. "Wait," she told them, "I'll help you." Then, over each lid, she put a large ball of cotton that was taped in place.

Their goodbyes were brief and without tears. Beatriz was about to cry, but Maruja stopped her with a coldness intended to give her courage. "Tell Alberto not to worry, that I love him and the children very much," she said. They kissed. Both were suffering: Beatriz, because she was filled with terror that at the moment of truth it might be easier to kill her than to let her go; Maruja, because of the double terror that they would kill Beatriz, and that she would be alone with the four guards. The only thing she did not think of was that she might be executed once Beatriz was released.

The door closed, and Maruja did not move, did not know what to do next until she heard the engines start up in the garage and the sound of the cars growing fainter in the night. A feeling of immense abandonment overwhelmed her. Only then did she remember that they had not kept their promise to return the television and the radio so she would know how the night ended.

The majordomo had left with Beatriz, but his wife promised to make a call and have the radio and television brought back before the 9:30 news. They were not returned. Maruja begged the guards to let her watch the television in the house, but neither they nor the majordomo dared to break the rules in so serious a matter. Less than two hours later an excited Damaris came in to tell her that Beatriz was safe at home, and had been very careful in her statements, not saying anything that could do anyone any harm. The entire family, including Alberto, of course, was with her. The house was overflowing with people.

Maruja still suspected it was not true. She insisted that they lend her a radio. She lost control and confronted the guards with no regard for the consequences. These were not serious, because the guards had witnessed the treatment she had received from the bosses and preferred to calm her down with renewed efforts to obtain a radio. Later the majordomo came in and gave her his word that Beatriz was all right and in a safe place, and that the entire country had seen and heard her with her family. But what Maruja wanted was a radio so she could hear Beatriz's voice with her own ears. The majordomo promised to bring her one, but did not. At midnight, devastated by exhaustion and rage, Maruja took two of the powerful barbiturates and did not wake up until eight the next morning.

THE GUARDS' ACCOUNTS were true. Beatriz had been taken to the garage through the courtyard. They had her lie down on the floor of a vehicle that must have been a Jeep because they had to help her climb into it. At first they bounced over very rough roads. As soon as they began driving along a smooth, paved surface, one of the men riding with Beatriz began to make senseless threats. She could tell from his voice that he was in a nervous state his harshness could not hide, and that he was not one of the bosses who had been in the house.

"A mob of reporters will be waiting for you," the man said. "Well, you just be very careful. One wrong word can cost your sister-in-law her life. Remember: We never talked to you, you never saw us, and this drive took more than two hours."

Beatriz listened in silence to these threats and many others that he seemed to repeat only to calm his own fear. In a three-way conversation she realized she did not recognize any of the voices except the majordomo's, and he barely spoke. She began to tremble uncontrollably: The most sinister of her forebodings was still a possibility.

"I want to ask a favor," she said without thinking, her voice steady. "Maruja has circulatory problems, and we'd like to send her some medicine. Will you make sure she gets it?"

"Affirmative," the man said. "Don't worry."

"Thank you so much," said Beatriz. "I'll follow your instructions. I won't make trouble for you."

There was a long pause, and in the background she could hear fast-moving cars, heavy trucks, fragments of music, and loud voices. The men whispered among themselves. Then one spoke to Beatriz.

"There are a lot of checkpoints along here," he said. "If we're stopped, we'll say you're my wife; you're so pale we can tell them we're taking you to the hospital."

Beatriz, who was feeling calmer, could not resist the temptation to gamble:

"With these patches on my eyes?"

"They operated on your eyes," the man said. "You'll sit beside me, and I'll put my arm around you."

The kidnappers' concern was not unfounded. At that moment seven buses were burning in various neighborhoods in Bogotá, set on fire by incendiary bombs placed by urban guerrillas. At the same time, the FARC had dynamited the electric tower in the municipality of Cáqueza, on the outskirts of the capital, and had tried to take over the town. For this reason the police were carrying out some raids in Bogotá, but they went almost unnoticed. And so the traffic at seven was no different from any other Thursday evening: heavy and noisy, with long traffic lights, sudden maneuvers to avoid collisions, the most violent insults. The tension was noticeable even in the kidnappers' silence.

"We're going to drop you off at a certain place. You get out fast and count to thirty, nice and slow. Then take off the tape, walk away and don't turn around, and grab the first cab you see."

She felt a folded bill being placed in her hand. "For the taxi," said the man. "It's five thousand pesos." Beatriz put it in her pants pocket, where she happened to find another tranquilizer, which she swallowed. After half an hour the car stopped. Then the same voice pronounced a final warning:

"If you tell the press that you were with doña Marina Montoya, we'll kill doña Maruja."

They had arrived. The men were very clumsy as they tried to get Beatriz out of the car without taking off her blindfold, and so nervous they got in one another's way in a tangle of orders and curses. Beatriz felt solid ground under her feet.

"It's okay," she said. "I'm fine now."

She stood motionless on the sidewalk until they climbed back in the car and immediately drove away. Only then did she hear another car behind them, pulling away at the same time. Beatriz did not count as ordered but took two steps with arms outstretched and realized she must be in the middle of the street. She pulled off the blindfold and knew right away that she was in the Normandía district, because she used to visit a friend who lived there and sold jewelry from her house. Beatriz looked at the houses with lights in the windows, trying to choose one where they would let her in, since she felt too shabby to take a cab and wanted to call home and have them pick her up. She had not made her decision yet when a yellow cab in very good condition stopped beside her. The driver, who was young and well dressed, asked:

"Taxi?"

Beatriz agreed, and realized only when she was inside that so opportune a cab could be no accident. And yet, the very certainty that he was a final link in the chain of captors filled her with a strange sense of security. The driver asked the address, and she answered in a whisper. She could not understand why he did not hear her until he asked the address for the third time. Then she repeated it in her natural voice.

The night was cold and clear, with a few stars. The driver and Beatriz spoke no more than necessary, but he kept looking at her in the rearview mirror. As they drove toward her house, Beatriz had the feeling that the traffic lights were longer and more frequent. When they were two blocks away, she asked the driver to slow down in case they had to get around the reporters her captors had warned about. There were none. She saw her building and was surprised that it did not cause the intense emotion she had expected.

The meter read six hundred pesos. Since the driver did not

have change for five thousand, Beatriz went into the building for help, and the old porter gave a shout and threw his arms around her in a wild embrace. During the interminable days and fearful nights of her captivity, Beatriz had imagined that moment as a seismic upheaval that would expend all the strength of her body and her soul. It was just the opposite: a kind of stillwater in which she could barely feel the slow, regular beat of her heart, calmed by tranquilizers. Then she let the porter pay her fare, and she rang the bell of her apartment.

Gabriel, her younger son, opened the door. His shout could be heard throughout the house: "Mamaaaaá!" Catalina, her fifteen-year-old daughter, came running with a cry and threw her arms around her neck, then let go in consternation.

"But Mommy, why are you talking like that?"

It was the fortunate detail that broke through her state of shock. Beatriz would need several days, amid crowds of visitors, to lose the habit of talking in whispers.

They had been waiting for her since morning. Three anonymous phone calls—no doubt from the kidnappers—had announced her release. Countless reporters had called to find out if they knew the precise time. A few minutes after noon, it was confirmed by Alberto Villamizar, who had received a call from Guido Parra. The press was left in the dark. A journalist who called three minutes before Beatriz arrived told Gabriel in a firm, reassuring voice: "Don't worry, they'll let her go today." Gabriel had just put down the receiver when the doorbell rang.

Dr. Guerrero had waited for her in the Villamizars' apartment, assuming that Maruja would be released as well and both women would go there. He drank three whiskeys while he waited, until the seven o'clock news. Since they had not come, he thought it was just another of the false reports circulating at the time and went back to his house. He put on his pajamas, poured another whiskey, got into bed, and turned on "Radio Recuerdo," hoping the boleros would lull him to sleep. Since the beginning of his calvary, he had not been able to read. He was half-asleep when he heard Gabriel's shout.

He walked out of the bedroom with admirable self-control. Beatriz and he—married for twenty-five years—exchanged an unhurried embrace, not shedding a tear, as if she were back from a short trip. Both had thought so much about this moment that when the time came to live it, their reunion was like a scene in a play, rehearsed a thousand times, capable of moving everyone but the actors.

As soon as Beatriz walked into her house she thought of Maruja, alone and deprived of news in that miserable room. She telephoned Alberto Villamizar, and he answered at the first ring in a voice prepared for anything.

"Hello," she said. "It's Beatriz."

She knew her brother had recognized her voice even before she said her name. She heard a deep, rough sigh, like the growl of a cat, and then a question asked without the slightest alteration in his voice:

"Where are you?"

"At my house."

"Perfect," said Villamizar. "I'll be there in ten minutes. In the meantime, don't talk to anybody."

He was punctual. Beatriz had called just as he was about to fall asleep. Beyond the joy of seeing his sister and having the first and only direct news about his captive wife, he was moved by the pressing need to prepare Beatriz before the reporters and the police arrived. His son Andrés, who has an irresistible calling to be a race-car driver, got him there in record time.

Everyone was feeling calmer. Beatriz sat in the living room with her husband and children, her mother and two sisters, who listened with avid interest to her story. Alberto thought she looked pale after her long confinement, and younger than before, like a schoolgirl in her sweatsuit, ponytail, and flat shoes. She almost cried but he stopped her, eager to know about Maruja. "Believe me, she's all right," Beatriz told him. "Things there are difficult, but bearable, and Maruja is very brave." And then she attempted to answer the question that had tormented her for two weeks.

"Do you know Marina's telephone number?" she asked.

Villamizar thought the least brutal thing would be the truth.

"They killed her," he said.

The pain of the bad news threw Beatriz off balance with retroactive terror. If she had known two hours earlier, she might not have been able to endure the drive to her own freedom. She cried until she had no more tears. Meanwhile, Villamizar took precautions to make sure no one came in until they had decided on a public version of the abduction that would not put the other hostages at risk.

Details of her captivity could give an idea of the house where they had been imprisoned. To protect Maruja, Beatriz had to tell the press that the trip home was a three-hour drive from somewhere in the temperate zone, though the truth was just the opposite: The real distance, the hilly roads, the music on the loudspeakers that blared all night on weekends, the noise of airplanes, the weather, everything indicated a neighborhood in the city. And questioning four or five priests in the district would have been enough to find out which one exorcised the house.

Other even more careless oversights on the part of her captors provided enough clues for an armed rescue attempt with minimum risk. It ought to take place at six in the morning, after the change in shifts, because the guards who came on duty then did not sleep well at night and they sprawled on the floor, exhausted, not concerned with their weapons. Another important piece of information was the layout of the house, in particular the courtyard gate, where they saw only an occasional armed guard, and the dog was easier to bribe than his barking would lead one to believe. It was impossible to know in advance if there was also a security cordon around the place, though the lax disorder inside made it doubtful, and in any case that would be easy enough to find out

once the house had been located. After the tragedy of Diana Turbay, Villamizar had less confidence than ever in the success of
armed rescues, but he kept it in mind in the event that became the
only alternative. This was, perhaps, the only secret he did not
share with Rafael Pardo.

These pieces of information created a moral dilemma for Beatriz. She had promised Maruja not to reveal any clues that might
lead to a raid on the house, but she made the grave decision to pass
these facts on to her brother when she saw that he realized with as
much clarity as Maruja and Beatriz herself how undesirable an
armed solution would be, above all when her release proved that
in spite of all the obstacles, the negotiation route was still open.
And so the next day, fresh and rested after a good night's sleep,
Beatriz held a press conference at her brother's house, where a forest of flowers made it almost impossible to walk. She gave the
journalists and the public an accurate picture of the horror of her
captivity, but not a single fact of use to those who might want to
act on their own, and endanger Maruja's life.

The following Wednesday, positive that by now Maruja knew
about the new decree, Alexandra decided to produce a program
to celebrate it. In recent weeks, as negotiations progressed, Villamizar had made significant changes in his apartment, hoping his
wife would find them to her liking when she was released. He had
put in a library where she had wanted one, replaced some furniture, hung some new pictures, and found a prominent place for
Maruja's prized possession, the Tang Dynasty horse she had
brought home from Jakarta. At the last minute he remembered
that she had complained about not having a decent rug in the
bathroom, and one was bought without delay. The bright, transformed house was the backdrop for an unusual television program
that allowed Maruja to know about the new decoration before she
returned. It turned out very well, though they did not even know
if Maruja saw it.

Beatriz soon took up her life again. In her captive's bag she kept the clothes she had worn when she was released, and it held the room's depressing odor that still woke her with a start in the middle of the night. She recovered her spiritual balance with her husband's help. The only ghost that still came to her from the past was the voice of the majordomo, who telephoned her twice. The first time it was the shout of a desperate man:

"The medicine! The medicine!"

Beatriz recognized his voice and her blood turned to ice in her veins, but she found enough breath to ask in the same tone:

"What medicine? What medicine?"

"The medicine for the señora!" shouted the majordomo.

Then it became clear that he wanted the name of the medicine Maruja took for her circulation.

"Vasotón," said Beatriz. And, having regained her composure, she asked: "How are things?"

"I'm fine, thanks," said the majordomo.

"Not you," Beatriz corrected him. "Her."

"Ah, don't worry," said the owner. "The señora is fine."

Beatriz hung up and burst into tears, overcome by the nausea of hideous memories: the wretched food, the dungheap of a bathroom, the days that were always the same, the horrific solitude of Maruja in the fetid room. In any case, a mysterious announcement appeared at the bottom of the screen during the sports segment of a television newscast: "Take Basotón." The spelling was changed to keep an uninformed laboratory from protesting the use of its product for mysterious purposes.

The second call from the majordomo, several weeks later, was very different. It took Beatriz a moment to identify the voice, distorted by some device. But the style was somewhat paternal.

"Remember what we talked about," he said. "You weren't with doña Marina. Or anybody."

"Don't worry," said Beatriz, and hung up.

Guido Parra, intoxicated by the first success after all his efforts, told Villamizar that Maruja's release was a matter of three days. Villamizar relayed this to Maruja in a press conference on radio and television. Moreover, Beatriz's accounts of the conditions of their captivity persuaded Alexandra that her messages were reaching their destination. And so she held a half-hour interview with Beatriz, who talked about everything Maruja wanted to know: how she had been freed, how the children were, and the house, and friends, and the hopes she should have for her release.

From that time on, Alexandra's program was based on trivia: the clothes they were wearing, the things they were buying, the people they were seeing. Someone would say, "Manuel cooked the pork roast," just so Maruja would know that the order she had left behind in her house was still intact. All of this, no matter how frivolous it might have seemed, had a reassuring significance for Maruja: Life was continuing.

The days passed, however, and no signs of her liberation could be seen. Guido Parra became entangled in vague explanations and puerile excuses; he stopped answering the phone; he dropped out of sight. Villamizar demanded an explanation. Parra wandered through long preambles. He said things had been complicated by an increase in the number of killings by the police in the Medellín slums. He asserted that until the government put an end to those barbaric methods, it would be very difficult for anybody to be released. Villamizar did not let him finish.

"This wasn't part of the agreement," he said. "Everything was based on the decree being explicit, and it is. This is a debt of honor, and nobody can play games with me."

"You don't know how fucked up it is being a lawyer for these guys," Parra said. "My problem isn't whether or not to charge them, my problem is that if things don't turn out right they'll kill me. What do you want me to do?"

"Let's talk straight, no more bullshit," said Villamizar. "What's going on?"

"If the police don't stop the killings and don't punish the ones responsible, there's no chance they'll let doña Maruja go. That's it in a nutshell."

Blind with rage, Villamizar cursed Escobar with a string of oaths and finished by saying:

"And you, you better get lost, because the man who's going to kill you is me."

Guido Parra vanished. Not only because of Villamizar's violent reaction but also because of Pablo Escobar's, who apparently did not forgive him for overstepping his authority as a negotiator. Hernando Santos could appreciate this when a terrified Guido Parra called to say that he had such an awful letter for him from Escobar that he did not even have the courage to read it to him.

"The man is crazy," he said. "Nobody can calm him down, and the only thing I can do is disappear from the face of the earth."

Hernando Santos, knowing this would cut off his only channel to Pablo Escobar, tried to convince him to stay on. He failed. The last favor Guido Parra asked was that he get him a visa for Venezuela and arrange for his son to finish his studies at the Gimnasio Moderno in Bogotá. Unconfirmed rumors say that he took refuge in a convent in Venezuela where one of his sisters was a nun. Nothing else was known about him until April 16, 1993, when he was found dead in Medellín, in the trunk of a car with no license plates, along with his son the secondary school graduate.

Villamizar needed time to recover from a terrible sense of defeat. He was crushed by remorse for having believed in Escobar's word. Everything seemed lost. During the negotiations he had kept Dr. Turbay and Hernando Santos informed, for they too had been left with no channels to Escobar. They saw one another almost every day, and little by little he stopped telling them about the setbacks and gave them only encouraging news. He spent long hours in the company of the former president, who endured the death of his daughter with heartrending stoicism; he retreated into himself and refused to make a statement of any kind: He became invisible. Hernando Santos, whose only hope of freeing his son had been based on Parra's mediation, slipped into a profound depression.

The murder of Marina, and in particular the brutal way it had been discovered and announced, gave rise to inevitable questions about what to do now. Every possibility for mediation of the kind provided by the Notables had been exhausted, yet no other intermediary seemed effective. Goodwill and indirect methods made no sense.

Villamizar was clearsighted about the situation, and he unburdened himself to Rafael Pardo. "Imagine how I feel," he said. "For all these years Escobar has been my family's cross, and mine. First he threatens me. Then he makes an attempt on my life, and it's a miracle I escape. He goes on threatening me. He assassinates Galán. He abducts my wife and my sister, and now he wants me to defend his rights." There was no consolation to be had, however, because his fate had been decided: The only certain road to freedom for the hostages led straight to the lion in his den. In plain language: The only thing left for him to do—and he was bound to do it—was fly to Medellín and find Pablo Escobar, wherever he might be, and discuss the situation face-to-face.

8

THE PROBLEM WAS how to find Pablo Escobar in a city martyrized by violence. In the first two months of 1991 there had been twelve hundred murders—twenty a day—and a massacre every four days. An agreement among almost all the armed groups had led to the bloodiest escalation of guerrilla violence in the history of the country, and Medellín was the center of urban terrorism. A total of 457 police had been killed in only a few months. The DAS had said that two thousand people in the slums were working for Escobar, many of them adolescents who earned their living hunting down police. For each dead officer they received five million pesos, for each agent a million and a half, and 800,000 for each one wounded. On February 16, 1991, three low-ranking officers and eight agents of the police were killed when a car was blown up with 150 kilos of dynamite outside the bullring in Medellín. Nine passersby were also killed and another 143, who had nothing to do with the war, were injured.

The Elite Corps, the frontline troops in the battle against drug trafficking, were branded by Pablo Escobar as the incarnation of all evil. The Corps had been created in 1989 by President Virgilio

Barco, when he was driven to despair by his inability to establish precise responsibility in entities as large as the army and the police. Its formation had been entrusted to the National Police in order to distance the military as much as possible from the deadly contagions of drug trafficking and paramilitarism. It began with only three hundred men, who had a special squadron of helicopters at their disposal and were trained by the Special Air Service (SAS) of the British government.

The new group had begun operations along the midsection of the Magdalena River, in the center of the country, at the time the paramilitary groups created by landowners to fight the guerrillas were most active. From there a group specializing in urban operations broke off and established itself in Medellín as a freewheeling body of legionnaires answerable only to the National Police Commission in Bogotá, without any intermediate jurisdictions, and, by its very nature, not overly meticulous regarding the limits of its authority. They sowed confusion among the criminals, and also among the local authorities, who were very reluctant to assimilate an autonomous force over which they had no control. The Extraditables fought them in a bloody war, and accused them of responsibility for every kind of human rights violation.

The people of Medellín knew that not all the Extraditables' denunciations of murder and abuse by the police were unfounded, because they witnessed them on the streets, though in most cases there was no official acknowledgment that they had occurred. National and international human rights organizations protested, and the government had no credible response. Months later it was decided that no raids could be made without the presence of a representative of the Prosecutor General's Office, leading to the inevitable bureaucratization of their operations.

There was little the judicial system could do. Judges and magistrates, whose low salaries were barely enough to live on, but not enough to pay for the education of their children, faced an insoluble dilemma: Either they sold themselves to the drug traffickers, or they were killed. The admirable and heartbreaking fact is that many chose death.

Perhaps the most Colombian aspect of the situation was the astonishing capacity of the people of Medellín to accustom themselves to everything, good and bad, with a resiliency that may be the cruelest form courage can take. Most did not seem aware that they were living in a city that had always been the most beautiful, the liveliest, the most hospitable in the country, and in recent years had become one of the most dangerous in the world. Until this time, urban terrorism had been a rare element in the centuries-old culture of Colombian violence. The same historical guerrilla groups who now practiced it had once condemned it, and with reason, as an illegitimate form of revolutionary struggle. People had learned to live with the fear of what had happened, but not with uncertainty about what might happen: an explosion that would blow up one's children at school, or disintegrate the plane in midair, or pulverize vegetables at the market. Random bombs that killed the innocent and anonymous threats on the telephone had surpassed all other causes of anguished anxiety in daily life. Yet the economy of Medellín was not affected in statistical terms.

Years earlier the drug traffickers had been popular because of their mythic aura. They enjoyed complete impunity and even a certain prestige because of their charitable works in the marginal neighborhoods where they had spent their impoverished childhoods. If anyone had wanted them arrested, he could have told the policeman on the corner where to find them. But a good part of Colombian society viewed them with a curiosity and interest that bore too close a resemblance to complacency. Politicians, industrialists, businesspeople, journalists, even ordinary freeloaders, came to the perpetual party at the Hacienda Nápoles, near Medellín, where Pablo Escobar kept a zoo with giraffes and hippos brought over from Africa, and where the entrance displayed, as if it were a national monument, the small plane used to export the first shipment of cocaine.

Luck and a clandestine life had left Escobar in charge of the henhouse, and he became a legend who controlled everything from the shadows. His communiqués, with their exemplary style and perfect cunning, began to look so much like the truth that one was mistaken for the other. At the height of his splendor, people put up altars with his picture and lit candles to him in the slums of Medellín. It was believed he could perform miracles. No Colombian in history ever possessed or exercised a talent like his for shaping public opinion. And none had a greater power to corrupt. The most unsettling and dangerous aspect of his personality was his total inability to distinguish between good and evil.

This was the invisible, improbable man Alberto Villamizar proposed to seek out in mid-February so that he could talk him into returning his wife. He would begin by making contact with the three Ochoa brothers in the high-security Itagüí prison. Rafael Pardo—with the president's approval—gave him the green light but reminded him of the limitations: This was not an official negotiation but an exploratory move. Pardo told him he could make no agreement in exchange for concessions from the government, but that the government was interested in the surrender of the Extraditables within the boundaries set by the capitulation policy. This new approach was the springboard for Villamizar's idea of also changing the thrust of his own efforts, centering them not on the release of the hostages—which had been the focus so far—but on the surrender of Pablo Escobar. One would be a simple consequence of the other.

And so began a second captivity for Maruja and a different kind of battle for Villamizar. Escobar probably intended to release her with Beatriz, but the Diana Turbay tragedy may have upset his plans. Aside from bearing responsibility for a death he had not ordered, the killing of Diana must have been a disaster for him, robbing him of an object of inestimable value and, in the end, complicating his life. Police activity flared up again with so much intensity that he was forced to submerge all the way to the bottom.

With Marina dead, he had been left with Diana, Pacho, Maruja, and Beatriz. If he had decided at that moment to execute one, perhaps it would have been Beatriz. With Beatriz free and Diana dead, he was left with two: Pacho and Maruja. Perhaps he would have preferred to keep Pacho for his exchange value, but Maruja had acquired an unforeseen and incalculable worth because of Villamizar's persistence in keeping contacts alive until the government decided to issue a more explicit decree. For Escobar too, the only lifesaver in the water was Villamizar's mediation, and the only thing that could guarantee it was holding on to Maruja. The two men were condemned to each other.

Villamizar began by visiting doña Nydia Quintero to learn the details of her experience. He found her generous, resolved, serene in her mourning. She recounted her conversations with the Ochoa sisters, with the old patriarch, with Fabio in prison. She gave the impression of having assimilated the awful death of her daughter, and she did not invoke it because of grief or for the sake of vengeance, but so that it might be useful in achieving peace. In that spirit she gave Villamizar a letter for Pablo Escobar in which she expressed her hope that Diana's death might help to prevent any other Colombian from ever feeling the sorrow she felt. She began by admitting that the government could not stop raids against criminals, but it could avoid attempts to rescue the hostages, for the families knew, the government knew, everyone knew that if they happened upon the captives during one of their raids, it could cause an irreparable tragedy, like the one that had befallen her daughter. "For this reason I come to you," the letter said, "my heart overflowing with pain, forgiveness, and goodwill, to implore you to free Maruja and Francisco." And she ended with a surprising request: "Give me your word that you did not want Diana to die." Months later, from prison, Escobar made public his astonishment at Nydia's having composed that letter free of recriminations or rancor. "How it grieves me," Escobar wrote, "that I did not have the courage to answer her."

Villamizar went to Itagüí to visit the three Ochoa brothers, carrying Nydia's letter and the government's unwritten authority. Two bodyguards from DAS accompanied him, and the Medellín police added six more. He found the Ochoas newly installed in the high-security prison, with three checkpoints that were slow, repetitive, and placed at regular intervals, and bare adobe walls that gave the impression of an unfinished church. The empty corridors, the narrow stairways with yellow pipe railings, the alarms in full view, ended at a cellblock on the third floor where the three Ochoa brothers whiled away the years of their sentences making fine leather goods: saddles and all kinds of equestrian trappings. The entire family was there: children, in-laws, sisters. Martha Nieves, the most active of them, and María Lía, Jorge Luis's wife, acted as hostesses with the exemplary hospitality of the Medellinese.

He arrived when it was time for lunch, which was served at the far end of the courtyard in a large open structure that had posters of movie stars on the walls, professional exercise equipment, and a dining table large enough to seat twelve. Under a security arrangement, the food was prepared at the nearby Hacienda La Loma, the family's official residence, and on that day it was a succulent display of local cuisine. While they were eating they followed the unbreakable Antioquian custom of discussing nothing but the food.

After the meal, with all the formality of a family council, the dialogue began. It was not as easy as the harmonious lunch might have led one to suppose. Villamizar started off in his slow, calculated, explanatory way that leaves little room for questions because everything seems to have been answered ahead of time. He gave a detailed account of his negotiations with Guido Parra and the abruptness with which they were broken off, and concluded with his conviction that only direct contact with Pablo Escobar could save Maruja.

"Let's try to stop this barbarism," he said. "Let's talk, instead of making more mistakes. First, let me assure you there is no possibility at all that we will attempt an armed rescue. I prefer to talk, to know what is going on and what people want."

Jorge Luis, the eldest brother, took the lead. He told about the losses suffered by the family in the turbulence of the dirty war, the reasons for their surrender and the difficulties surrounding it, and the unbearable fear that the Constituent Assembly would not prohibit extradition.

"This has been a very hard war for us," he said. "You can't imagine what we have suffered, what the family and our friends have suffered. Everything has happened to us."

He gave precise details: his sister, Martha Nieves, abducted; his brother-in-law, Alonso Cárdenas, abducted and murdered in 1986; his uncle, Jorge Iván Ochoa, abducted in 1983; and his cousins, Mario Ochoa and Guillermo León Ochoa, abducted and murdered.

Villamizar, in turn, tried to show that he was as victimized by the war as they, to make them understand they would all have to pay equally for anything that happened from then on. "It's been as hard for me as for you," he said. "The Extraditables tried to assassinate me in '86, I had to go to the ends of the earth and even there they pursued me, and now they've abducted my wife and my sister." He was not there to complain, however, but to put himself on an equal footing with them.

"It's an abuse," he concluded, "and the time has come for us to begin to understand one another."

Only the two men spoke. The rest of the family listened in the mournful silence of a funeral, while the women plied the visitor with attentions but did not take part in the conversation.

"We can't do anything," said Jorge Luis. "Doña Nydia was here. We understood her situation but we told her the same thing. We don't want any problems."

"As long as this war lasts, you are all in danger, even behind these fortified walls," Villamizar insisted. "But if it ends now, you'll have your father and mother, your entire family intact. And that won't happen until Escobar surrenders to the authorities and Maruja and Francisco return home safe and sound. But you can be sure that if they're killed, you'll pay too, your families, everyone will pay."

During the three long hours of their interview in the prison, each man demonstrated his courage at the very edge of the abyss. Villamizar appreciated the Medellinese realism in Ochoa. The Ochoas were impressed by the direct, frank manner in which their visitor analyzed all aspects of the subject. They had lived in Cúcuta—Villamizar's home region—knew many people there, and got along well with them. At last, the other two Ochoas spoke, and Martha Nieves lightened the atmosphere with her native grace. The men had seemed firm in their refusal to intervene in a war from which they now felt safe, but little by little they became more thoughtful.

"All right, then," Jorge Luis concluded. "We'll send the message to Pablo and tell him you were here. But my advice to you is to speak to my father. He's at La Loma, and he'll enjoy talking to you."

And so Villamizar went to the hacienda with the entire family, and with only the two bodyguards he had brought from Bogotá, since the full security team seemed too conspicuous to the Ochoas. They drove to the entrance and then continued on foot, walking about a kilometer to the house along a path lined with leafy, well-tended trees. Several men without visible weapons blocked the way of the bodyguards and asked them to take a different direction. It was an anxious moment, but the men from the house reassured the strangers with good manners and even better words.

"Walk around, have something to eat," they said. "The doctor has to talk with don Fabio."

The path ended in a small square, and on the other side stood the large, well-kept house. On the terrace overlooking fields that stretched to the horizon, the old patriarch was waiting for his visitor. With him was the rest of the family, all women, and almost all of them wearing mourning for their dead, casualties of the war. Although it was the siesta hour, they had prepared an assortment of food and drink.

They exchanged greetings, and Villamizar knew that don Fabio already had a complete report on the conversation held in the prison. That made the preliminaries shorter. Villamizar limited himself to repeating what he had said before: A flare-up in the war could cause much more harm to his large, prosperous family, who were not accused of either murder or terrorism. For the moment three of his sons were safe, but the future was unpredictable, which meant that no one ought to be more interested than they in achieving peace, and peace would not be possible until Escobar followed the example of don Fabio's sons.

Don Fabio listened with placid attention, approving with gentle nods when something seemed correct. Then, in sentences as brief and definitive as epitaphs, he said what he thought in five minutes. No matter what was done, he said, in the end they would find that the most important element was missing: talking to Escobar in person. "So the best thing is to start there," he said. He thought Villamizar was the right man to try it, because Escobar only trusted men whose word was as good as gold.

"And you are one of those men," don Fabio concluded. "The problem is proving it to him."

The visit had begun in the prison at ten in the morning and ended at six at La Loma. Its great achievement was breaking the ice between Villamizar and the Ochoas for the common goal—already agreed to by the government—of having Escobar turn himself in to the authorities. That certainty made Villamizar want to convey his impressions to the president. But when he reached Bogotá he was met with bad news: The president too had been wounded in his own flesh by an abduction.

This is what happened: Fortunato Gaviria Botero, his first cousin and dearest friend since childhood, had been taken at his country house in Pereira by four hooded men armed with rifles.

The president did not change his plans to attend a regional conference of governors on the island of San Andrés, and he left on Friday afternoon still not knowing if his cousin had been abducted by the Extraditables. On Saturday he woke at dawn to go diving, and when he came out of the water he was told that Fortunato's captors—who were not drug traffickers—had killed him and buried his body, without a coffin, in an open field. The autopsy showed earth in his lungs, and this was interpreted to mean that he had been buried alive.

The president's first reaction was to cancel the regional conference and return immediately to Bogotá, but he was stopped by physicians who told him he should not fly for twenty-four hours since he had spent more than an hour at a depth of sixty feet. Gaviria followed their recommendations, and the nation saw him on television presiding over the conference with his most mournful face. But at four that afternoon he ignored medical advice and returned to Bogotá to arrange the funeral. Some time later, recalling the day as one of the most difficult in his life, he said with acid humor:

"I was the only Colombian who didn't have a president to complain to."

As soon as his prison lunch with Villamizar had ended, Jorge Luis Ochoa sent Escobar a letter encouraging him to change his mind about surrender. He depicted Villamizar as a serious Santanderean who could be believed and trusted. Escobar's reply was immediate: "Tell that son of a bitch not to talk to me." Villamizar learned about it in a phone call from Martha Nieves and María Lía, who asked him to come back to Medellín anyway to continue to look for a solution. This time he went without an escort. He took a cab from the airport to the Hotel Intercontinental, and some fifteen minutes later he was picked up by an Ochoa driver. He was an amiable, bantering twenty-year-old from Medellín who observed him for some time in the rearview mirror. At last he asked:

"Are you scared?"

Villamizar smiled at him in the mirror.

"Don't worry, Doctor," the boy continued. And added, with a good deal of irony: "Nothing will happen to you while you're with us. How could you even think such a thing?"

The joke gave Villamizar a confidence and sense of security that remained with him during all of his subsequent trips. He never knew if he was followed, not even at a much more advanced stage, but he always felt sheltered by a supernatural power.

Escobar did not seem to feel he owed Villamizar anything for the decree that made his escape from extradition a certainty. As a hard-core gambler who kept track of every penny, he probably thought the favor had been paid for with the release of Beatriz, but that the old debt was still intact. The Ochoas, however, believed that Villamizar had to persevere.

And so he ignored the insults and decided to move ahead. The Ochoas supported him. He returned two or three times and together they devised a plan of action. Jorge Luis wrote Escobar another letter in which he stated that the guarantees for his surrender were in place, that his life would be protected, and that under no circumstances would he be extradited. But Escobar did not reply. Then they decided that Villamizar himself should write to Escobar explaining his situation and his offer.

The letter was written on March 4, in the Ochoas' cell, with the help of Jorge Luis, who told him what should be said and what might be out of place. Villamizar began by acknowledging that respect for human rights was fundamental to achieving peace. "There is a fact, however, that cannot be ignored: Those who violate human rights have no better excuse for continuing to do so than citing the same violations committed by others." This was an obstacle to action on both sides, and to whatever he had achieved in that regard during the months he had worked for his wife's release. The Villamizar family had been the target of a persistent violence for which it bore no responsibility: the attempt on his life, the murder of his sister-in-law's husband, Luis Carlos Galán, and the abduction of his wife and sister. "My sister-in-law, Gloria Pachón de Galán, and I," he added, "do not understand and cannot accept so many unjustified and inexplicable attacks." On the contrary: The release of Maruja and the other journalists was indispensable to finding the road to true peace in Colombia.

Escobar's reply two weeks later began with a bitter blow: "My dear Doctor, I regret that I cannot oblige you." He proceeded to call his attention to reports that certain members of the Constituent Assembly in the official sector, with the consent of the hostages' families, were proposing not to consider the subject of extradition if the captives were not freed. Escobar considered this inappropriate, for the abductions could not be thought of as a means of exerting pressure on members of the Constituent Assembly since the abductions predated the election. In any event, he allowed himself to issue a terrible warning: "Remember, Dr. Villamizar, extradition has taken many victims, and adding two more will not change the process or the continuing struggle very much."

The warning was a complete surprise, because Escobar had not referred again to extradition as a reason for war after the decree undermined that argument for anyone who surrendered, and had focused instead on human rights violations by the special forces that were fighting him. It was his grand strategy: to gain ground with partial victories, continue the war for other reasons that could go on multiplying forever, and not have to surrender.

In his letter, in fact, he claimed to understand that Villamizar's struggle was the same as his in the sense that both wanted to protect their families, but once again he insisted that the Elite Corps had killed some four hundred boys from the slums of Medellín and no one had been punished for it. Such actions, he said, justified the abduction of the journalists as a means of pressing for sanctions on the police who were guilty. He also expressed surprise that no public official had attempted to make direct contact with him concerning the hostages. In any event, he went on, calls and pleas for their freedom would be useless, since what was at stake were the lives of the Extraditables' families and associates. And he concluded: "If the government does not intervene and does not listen to our proposals, we will proceed to execute Maruja and Francisco, about that there can be no doubt."

The letter showed that Escobar was seeking contacts with public officials. Surrender had not been discarded, but it would come at a higher price than anyone had expected, and he was prepared to demand payment with no sentimental discounts. Villamizar understood this, and that same week he visited the president and brought him up-to-date. The president did no more than take careful notes.

At this time Villamizar also met with the prosecutor general, trying to find a different way to proceed in a new situation. The meeting was very productive. The prosecutor general told him that at the end of the week he would issue a report on the death of Diana Turbay holding the police responsible for acting without prudence or orders, and that he was filing charges against three officers of the Elite Corps. He also disclosed that he had investigated eleven agents whom Escobar had accused by name, and had filed charges against them as well.

He kept his word. On April 3 the president received an investigative study from the Prosecutor General's Office regarding the circumstances surrounding Diana Turbay's death. The operation—the study says—began to take shape on January 23, when the intelligence services of the Medellín police received a series of anonymous calls of a generic nature regarding the presence of armed men in the hilly areas of the municipality of Copacabana. Activity was centered—according to the phone calls—in the region of Sabaneta, in particular on the farm properties of Villa del Rosario, La Bola, and Alto de la Cruz. At least one of the calls suggested that this was where the journalists were being held hostage, and that the Doctor—that is, Pablo Escobar—might even be there as well. This piece of information was mentioned in the analysis that served as the basis for the next day's operations, but there was no mention of the probable presence of the abducted journalists. General Miguel Gómez Padilla, head of the National Police, stated that he had been informed on the afternoon of January 24 that on the following day a search-and-seizure verification operation would be carried out, "and the possible capture of Pablo Escobar and a group of drug traffickers." But, it seems, there was no mention at this time either of a possible encounter with the two hostages, Diana Turbay and Richard Becerra.

The operation began at eleven o'clock on the morning of January 25, when Captain Jairo Salcedo García left the Carlos Holguín Academy in Medellín with seven officers, five noncommissioned officers, and forty agents. An hour later, Captain Eduardo Martínez Solanilla was accompanied by two officers, two noncommissioned officers, and seventy-one agents. The report pointed out that in the relevant memorandum no record had been made of the departure of Captain Helmer Ezequiel Torres Vela, who was in charge of the raid on La Bola farm, where Diana and Richard were in fact being held. But in his subsequent statement to the Prosecutor General's Office, the same captain confirmed that he had set out at eleven in the morning with six officers, five noncommissioned officers, and forty agents. Four combat helicopters were assigned to the entire operation.

The raids on Villa del Rosario and Alto de la Cruz were carried out with no difficulty. At about one o'clock, the raid on La Bola began. Second Lieutenant Iván Díaz Alvarez stated that he was coming down from the mesa where the helicopter had left him when he heard shooting on the side of the mountain. Racing in that direction, he caught a glimpse of nine or ten men armed with rifles and submachine guns and running for their lives. "We stayed there a few minutes to see where the attack was coming from," the second lieutenant declared, "when much further down the slope we heard someone calling for help." The second lieutenant said he had hurried down and found a man who shouted: "Please help me." The second lieutenant shouted back: "Halt! Who are you?" The man replied that he was Richard, the journalist, and needed help because Diana Turbay had been wounded. The second lieutenant said that then, without knowing why, he asked the question: "Where's Pablo?" Richard answered: "I don't know, but help me, please." Then the soldier approached, taking all precautions, and then other men from his unit appeared. The second lieutenant concluded: "For us it was a surprise to find the journalists there because that wasn't our objective."

This account agrees almost point by point with the one given by Richard Becerra to the Attorney General's Office. Richard later amplified his statement, saying he had seen the man who shot at him and Diana, and that he had been standing to the left with both hands extended, at a distance of about fifteen meters. "By the time the shooting stopped," Richard concluded, "I had already dropped to the ground."

With regard to the single bullet that caused Diana's death, tests showed that it had entered the left iliac region and moved upward and to the right. The characteristics of the micrological damage indicated that it was a high-velocity bullet, traveling between two and three thousand feet per second, or some three times faster than the speed of sound. It could not be recovered because it shattered into three parts, which lessened its weight, altered its shape, and reduced it to an irregular fragment that continued its trajectory, causing damage of an essentially fatal nature. It was almost certainly a 5.56-caliber bullet, perhaps fired by a rifle similar, if not identical, to an Austrian AUG that had been found on the scene and was not a standard-issue police weapon. In a marginal note, the autopsy report indicated: "Diana had an estimated life expectancy of fifteen more years."

The most intriguing fact in the raid was the presence of a handcuffed civilian in the same helicopter that transported the wounded Diana to Medellín. Two police agents agreed he was a man who looked like a campesino, about thirty-five or forty years old, dark skin, short hair, rather robust, about five feet, seven inches tall, and wearing a cloth cap. They said he had been detained during the raid, and that they were trying to find out who he was when the shooting began, so they had to handcuff him and take him along to the helicopters. One of the agents added that they had left him with their second lieutenant, who questioned him in their presence and released him near the place where he had been picked up. "The gentleman had nothing to do with it," they said, "since the shots came from lower down and he was up there with us." These versions denied that the civilian had been on board the helicopter, but the crew of the aircraft contradicted this. Other statements were more specific. Corporal Luis Carlos Ríos Ramírez, the helicopter gunner, had no doubt that the man had been on board and was returned that same day to the zone of operations.

The mystery carried over to January 26 with the discovery of the body of one José Humberto Vázquez Muñoz, in the municipality of Girardota, near Medellín. He had been killed by three 9mm bullets in the thorax, and two in the head. In the files of the intelligence services, he was described as having a long criminal record as a member of the Medellín cartel. The investigators marked his photograph with the number 5, mixed it in with photographs of other known criminals, and showed them to those who had been held hostage with Diana Turbay. Hero Buss said: "I don't recognize any of them, but I think the person in number five looks a little like one of the thugs I saw a few days after the kidnapping." Azucena Liévano stated that the man in photograph number five, but without a mustache, resembled one of the guards on night duty at the house where she and Diana were held during the first few days of their captivity. Richard Becerra recognized number five as the handcuffed man in the helicopter, but he qualified this: "I think so, because of the shape of his face, but I'm not sure." Orlando Acevedo also recognized him.

Finally, Vázquez Muñoz's wife identified his body and said in a sworn statement that on January 25, 1991, at eight in the morning, her husband had left the house to find a taxi when he was seized by two men on motorcycles wearing police uniforms, and two men in civilian clothes, and put into a car. He managed to shout her name: "Ana Lucía." But they had already driven away. This statement, however, could not be admitted because there were no other witnesses to the abduction.

"In conclusion," said the report, "and on the basis of the evidence brought forward, it is reasonable to affirm that prior to the raid on the La Bola farm, certain members of the National Police in charge of the operation had learned from Mr. Vázquez Muñoz, a civilian in their custody, that some journalists were being held captive in the area, and that, subsequent to these events, he most surely was killed by their hand." Two other unexplained deaths at the site were also confirmed.

The Office of Special Investigations went on to conclude that there were no reasons to assume that General Gómez Padilla or any other high-ranking director of the National Police had been informed; that the weapon that caused Diana's wounds was not fired by any of the members of the special corps of the National Police in Medellín; that members of the unit that raided La Bola should be held accountable for the deaths of three persons whose bodies were found there; that a formal disciplinary investigation would be made into irregularities of a substantive and procedural nature on the part of magistrate 93 for Military Penal Investigation, Dr. Diego Rafael de Jesús Coley Nieto, and his secretary, as well as responsible parties of the DAS in Bogotá.

With the publication of this report, Villamizar felt he was on firmer ground for writing a second letter to Escobar. He sent it, as always, through the Ochoas, along with a letter to Maruja, and asked him to see that she got it. He took the opportunity to give Escobar a textbook explanation of the division of governmental powers into executive, legislative, and judicial, and to make him

understand how difficult it was for the president, within these constitutional and legal mechanisms, to control entities as large and
complex as the Armed Forces. However, he did acknowledge that
Escobar was correct to denounce human rights violations by law
enforcement agencies, and to insist on guarantees for himself, his
family, and his people when they surrendered. "I share your opinion," he said, "that you and I are engaged in essentially the same
struggle: to protect our families' lives and our own, and to achieve
peace." On the basis of these two objectives, he proposed that they
adopt a joint strategy.

Escobar, his pride wounded by the civics lesson, replied a few
days later. "I know that the country is divided into President, Congress, Police, Army," he wrote. "But I also know that the president
is in charge." The rest of the letter consisted of four pages that
reiterated the actions of the police, adding new facts but no new
arguments to what had been said earlier. He denied that the
Extraditables had executed Diana Turbay or had any intention to
do so, because if that were the case they would not have taken her
out of the house where she was being held or dressed her in black
so that she would look like a campesina from the helicopters. "A
dead hostage has no value," he wrote. Then, without transitions or
formulaic courtesies, he closed with these unexpected words:
"Don't worry about [having made] statements to the press demanding my extradition. I know everything will work out, and that
you will bear me no grudge, because your battle to defend your
family has the same objectives as the one I am waging to defend
mine." Villamizar related this statement to an earlier one of Escobar's in which he claimed to feel some embarrassment at holding
Maruja prisoner when his quarrel was not with her but with her
husband. Villamizar had said the same thing in a different way:
"Why is it that if you and I are the ones doing battle, my wife is
the one held prisoner?" and he proposed that Escobar take him in
exchange for Maruja so they could negotiate in person. Escobar
did not accept his offer.

By now Villamizar had been in the Ochoas' prison more than twenty times. He enjoyed the gems of local cuisine that the women from La Loma brought in, taking every possible security precaution. It was a reciprocal process of learning about one another and establishing mutual trust, and they devoted most of their time to dissecting every one of Escobar's sentences and actions to discover his hidden intentions. Villamizar would almost always take the last plane back to Bogotá. His son Andrés would meet him at the airport, and often had to drink mineral water while his father relieved his tension with slow, solitary whiskeys. He had kept his promise not to attend any public function, not to see friends: nothing. When the pressure grew intense, he would go out to the terrace and spend hours staring in the direction where he supposed Maruja was, sending her mental messages until he was overcome by exhaustion. At six in the morning he was on his feet, ready to start all over again. When they had an answer to a letter, or anything else of interest, Martha Nieves or María Lía would call and only have to say a single sentence:

"Doctor, tomorrow at ten."

When there were no calls, he spent his time and efforts on "Colombia Wants Them Back," the television campaign based on the information Beatriz had given them regarding conditions in captivity. The idea had originated with Nora Sanín, the head of the National Association of Media (ASOMEDIOS), and was produced by María del Rosario Ortiz—a close friend of Maruja's, and Hernando Santos's niece—in collaboration with her husband, who was a publicist, and with Gloria Pachón de Galán and other members of the family: Mónica, Alexandra, Juana, and their brothers.

The idea was for a daily succession of well-known personalities in film, the theater, television, soccer, science, or politics to deliver the same message, calling for the release of the hostages and respect for human rights. From the first it had provoked an overwhelming public response. Alexandra traveled from one end of the country to the other with a cameraman, chasing down celebrities. The campaign lasted three months, and some fifty people participated. But Escobar did not budge. When the harpsichordist Rafael Puyana said he was ready to get down on his knees to beg for the release of the hostages, Escobar responded: "Thirty million Colombians can come to me on their knees, and I still won't let them go." But in a letter to Villamizar he praised the program because it demanded not only freedom for the hostages but respect for human rights.

The ease with which Maruja's daughters and their guests trooped across television screens was disturbing to María Victoria, Pacho Santos's wife, because of her unconquerable stage fright. The unexpected microphones put in front of her, the indecency of the lights, the inquisitorial eye of the cameras, the same questions asked with the expectation of hearing the same answers, made her gorge rise with panic, and it was all she could do to swallow her nausea. Her birthday was observed on television; Hernando Santos spoke with professional ease, and then took her arm: "Say a few words." She often managed to escape, but sometimes she had to face it and not only thought she would die in the attempt, but felt awkward and stupid when she saw and heard herself on screen.

Then she reacted against this public servitude. She took a course in small business and another in journalism. By her own decision she became free, accepting invitations she had once despised, attending lectures and concerts, wearing cheerful clothing, staying out late, and at last destroying her image as a pitiful widow. Hernando and his closest friends understood and supported her, helped her to do as she chose. But before long she experienced social disapproval. She knew that many of those who praised her to her face were criticizing her behind her back. She began to receive bouquets of roses with no card, boxes of chocolates with no name, declarations of love with no signature. She enjoyed the illusion that they were from her husband, that perhaps he had managed to find a secret route to her from his prison. But the sender soon identified himself by phone: a madman. A woman also used the phone to tell her straight out: "I'm in love with you."

During those months of creative freedom, Mariavé happened to meet a clairvoyant she knew who had foretold Diana Turbay's tragic end. She was terrified by the mere thought that she too would hear some sinister prediction, but the psychic reassured her. Early in February Mariavé saw her again, and the clairvoyant murmured in her ear, without having been asked a question, and without waiting for a response: "Pacho's alive." She spoke with so much conviction that Mariavé believed it as if she had seen him with her own eyes.

THE TRUTH in February seemed to be that Escobar had no faith in decrees even when he said he did. Distrust was a vital state for him, and he often said he was still alive because of it. He delegated nothing essential. He was his own military commander, his own head of security, intelligence, and counterintelligence, an unpredictable strategist, and an unparalleled purveyor of disinformation. In extreme circumstances he changed his eight-man team of personal bodyguards every day. He was familiar with the latest technology in communications, wiretapping, and tracking devices. He had employees who spent the day engaging in lunatic conversations on his telephones so that the people monitoring his lines would become entangled in mangrove forests of non sequiturs and not be able to distinguish them from the real messages. When the police gave out two phone numbers for receiving information regarding his whereabouts, he hired whole schools of children to anticipate any callers and keep the lines busy twenty-four hours a day. His cunning in never leaving any clues was boundless. He consulted with no one, and provided strategies for his attorneys, whose only work was to outwit the judicial system.

His refusal to see Villamizar was based on his fear that he

might be carrying an electronic tracking device implanted under his skin. This was a tiny radio transmitter powered by a microscopic battery, whose signal could be picked up at great distances by a special receiver—a radiogonometer—that allows the approximate location of the signal to be established. Escobar had so much regard for the sophistication of this device that the idea of someone carrying a subcutaneous receiver did not seem fantastic to him. The gonometer can also be used to determine the coordinates of a radio transmission or a mobile or line telephone. This was why Escobar used phones as little as possible, and if he did, he preferred to be in moving vehicles. He employed couriers to deliver written notes. If he had to see someone, he went to the other person, they did not come to him. And when the meeting was over, he left in the most unpredictable ways. Or he went to the other extreme of technology and traveled in a public minibus that had false plates and markings and drove along established routes but made no stops because it always carried a full complement of passengers, who were his bodyguards. One of Escobar's diversions, in fact, was to act as driver from time to time.

In February, the possibility that the Constituent Assembly would decide in favor of non-extradition and an amnesty was becoming a probability. Escobar knew it and concentrated more energies in that direction than on the government. Gaviria must have turned out to be tougher than he had supposed. Everything relating to the capitulation decrees was kept current in the Office of Criminal Investigation, and the justice minister was prepared to deal with any judicial emergency. For his part, Villamizar acted not only on his own but at his own risk, though his close collaboration with Rafael Pardo kept open a direct channel to the government, which did not compromise him, and in fact allowed him to move forward without making concessions. At this time Escobar must have realized that Gaviria would never appoint an official representative to hold talks with him—which was his golden dream—and he clung to the hope that the Constituent Assembly would issue him a pardon, either as a repentant trafficker, or under the aegis of some armed group. It was not a foolish calculation. Before the swearing-in of the Constituent Assembly, the political parties had agreed on an agenda of closed subjects, and the government, using legal arguments, had succeeded in keeping extradition off the list because they needed it as a bargaining chip for their capitulation policy. But when the Supreme Court reached the spectacular decision that the Constituent Assembly could deal with any subject, without any restrictions whatsoever, the question of extradition reemerged from the ruins. Amnesty was not mentioned, but it was also possible: There was room for everything in the infinite.

PRESIDENT GAVIRIA was not one of those men who could leave a subject hanging and go on to another. In six months he had imposed on his colleagues a personal system of communicating by means of notes written on scraps of paper in cryptic sentences that summarized everything. Sometimes only the name of the individual he was writing to was on the note, which was handed to the closest person, and the addressee knew what he had to do. For his advisers, this method also had the terrifying virtue of making no distinction between work and leisure. Gaviria could not conceive of the difference, since he rested with the same discipline he applied to work, and continued sending his scraps of paper when he was at a cocktail party or as soon as he came up from diving. "A tennis game with him was like a meeting of the Council of Ministers," said one of his advisers. He could fall into a deep sleep for five or ten minutes, even sitting at his desk, and wake refreshed, while his colleagues collapsed with exhaustion. This method, however random it might appear, could trigger action with more urgency and energy than formal memos.

The system proved very useful when the president tried to parry the Supreme Court's blow against extradition with the argument that it was a question of law, not a constitutional issue. At first the government minister, Humberto de la Calle, succeeded in convincing the majority. But in the end, the things that interest individuals become more important than the things that interest governments, and people had been correct in identifying extradition as a contributing factor to social unrest, and in particular to the savagery of terrorism. And so, after much twisting and turning, it was at last included on the agenda of the Commission on Rights.

In the meantime, the Ochoas still feared that Escobar, pursued by his own demons, would decide to immolate himself in a catastrophe of apocalyptic proportions. Their fear was prophetic. Early in March, Villamizar received an urgent message from them: "Come immediately. Something very serious is going to happen." They had received a letter from Pablo Escobar threatening to set off fifty tons of dynamite in the historic district of Cartagena de Indias if there were no sanctions against the police who were devastating the slums of Medellín: 100 kilos for each boy killed outside of combat.

The Extraditables had considered Cartagena an untouchable sanctuary until September 28, 1989, when an explosion shook the foundations of the Hotel Hilton, blowing out windows and killing two physicians at a convention in session on another floor. From then on, it was clear that not even this historical treasure was safe from the war. The new threat did not permit a moment's hesitation.

Villamizar informed Gaviria a few days before the deadline. "Now we're not fighting for Maruja but to save Cartagena," he said, to provide the president with an argument. Gaviria's response was that he thanked him for the information, said the government would take steps to prevent the disaster, but under no circumstances would he give in to blackmail. And so Villamizar traveled to Medellín one more time, and with the help of the Ochoas succeeded in dissuading Escobar. It was not easy. Days before the deadline, Escobar guaranteed in a hurried note that for the moment nothing would happen to the captive journalists, and postponed the detonation of bombs in large cities. But he was also categorical: If police operations in Medellín continued past April, no stone would be left standing in the very ancient and noble city of Cartagena de Indias.

9

ALONE IN THE ROOM, Maruja knew she was in the hands of the same men who may have killed Marina and Beatriz, and were refusing to return the radio and television to keep her from finding that out. She moved from earnest pleading to enraged demands; she confronted her guards, shouting loud enough for the neighbors to hear; she refused to walk and threatened to stop eating. The majordomo and the guards, surprised by the unthinkable, did not know what to do. They conferred in whispers, went out to make phone calls, and came back even more indecisive. They tried to reassure Maruja with illusory promises, or intimidate her with threats, but they could not break her resolve not to eat.

She had never felt more self-possessed. It was clear that her guards had instructions not to mistreat her, and she gambled on their needing her alive at any cost. Her calculations were correct: Three days after Beatriz's release, the door opened very early in the morning and the majordomo came in carrying the radio and the television. "You'll learn something now," he said. And in an unemotional voice he announced:

"Doña Marina Montoya is dead."

In contrast to what she herself had expected, Maruja heard the news as if she had always known it. The astonishing thing for her would have been if Marina were alive. When the truth reached her heart, however, she realized how much she had loved her, how much she would have given to have it not be true.

"Murderers!" she screamed at the majordomo. "That's all you are: murderers!"

At that moment the "Doctor" appeared in the doorway and tried to calm Maruja with the news that Beatriz was safe at home, but she would not believe him until she saw it with her own eyes on television or heard it on the radio. Yet he seemed to have been sent to allow her to give vent to her feelings.

"You haven't been back," she said. "And I can understand that: You must be very ashamed of what you did to Marina."

He needed a moment to recover from his surprise.

"What happened?" Maruja provoked him. "Was she condemned to death?"

Then he said it had been a question of taking revenge for a double betrayal. "Your case is different," he said. And repeated what he had said earlier: "It's political." Maruja listened to him with the strange fascination that the idea of death holds for those who believe they are going to die.

"At least tell me how it happened," she said. "Did Marina know?"

"I swear to you she didn't," he said.

"How could that be?" Maruja insisted. "How could she not know?"

"They told her they were taking her to another house," he said with the urgency of someone who wants to be believed. "They told her to get out of the car, and she kept walking and they shot her in the back of the head. She couldn't have known anything."

The image of Marina with her hood on backward stumbling blindly toward an imaginary house would pursue Maruja through many sleepless nights. More than death itself, she feared the lucidity of the final moment. The only thing that gave her some consolation was the box of sleeping pills that she had saved as if they were precious pearls, and would swallow by the handful before allowing herself to be dragged off to the slaughter.

At last, on the midday news, she saw Beatriz surrounded by her family in a flower-filled apartment that she recognized in spite of all the changes: It was her own. But her joy at seeing it was ruined by her dislike for the new decoration. She thought the library was well done and just in the place she wanted it, but the colors of the walls and carpets were awful, and the Tang Dynasty horse was placed precisely where it would most be in the way. "How stupid they are!" she shouted. "It's just the opposite of what I said!" Her longing to be free was reduced for a moment to wanting to scold them for the poor job they had done.

In this whirlwind of contrary sensations and feelings, the days became intolerable, the nights interminable. Sleeping in Marina's bed unnerved her: Covered by her blanket, tormented by her odor, as she began to fall asleep she could hear in the darkness, beside her in the bed, the buzz of Marina's whispering. One night it was not a hallucination but miraculous and real. Marina grasped her arm with her warm, gentle, living hand, and breathed into her ear in her natural voice: "Maruja."

She did not consider it a hallucination because in Jakarta she had also had what seemed to be a fantastic experience. At an antiques fair she had bought the life-size sculpture of a beautiful youth who had one foot resting on the head of a conquered boy. Like the statues of Catholic saints, the figure had a halo, but this one was tin, and the style and material made it look like a shoddy afterthought. Only after keeping it for some time in the best spot in her house did she learn it was the God of Death.

One night Maruja dreamed she was trying to pull the halo off the statue because it seemed so ugly, but could not. It was soldered onto the bronze. She woke feeling troubled by the bad memory, hurried to look at the statue in the living room, and found the god uncrowned and the halo on the floor, as if this were the conclusion of her dream. Maruja—who is a rationalist and an agnostic—accepted the idea that she herself, in an episode of sleepwalking she could not recall, had torn the halo off the God of Death.

At the beginning of her captivity, she had been sustained by the rage she felt at Marina's submissiveness. Later it became compassion for her bitter fate and a desire to give her the will to live. She was sustained by having to pretend to a strength she did not have when Beatriz began to lose control, and the need to maintain her own equilibrium when adversity overwhelmed them. Someone had to take command to keep them from going under, and she had been the one to do it, in a grim, foul-smelling space that measured three meters by two and a half meters, where she slept on the floor, ate kitchen scraps, and never knew if she would live to see the next minute. But when no one else was left in the room, she no longer had any reason to pretend: She was alone with herself.

The certainty that Beatriz had told her family how to communicate with her on radio and television kept her alert. In fact, Villamizar appeared several times with his words of encouragement, and her children comforted her with their imagination and wit. Then, with no warning, that contact had been broken off for two weeks. This was when a sense of abandonment paralyzed her. She caved in. She stopped walking. She lay with her face to the wall, removed from everything, eating and drinking only enough to keep from dying. She experienced the same distress she had felt in December, the same cramps and shooting pains in her legs that had made the doctor's visit necessary. But this time she did not even complain.

The guards, involved in their personal conflicts and internecine quarrels, paid no attention to her. Her food grew cold on the plate, and both the majordomo and his wife seemed oblivious. The days became longer and emptier, so much so that she sometimes missed the worst moments of the early days. She lost interest in life. She cried. One morning she woke to discover in horror that her right arm had lifted by itself.

The change of guards in February was providential. As replacements for Barrabás's crew, they sent four new boys who were serious, well disciplined, and talkative. They had good manners and an ease of expression that were a relief to Maruja. As soon as they came in they invited her to play Nintendo and other video games. The games brought them together. From the start she knew they shared a common language, and that facilitated communication. They had, no doubt, been instructed to overcome her resistance and raise her morale with a different kind of treatment, for they tried to persuade her to follow the doctor's orders and walk in the courtyard, to think of her husband and children and not disappoint them when they were hoping to see her soon, and in good condition.

The atmosphere lent itself to confidences. Aware that they too were prisoners, and perhaps needed her as well, Maruja told them stories about her three sons, who had already gone through adolescence. She recounted the significant events in their lives as they were growing up and going to school, and talked about their habits and tastes. And the guards, feeling more confident, told her about themselves.

They had all finished secondary school, and one had completed at least a semester of college. In contrast to the previous guards, they said they were from middle-class families, but in one way or another had been marked by the culture of the Medellín slums. The oldest, a twenty-four-year-old whom they called Ant, was tall, good-looking, and rather reserved. His university studies had been interrupted when his parents died in a car accident, and his only recourse had been to join a gang of killers. Another, called Shark, recounted with amusement that he had passed half his courses in secondary school by threatening his teachers with a toy revolver. The most cheerful of this team, and of all the guards who had worked there, was called Top, and that, in effect, was what he resembled. He was very fat, with short, thin legs, and his love of dancing bordered on the maniacal. Once, after breakfast, he put a salsa tape in the cassette player and danced without a break, and with frenetic energy, until the end of his shift. The quietest one, whose mother was a schoolteacher, read books and newspapers and was well informed on current events. He had only one explanation for being in that life: "Because it's so cool."

Just as Maruja had first suspected, however, they were not insensible to human relationships. This, in turn, not only gave her back the will to live, but also the wit to gain advantages that the guards themselves may not have foreseen.

"Don't think I'm going to try anything stupid with you," she told them. "Believe me, I won't do any of the things I'm not allowed to, because I know this business will be over soon and turn out fine. So it doesn't make sense to put so many restrictions on me."

With an autonomy that none of the earlier guards—not even their bosses—had shown, the new guards dared to relax the rules much more than even Maruja had hoped. They let her move around the room, speak in a more natural voice, go to the bathroom without following a fixed schedule. The new regime gave her back the desire to take care of herself, which she attributed to her experience with the statue in Jakarta. She made good use of classes on Alexandra's program that had been prepared for her by a gymnastics teacher and were called, with her in mind, exercises in confined spaces. Her enthusiasm was so great that one of the guards asked with a suspicious look: "Is that program sending you some message?" Maruja had a hard time convincing him that it was not.

During this time she was also moved by the unexpected appearance of "Colombia Wants Them Back," which seemed not only well conceived and well produced, but also the best way to keep up the morale of the last two hostages. She felt more in touch with her family and friends. She thought about how she would have done the program, as a campaign, as a remedy, as a means of swaying public opinion, and began to make bets with the guards about who would appear on the screen the next day. Once she wagered it would be Vicky Hernández, the great actress and her close friend, and she won. The greater prize, in any case, was that just seeing Vicky and listening to her message produced one of the few happy moments of her captivity.

Her walks in the courtyard also began to bear fruit. The German shepherd, overjoyed at seeing her again, tried to squeeze under the gate to play with Maruja, but she calmed him down, petting and talking to him, afraid the guards would become suspicious. Marina had told her that the gate led to a quiet yard with sheep and chickens. Maruja confirmed this with a rapid glance in the moonlight. But she also saw a man with a rifle standing guard outside the enclosure. The hope of escaping with the complicity of the dog had been canceled.

On February 20, when life seemed to have reestablished its rhythm, the radio reported that the body of Dr. Conrado Prisco Lopera—a cousin of the gang's bosses, who had disappeared two days earlier—had been found in a field in Medellín. Another cousin, Edgar de Jesús Botero Prisco, was murdered four days later. Neither man had a criminal record. Dr. Prisco Lopera was the physician who had tended to Juan Vitta without concealing his name or his face, and Maruja wondered if he was the same masked doctor who had examined her earlier.

Like the death of the Prisco brothers in January, these killings had a serious effect on the guards and increased the anxiety of the majordomo and his family. The idea that the cartel would exact the life of a hostage as payment for their deaths, as it had with Marina Montoya, moved through the room like an ominous shadow. The majordomo came in the next day for no apparent reason, and at an unusual hour.

"I'm not trying to scare you," he told Maruja, "but something very serious has happened: A butterfly's been on the courtyard gate since last night."

Maruja, a skeptic regarding invisible forces, did not understand what he meant. The majordomo explained with calculated theatricality.

"You see, when they killed the other Priscos, the same thing happened," he said. "A black butterfly stayed on the bathroom door for three days."

Maruja recalled Marina's dark presentiments, but pretended not to understand.

"And what does that mean?" she asked.

"I don't know," replied the owner, "but it must be a very bad omen because that's when they killed doña Marina."

"The one now, is it black or tan?" Maruja asked.

"Tan," said the owner.

"Then it's a good omen," said Maruja. "It's the black ones that are unlucky."

His attempt to frighten her did not succeed. Maruja knew her husband, the way he thought and acted, and did not believe he would do anything rash enough to rob a butterfly of its sleep. She knew, above all, that neither he nor Beatriz would let slip any detail that could be of use in an armed rescue attempt. And yet, accustomed to interpreting changes in her inner state as reflections of the external world, she did not discount the fact that five deaths in the same family in one month might have terrible consequences for the last two hostages.

On the other hand, the rumor that the Constituent Assembly had certain doubts regarding extradition must have been some consolation to the Extraditables. On February 28, on an official visit to the United States, President Gaviria declared his firm commitment to maintaining it at all costs, but this caused no alarm: By now non-extradition had deep-rooted support throughout the country and required neither bribes nor intimidation to be enacted.

Maruja followed these events with close attention, in a routine that seemed to be the same day repeated over and over again. Then, without warning, while she was playing dominoes with the guards, the Top ended the game and picked up the tiles for the last time.

"We're leaving tomorrow," he said.

Maruja refused to believe him, but the schoolteacher's son confirmed the news.

"Really," he said. "Barrabás's crew is coming tomorrow."

This was the beginning of what Maruja would remember as her black March. Just as the guards who were leaving seemed to have been instructed to make her imprisonment a little easier, the ones who arrived had no doubt been told to make it unbearable again. They burst into the room like an earthquake: the Monk, tall, thin, more somber and introverted than last time; the others, the same ones, as if they had never left. Barrabás acted like a movie gangster, barking military orders at them to find the hiding place of something that did not exist, or pretending to search for it himself in order to terrorize his victim. They turned the room inside out with methodical brutality. They pulled the bed apart, emptied the mattress, and restuffed it so badly the lumps made it difficult to sleep on.

Daily life returned to the old style of keeping weapons at the ready if orders were not obeyed instantly. Barrabás never spoke to Maruja without aiming his submachine gun at her head. She, as always, responded by threatening to denounce him to his superiors.

"I'm not going to die just because you fire a bullet by mistake," she said. "You take it easy or I'll complain."

This time the strategy did not work. It seemed clear, however, that the disorder was not deliberate or meant to intimidate, but was the result of a system corroded from within by profound demoralization. Even the frequent, colorful arguments between the majordomo and Damaris became frightening. He would come home at all hours—if he came home at all—stupefied by drink, and have to confront his wife's obscene recriminations. Their screams and shouts, and the crying of their young daughters wakened from sleep, could be heard all over the house. The guards made fun of them with theatrical imitations that added to the noise. It seemed inconceivable that with all the uproar, no one was curious enough to come to the house.

The majordomo and his wife each came to Maruja for advice: Damaris, because of a plausible jealousy that gave her no peace, and he, to find some way to calm her down without giving up his escapades. But Maruja's good offices did not last beyond the majordomo's next fling.

During one of their many fights, Damaris clawed at her husband's face like a cat, and it was a long time before the marks disappeared. He hit her so hard she went through the window. It was a miracle he did not kill her, but she managed to hold on at the last minute and was left dangling from the balcony over the courtyard. It was the end. Damaris packed her bags and left with the girls for Medellín.

The house was now in the sole care of the majordomo, who sometimes stayed away until nightfall, when he showed up with yogurt and bags of potato chips. Every once in a while he would bring back a chicken. The guards, tired of waiting, would ransack the kitchen and come back to the room with stale crackers and some raw sausage for Maruja. Boredom made them touchy, and more dangerous. They railed against their parents, the police, society in general. They told about their gratuitous crimes and deliberate sacrileges to prove to one another that God did not exist, and went to insane lengths in recounting their sexual exploits. One of them described the aberrations he had inflicted on one of his girlfriends as revenge for her mocking and humiliating him. Resentful and out of control, they took to smoking marijuana and crack until the dense air in the room became unbreathable. They played the radio at ear-splitting volume, slammed the door when they went in or out, shouted, sang, danced, cavorted in the courtyard. One of them looked like a professional acrobat in a traveling circus. Maruja warned them that the noise would attract the attention of the police.

"Let them come and kill us," they shouted in chorus.

Maruja felt ready to snap, above all because of the crazed Barrabás, who liked to wake her by pressing the barrel of his machine gun against her temple. Her hair began to fall out. The pillow covered with strands of hair depressed her from the moment she opened her eyes at dawn.

She knew that each of the guards was different, but they all were susceptible to insecurity and mutual distrust. Maruja's fear exacerbated these feelings. "How can you live like this?" she would demand without warning. "What do you believe in? Do you have any idea of what friendship means?" Before they could respond she cornered them: "Does the word loyalty mean anything to you?" They did not reply, but the answers they gave themselves must have been disquieting, because instead of becoming defiant they deferred to Maruja. Only Barrabás stood up to her. "You rich motherfuckers!" he once shouted. "Did you really think you'd run things forever? Not anymore, damn it: It's all over!" Maruja, who had been so afraid of him, met the challenge with the same rage.

"You kill your friends, your friends kill you, you all end up killing each other," she screamed. "Who can understand you? Find me one person who can say what kind of animals you people are."

Driven, perhaps, to desperation because he could not kill her, Barrabás smashed his fist into the wall and damaged the bones in his wrist. He bellowed like a savage and burst into tears of fury. Maruja would not allow herself to be softened by compassion. The majordomo spent the entire afternoon trying to calm her down, and made an unsuccessful effort to improve supper.

Maruja asked herself how, with so much commotion, they could still believe it made sense to talk in whispers, confine her to the room, ration out the radio and television for reasons of security. Tired of all the madness, she rebelled against the meaningless rules of her captivity, spoke in her natural voice, went to the bathroom whenever she wanted. But her fear of sexual attack intensified, above all when the majordomo left her alone with the two guards on duty. It culminated one morning when a masked guard burst into the bathroom while she was in the shower. Maruja managed to cover herself with a towel, and her terrified scream must have been heard for miles around. He froze and stood like a statue, his heart in his mouth for fear of how the neighbors would react. But no one came, not a sound was heard. He backed out of the room on tiptoe, as if he had opened the bathroom door by mistake.

The majordomo showed up one day with another woman to run the house. But instead of controlling the disorder, they both helped to increase it. The woman joined him in his fierce bouts of drinking that tended to end in blows and smashed bottles. Meals were served at improbable hours. On Sundays they went out carousing and left Maruja and the guards with nothing to eat until the next day. One night, while Maruja was walking alone in the courtyard, the four guards went to raid the kitchen and left the machine guns in the room. An idea made her shudder. She relished it as she talked to the dog, petted him, whispered to him, and the overjoyed animal licked her hands with complicitous growls. A shout from Barrabás brought her back to reality.

It was the end of an illusion. They replaced the dog with a new one that had the face of a killer. They prohibited her walks, and Maruja was subjected to a regime of constant surveillance. What she feared most then was that they would shackle her to the bed with a plastic-wrapped chain that Barrabás moved back and forth in his hands like an iron rosary. Maruja tried to anticipate their next move.

"If I had wanted to leave, I would have done it a long time ago," she said. "I've been left alone lots of times, and if I didn't run away it's because I didn't want to."

Somebody must have complained, because one morning the majordomo appeared in the room, full of suspect humility and all kinds of excuses: that he could die of shame, that the boys would behave themselves from now on, that he had sent for his wife and she was coming back. And it was true: Damaris returned, the same as always, with her two girls, her Scottish bagpiper's miniskirts, and her endless lentils. Two bosses with masks and the same conciliatory attitude arrived the next day, shoved the four guards out, and imposed order. "They won't be back again," one of them said with hair-raising decisiveness. And it was over.

That same afternoon they sent the crew of high school graduates, and it was like a magical return to the peace of February: unhurried time, entertainment magazines, the music of Guns N' Roses, and Mel Gibson movies watched with hired gunmen well versed in unrestrained passions. Maruja was moved by the fact that the adolescent killers watched and listened with as much devotion as her children.

Toward the end of March, without any announcement, two strangers appeared, their faces hidden under hoods lent them by the guards. One, with barely a greeting, began to measure the floor with a tailor's metric tape, while the other tried to ingratiate himself with Maruja.

"I'm delighted to make your acquaintance, Señora," he said. "We're here to carpet the room."

"Carpet the room!" Maruja shouted in a blind fury. "You can go to hell! What I want is to get out of here! Right now!"

What troubled her was not the carpet but what it could mean: an indefinite postponement of her release. One of the guards would say later that Maruja's interpretation had been mistaken, since it could have meant she would be leaving soon and they were renovating the room for more important hostages. But at that moment Maruja was sure a carpet could only mean another year of her life.

PACHO SANTOS ALSO had to use all his wits to keep his guards occupied, because when they were bored with playing cards, seeing the same movie ten times in a row, and recounting their sexual exploits, they began to pace the room like caged lions. Through the holes in their hoods he could see their reddened eyes. The only thing they could do then was take a few days off—that is, stupefy themselves with alcohol and drugs during a week of nonstop parties, and come back worse than before. Drugs were prohibited and their use was punished with great severity, and not only during working hours, but the addicts always found a way around the vigilance of their superiors. The most common drug was marijuana, but their prescription for difficult times were Olympiads of crack that made him fear a calamity. One of the guards, after a night of carousing in the street, burst into the room and woke Pacho with a shout. He saw the devil's mask almost touching his face, the bloodshot eyes, the coarse hairs bristling from his ears, and smelled the sulfurous stink of hell. One of his guards wanted to finish up the party with Pacho. "You don't know how bad I am," he said while they drank a double *aguardiente* together at six in the morning. For the next two hours the guard, without being asked, told Pacho the story of his life, driven by the uncontrollable compulsion of his conscience. At last he passed out, and if Pacho did not escape then it was because he lost his courage at the last minute.

His most heartening reading in captivity were the personal notes that *El Tiempo*, on María Victoria's initiative, published for him, without concealment or reticence, on its editorial pages. One was accompanied by a recent photograph of his children, and in the heat of the moment he wrote them a letter filled with those thunderous truths that seem ridiculous to anyone who has not lived through them: "I'm sitting here in this room, chained to a bed, my eyes full of tears." From then on he wrote his wife and children a series of letters from the heart, which he could never send.

Pacho had lost all hope after the deaths of Marina and Diana, and then the possibility of escape came out to meet him without his looking for it. By now he was certain he was in one of the neighborhoods near Avenida Boyacá, to the west of the city. He knew these districts because he would make detours through them when traffic was very heavy on his way home from the newspaper, and he had been driving that route on the night he was abducted. Most of its structures were clusters of residences built in rows, the same house repeated many times over: a large door to the garage, a tiny garden, a second floor overlooking the street, and all the windows protected by wrought-iron gates painted white. And in one week he managed to find out the exact distance to the pizzeria, and learned that the factory was none other than the Bavaria Brewery. A disorienting detail was the demented rooster that at first crowed at any hour, and as the months passed crowed at the same hour in different places: sometimes far away at three in the afternoon, other times next to his window at two in the morning. It would have been even more disorienting if he had known that Maruja and Beatriz also heard it in a distant section of the city.

At the end of the hallway, to the right of his room, he could jump from a window that opened onto a small, enclosed courtyard, and then climb the vine-covered adobe wall next to a tree with sturdy branches. He did not know what lay on the other side of the wall, but since it was a corner house, it had to be a street. And almost certainly it was the street with the grocery store, the pharmacy, and an auto repair shop. This shop, however, could be a negative factor, since it might be a front for the kidnappers. In fact, Pacho once heard a conversation about soccer coming from that direction, and was sure the two voices belonged to his guards. In any case, climbing the wall would be easy, but the rest was unpredictable. The better alternative was the bathroom, which had the undeniable advantage of being the only place they let him go without the chain.

It seemed clear that his escape had to take place in the middle of the day, because he never went to the bathroom after getting into bed for the night—even if he stayed awake watching television or writing—and any deviation could betray him. Then too, the businesses closed early, the neighbors were in for the night after the seven o'clock news, and by ten there was not a soul on the streets. Even on Friday nights, which are very noisy in Bogotá, one heard only the slow wheeze of the brewery or the sudden wail of an ambulance speeding down Avenida Boyacá. And at night it would not be easy to find immediate refuge on the deserted streets, and the doors of businesses and houses would be locked and bolted against the dangers of the night.

However, the opportunity—stark and plain—presented itself on March 6, and it came at night. One of the guards had brought in a bottle of *aguardiente* and invited him to have a drink while they watched a program about Julio Iglesias on television. Pacho drank little and only to humor him. The guard, who had come on duty in the afternoon, had already been drinking and passed out before the bottle was emptied, and before he could put the chain on Pacho, who was collapsing with fatigue and did not see the chance that had fallen from the skies. Whenever he wanted to go to the bathroom at night, the guard on duty had to accompany him, but Pacho preferred not to disturb his blissful drunken stupor. He went out into the hallway in all innocence, just as he was, barefoot and in his underwear, and held his breath as he passed the room where the other guards were sleeping. One was snoring like a chainsaw. Pacho had not been aware until then that he was running away without realizing it, and that the most difficult part was over. A wave of nausea rose from his stomach, froze his tongue, and emptied out his heart. "It wasn't the fear of escaping but the fear of not daring to," he would say later. He went into the darkened bathroom and closed the door, his decision irrevocable. Another guard, still half-asleep, pushed the door open and shined a flashlight in his face. Both were astonished.

"What are you doing?" asked the guard.

Pacho responded in a firm voice:

"Taking a shit."

It was the only thing that occurred to him. The guard shook his head, not knowing what to think.

"Okay," he said at last. "Enjoy yourself."

He stayed at the door, shining the flashlight on him, not blinking, until Pacho pretended he had finished.

During that week, in the throes of depression at his failure, he resolved to escape in a radical and irremediable way. "I'll take the blade from the razor, cut my veins, and they'll find me dead in the morning," he told himself. The next day, Father Alfonso Llanos Escobar published his weekly column in *El Tiempo*, addressed it to Pacho Santos, and ordered him in the name of God not to even consider suicide. The article had been on Hernando Santos's desk for three weeks; without really knowing why, he had been unable to decide if he should publish it, and on the previous day—again without knowing why—he resolved at the last minute to use it. Each time he tells the story, Pacho again experiences the stupefaction he felt that day.

A LOW-RANKING BOSS who visited Maruja at the beginning of April promised to intercede to allow her to receive a letter from her husband, something she needed as if it were a medicine for her soul and her body. The response was astounding: "No problem." The man left around seven in the evening. At twelve-thirty, after her walk in the courtyard, the majordomo knocked with some urgency at the door, which was locked on the inside, and handed her the letter. It was not one of several sent by Villamizar with Guido Parra, but the one sent through Jorge Luis Ochoa, to which Gloria Pachón de Galán had added a consolatory postscript. On the back of the paper, Pablo Escobar had written a note in his own hand: "I know this has been terrible for you and your family, but my family and I have also suffered a great deal. But don't worry, I promise that nothing will happen to you, whatever else happens." And he concluded with a marginal confidence that Maruja found unbelievable: "Don't pay attention to my press communiqués, they're only to keep up the pressure."

Her husband's letter, however, disheartened her with its pessimism. He said that things were going well, but that she must be patient because the wait might be even longer. Certain that someone else would read it before it was delivered to her, Villamizar had concluded with words meant more for Escobar than Maruja: "Offer up your sacrifice for the peace of Colombia." She became furious. She had often intercepted the mental messages that Villamizar sent to her from their terrace, and she had responded with all her heart: "Get me out of here, I don't know who I am anymore after so many months of not seeing myself in a mirror."

The letter gave her one more reason for writing in her reply that what the hell did he mean by patience, damn it, she'd already shown more than enough and suffered more than enough during hideous nights when the icy fear of death would wake her with a start. She did not know it was an old letter, written between his failure with Guido Parra and his first interviews with the Ochoas, at a time when he saw no glimmer of hope. Not the kind of optimistic letter he would have written now, when the road to her freedom seemed clear and defined.

Fortunately, the misunderstanding allowed Maruja to realize that her anger was caused not so much by the letter as by an older, less conscious rancor toward her husband: Why had Alberto permitted them to release only Beatriz if he was the one handling the process? In the nineteen years of their life together, she had not had time, or reason, or courage to ask herself that kind of question, and her answer to herself made Maruja see the truth: She had been able to withstand captivity because of the absolute certainty that her husband was devoting every moment of his life to her release, and that he did this without rest and even without hope because of his absolute certainty that she knew what he was doing. It was—though neither of them realized it—a pact of love.

They had met nineteen years earlier at a business meeting

when they were both young publicists. "Alberto appealed to me right away," Maruja says. Why? She doesn't have to think twice: "Because he looks so helpless." It was the last answer one would expect. At first glance, Alberto seemed a typical nonconformist university student of the time, with hair down to his shoulders, a two-day growth of beard, and one shirt that was washed when it rained. "Sometimes I bathed," he says today, with a laugh. At second glance, he was a drinker and a womanizer, and had a short temper. But at third glance, Maruja saw a man who could lose his head over a beautiful woman, especially if she was intelligent and sensitive, and most especially if she had more than enough of the only thing lacking to turn the boy into a man: an iron hand and a tender heart.

Asked what he had liked about her, Villamizar answers with a growl. Perhaps because Maruja, apart from her visible charms, was not the best-qualified person to fall in love with. In the bloom of her early thirties, she had married in the Catholic Church at the age of nineteen, and had given her husband five children—three girls and two boys—born fifteen months apart. "I told Alberto everything right away," Maruja says, "so he'd know he was entering a mine field." He listened with another growl, and instead of asking her to lunch, he had a mutual friend ask them both. The next day he asked her to lunch, along with the same friend, on the third day he asked her alone, and on the fourth day they saw each other without having lunch. And so they continued to meet every day, with the best of intentions. When Villamizar is asked if he was in love or only wanted to take her to bed, he answers in pure Santanderese: "Don't screw around, it was serious." Perhaps not even he imagined just how serious it was.

Maruja had a marriage with no surprises, no arguments, a perfect marriage, but perhaps it was missing the gram of inspiration and risk she needed to feel alive. She made time for Villamizar by saying she was at the office. She invented more work than she had, even on Saturdays from noon until ten at night. On Sundays and holidays they improvised children's parties, lectures on art, midnight cinema clubs, anything, just so they could be together. He had no problems: He was single and available, came and went as he pleased, and had so many Saturday sweethearts it was as if he had none at all. He needed only to write his final thesis to be a surgeon like his father, but the times favored living one's life more than curing the sick. Love had escaped the confines of boleros, the perfumed love letters that had endured for four centuries were a thing of the past, as were tearful serenades, monogrammed handkerchiefs, the language of flowers, and empty movie theaters at three in the afternoon, and the whole world seemed protected from death by the inspired lunacy of the Beatles.

A year after they met they began to live together, with Maruja's children, in an apartment that measured a hundred square meters. "It was a disaster," says Maruja. And with reason: They lived amid free-for-all quarrels, the crash of breaking plates, jealousies and suspicions on the part of both children and adults. "Sometimes I hated him with all my heart," says Maruja. "I felt the same about her," says Villamizar. "But never for more than five minutes," Maruja laughs. In October 1971, they were married in Ureña, Venezuela, and it was as if they had added one more sin to their life, because divorce did not exist and very few believed in the legality of civil ceremonies. After four years Andrés was born, the only child they had together. The difficulties continued but caused them less grief: Life had taken on the task of teaching them that the joy of love was not meant to lull you to sleep, but to keep you struggling together.

Maruja was the daughter of Alvaro Pachón de la Torre, a star reporter of the 1940s who died with two well-known colleagues in a car crash of historic importance to the profession. Her mother was dead, and she and her sister Gloria had been on their own from the time they were very young. Maruja had been a draftsman and painter at the age of twenty, a precocious publicist, a director and scriptwriter for radio and television, the head of public relations or advertising for major companies, and always a journalist. Her artistic talent and impulsive nature attracted immediate attention, helped along by a gift for command that was concealed behind the quiet pools of her Gypsy eyes. Villamizar, for his part, forgot about medicine, cut his hair, threw out his one shirt, put on a tie, and became an expert in the mass marketing of anything they gave him to sell. But he did not change his nature. Maruja acknowledges that more than any of life's blows, it was he who cured her of the formalism and inhibitions of her social milieu.

They had separate, successful careers while the children were in school. Maruja came home every night at six to spend time with them. Smarting from her own strict, conventional upbringing, she wanted to be a different kind of mother who did not attend parents' meetings at school or help with homework. The girls complained: "We want a mommy like all the others." But Maruja pushed them in the opposite direction toward the independence and education to do whatever they wanted. The curious thing is that they all wanted to do precisely what she would have chosen for them. Mónica studied at the Academy of Fine Arts in Rome, and is a painter and graphic designer. Alexandra is a journalist and a television producer and director. Juana is a scriptwriter and director for television and films. Nicolás composes music for movies and television. Patricio is a psychologist. Andrés, a student of economics, was bitten by the scorpion of politics thanks to his father's bad example, and at the age of twenty-one was elected by popular vote to the alderman's seat on the town council of Chapinero, in northern Bogotá.

The complicity of Luis Carlos Galán and Gloria Pachón, dating back to the days before their marriage, proved decisive in the political career that Alberto and Maruja never expected. Galán, at the age of thirty-seven, ran for the presidential candidacy of the New Liberalism Party. His wife, Gloria, who was also a journalist, and Maruja, experienced in promotion and publicity, conceived and directed advertising strategies for six electoral campaigns. Villamizar's experience in mass marketing had given him a logistical knowledge of Bogotá that very few politicians possessed. As a team, the three of them created, in one frantic month, the first New Liberalism campaign in the capital, and swept away more seasoned candidates. In the 1982 elections, Villamizar was listed sixth in a slate that did not expect to elect more than five representatives to the Chamber, but in fact elected nine. Unfortunately, that victory was the prelude to a new life that would lead Alberto and Maruja—eight years later—to her abduction and its gruesome test of their love.

SOME TEN DAYS after the letter, the important boss they called the "Doctor"—acknowledged by now as the man in charge of her abduction and captivity—paid Maruja an unannounced visit. After seeing him in the house where she had been taken on the night of the kidnapping, he had come back about three times prior to Marina's death. He and Marina would have long whispered conversations together, as if they were old friends. His relationship to Maruja had always been strained. For any remark of hers, no matter how simple, he had a haughty, brutal reply: "You have nothing to say here." When the three hostages were still together, she tried to register a complaint with him about the wretched conditions in the room, to which she attributed her persistent cough and erratic pains.

"I've spent worse nights in places a thousand times worse than this," he answered in an angry tone. "Who do you people think you are?"

His visits were preludes to great events, good or bad, but always decisive. This time, however, encouraged by Escobar's letter, Maruja had the heart to confront him.

Their communication was immediate and surprisingly untroubled. She began by asking, with no resentment, what Escobar wanted, how the negotiations were going, what the chances were of his surrendering soon. He told her in a frank manner that nothing would be easy unless there were sufficient guarantees of safety for Pablo Escobar, his family, and his people. Maruja asked about Guido Parra, whose efforts had brought her hope and whose sudden disappearance intrigued her.

"Well, he didn't behave very well," he said in an unemotional way. "He's out of it now."

That could be interpreted in three ways: either he had lost his power, or he had really left the country—which was the public story—or he had been killed. The "Doctor" evaded the issue, saying that in fact he did not know.

In part to satisfy her irresistible curiosity, and in part to gain his confidence, Maruja also asked who had written a recent letter from the Extraditables to the ambassador of the United States regarding extradition and the drug trade. She had found it striking not only because of the strength of its arguments but because it was so well written. The "Doctor" was not certain, but he assured her that Escobar wrote his letters himself, rethinking and revising drafts until he said what he wanted to say without equivocations or contradictions. At the end of their conversation, which lasted almost two hours, the "Doctor" again raised the subject of surrender. Maruja realized he was more interested than he had first appeared to be, thinking not only about Escobar's future but about his own. She had a well-reasoned opinion about the controversies surrounding the decrees, knew the details of the capitulation policy, and was familiar with the tendencies of the Constituent Assembly regarding extradition and amnesty.

"If Escobar isn't willing to spend at least fourteen years in jail," she said, "I don't believe the government will accept his surrender."

He thought so much of her opinion that he had a startling idea: "Why don't you write a letter to the Chief?" And he repeated it when he saw how disconcerted Maruja became.

"I mean it, write to him," he said. "It could be very helpful."

And she did. He brought her paper and pencil, and waited without impatience, walking from one end of the room to the other. Maruja smoked half a pack of cigarettes from the start of the letter to the finish, sitting on the bed and writing on a board she held on her lap. In simple terms she thanked Escobar for the sense of security his words had given her. She said she had no desire for revenge against him or the people managing her captivity, and she thanked all of them for the respect with which she had been treated. She hoped Escobar could accept the government's decrees and provide a good future for himself and his children in their own country. She concluded with the formula that Villamizar had suggested in his letter, offering up her sacrifice for peace in Colombia.

The "Doctor" was hoping for something more concrete regarding the terms of the surrender, but Maruja convinced him that the effect would be the same without going into details that might seem impertinent or be misinterpreted. She was right: The letter was given to the press by Pablo Escobar, who had their ear just then because of the interest in his surrender.

Maruja also gave the "Doctor" a letter for Villamizar, one very different from the letter she had written under the effects of her rage, and as a result he appeared on television again after many weeks of silence. That night she took the powerful sedative and dreamed, in a futuristic version of a western movie, that Escobar was getting out of a helicopter and using her as a shield against a barrage of bullets.

At the end of his visit, the "Doctor" had instructed the people in the house to take greater pains in their treatment of Maruja. The majordomo and Damaris were so pleased with the new orders that they sometimes went overboard in complying with them. Before leaving, the "Doctor" had wanted to change the guards. Maruja asked him not to. The young high-school graduates on duty in April had been a relief after the excesses of March, and they continued to maintain peaceful relations with her. Maruja had gained their confidence. They told her what they heard from the majordomo and his wife, and kept her informed about the internal conflicts that had once been state secrets. They even promised— and Maruja believed them—that if anyone tried to do anything to her, they would be the first to stop him. They showed their affection with treats they stole from the kitchen, and they gave her a can of olive oil to help disguise the abominable taste of the lentils.

The only difficulty was the religious anxiety that troubled them and which she could not resolve because of her innate lack of belief and her ignorance in matters of faith. She often risked shattering the harmony in the room. "Let's see what this is all about," she would ask them. "If killing is a sin, why do you kill?" She would challenge them: "All those six o'clock rosaries, all those candles, all that business with the Holy Infant, and if I tried to escape you wouldn't think twice about shooting me." The debates became so virulent that one of them shouted in horror:

"You're an atheist!"

She shouted back that she was. She never thought it would cause such stupefaction. Knowing she might have to pay dearly for her idle iconoclasm, she invented a cosmic theory of life and the world that allowed them to talk without quarreling. And so the idea of replacing them with guards she did not know was not something she favored. But the "Doctor" explained:

"It'll take care of the machine guns."

Maruja understood what he meant when the new crew arrived. They were unarmed housekeepers who cleaned and mopped all day until they became more of a nuisance than the trash and dirt had been before. But Maruja's cough began to disappear, and the new order allowed her to watch television with a serenity and concentration that were beneficial to her health and stability.

Maruja the unbeliever did not pay the slightest attention to "God's Minute," a strange sixty-second program in which the eighty-two-year-old Eudist priest, Rafael García Herreros, would offer a reflection that was more social than religious, and often tended to be cryptic. Pacho Santos, however, who is a devout practicing Catholic, was very interested in his messages, so unlike those of professional politicians. Father García Herreros had been one of the best-known faces in the country since January 1955, when he began to air his program on Televisora Nacional's channel 7. Before that he had been a familiar voice on a Cartagena radio station since 1950, on a Cali station since January of 1952, in Medellín since September of 1954, and in Bogotá since December of the same year. He started on television at almost the same time that the system began operating. He was distinguished by his direct, sometimes brutal style, and as he spoke he fixed his falcon eyes on the viewer. Every year since 1961 he had organized the Banquet for a Million, attended by famous people—and those who aspired to fame—who paid a million pesos for a cup of consommé and a roll served by a beauty queen. The proceeds were used for the charity that had the same name as the program. The most controversial invitation was the one he sent in 1968 in a personal letter to Brigitte Bardot. Her immediate acceptance scandalized the local prudes, who threatened to sabotage the banquet. The priest stood firm. An opportune fire at the Boulogne studios in Paris, and the fantastic explanation that no seats were available on the planes, were the two excuses that saved the nation from utter embarrassment.

Pancho Santos's guards were faithful viewers of "God's Minute," but they were more interested in its religious content than in its social message. Like most families from the shantytowns of Antioquia, they had blind faith in the priest's saintliness. His tone was always abrupt, the content sometimes incomprehensible. But the April 18 program—directed beyond a doubt to Pablo Escobar, though his name was not mentioned—was indecipherable.

Looking straight into the camera, Father García Herreros said:

They have told me you want to surrender. They have told me you would like to talk to me. Oh sea! Oh sea of Coveñas at five in the evening when the sun is setting! What should I do? They tell me he is weary of his life and its turmoil, and I can tell no one my secret. But it suffocates me internally. Tell me, oh sea: Can I do it? Should I do it? You who know the history of Colombia, you who saw the Indians worshipping on this shore, you who heard the sound of history: Should I do it? Will I be rejected if I do it? Will I be rejected in Colombia? If I do it: Will there be shooting when I go with them? Will I fall with them in this adventure?

Maruja heard the program too, but it seemed less strange to her than to many Colombians because she always thought that the priest liked to wander until he lost his way among the galaxies. She viewed him as an inescapable prelude to the seven o'clock news. That night she paid attention because everything that concerned Pablo Escobar concerned her too. She was perplexed, intrigued, and very troubled by doubts about what lay behind that divine rigmarole. Pacho, however, was sure the priest would get him out of that purgatory, and he embraced his guard with joy.

10

FATHER GARCÍA HERREROS's message created an opening in the impasse. It seemed a miracle to Alberto Villamizar, for at the time he had been going over the names of possible mediators whose image and background might inspire more trust in Escobar. Rafael Pardo heard about the program and was disturbed by the idea that there could be a leak in his office. In any case, both he and Villamizar thought Father García Herreros might be the right person to mediate Escobar's surrender.

By the end of March, in fact, the letters going back and forth had nothing left to say. Worse yet: It was evident that Escobar was using Villamizar as a means of sending messages to the government and not giving anything in return. His last letter was nothing more than a list of interminable complaints—that the truce had not been broken but he had given his people permission to defend themselves against the security forces, that these forces were on the list of people to be killed, that if solutions were not forthcoming then indiscriminate attacks against police and the civilian population would increase. He complained that the prosecutor had discharged only two officers, when twenty had been accused by the Extraditables.

When Villamizar reached a dead end he discussed it with Jorge Luis Ochoa, but for more delicate matters Jorge Luis would send him to his father's house for advice. The old man would pour him half a glass of his sacred whiskey. "Drink it all up," he would say. "I don't know how you stand so much tragedy." This was the situation at the beginning of April when Villamizar returned to La Loma and gave don Fabio a detailed accounting of his failures with Escobar. Don Fabio shared his disillusionment.

"We won't screw around anymore with letters," he decided. "At this rate it will take a hundred years. The best thing is for you to meet with Escobar and for the two of you to agree on whatever conditions you like."

Don Fabio himself sent the proposal. He let Escobar know that Villamizar was prepared to be taken to him, with all the risks this entailed, in the trunk of a car. But Escobar did not accept. "Maybe I'll talk to Villamizar, but not now," was his reply. Perhaps he was still wary of the electronic tracking device that could be hidden anywhere, even under the gold crown of a tooth.

In the meantime, he continued to insist on sanctions for the police and to repeat his accusations that General Maza Márquez had allied himself with the paramilitary forces and the Cali cartel to kill his people. This accusation, and his charge that the general had killed Luis Carlos Galán, were two of Escobar's fierce obsessions with Maza Márquez. The general's reply, in public or in private, always was that for the moment he was not waging war against the Cali cartel because his priority was terrorism by drug traffickers and not the drug traffic itself. Escobar, for his part, had written this aside in a letter to Villamizar: "Tell doña Gloria that Maza killed her husband, there can be no doubt about it." Maza's response to the repeated accusation was always the same: "Escobar knows better than anyone else that it isn't true."

In despair over this brutal, pointless war that vanquished all intelligent initiatives, Villamizar made one final effort to persuade the government to declare a truce in order to negotiate. It was impossible. Rafael Pardo told him that while the families of the hostages were opposing the government's decision not to make any concessions, the enemies of the capitulation policy were accusing the government of handing the country over to the traffickers.

Villamizar—accompanied on this occasion by his sister-in-law, doña Gloria Pachón de Galán—also visited General Gómez Padilla, director general of the National Police. She asked the general for a month's truce to allow them to attempt personal contact with Escobar.

"I cannot tell you how sorry we are, Señora," the general said, "but we cannot halt operations against this criminal. You are acting at your own risk, and all we can do is wish you luck."

This was all they accomplished with the police, whose hermeticism was meant to stop the inexplicable leaks that had allowed Escobar to escape the best-planned sieges. But doña Gloria did not leave empty-handed, for as they were saying goodbye an officer told her Maruja was being held somewhere in the department of Nariño, on the Ecuadoran border. She had learned from Beatriz that the house was in Bogotá, which meant that the police's misinformation lessened her fear of a rescue operation.

By this time speculation in the press regarding the terms of Escobar's surrender had reached the proportions of an international scandal. Denials from the police and explanations from all segments of the government, even from the president, had not convinced many people that there were no negotiations or secret agreements for his capitulation.

General Maza Márquez believed it to be true. What is more, he had always been certain—and said so to anyone who wanted to listen—that his removal would be one of Escobar's primary conditions for surrender. For a long time President Gaviria seemed angered by certain statements made by Maza Márquez to the press, and by unconfirmed rumors that the general was responsible for some of the sensitive leaks. But at this time—considering his many years in the position, his immense popularity because of the hard line he had taken against crime, and his ineffable devotion to the Holy Infant—it was not likely that the president would remove him without good reason. Maza had to be conscious of his power, but he also had to know that sooner or later the president would exercise his, and the only thing he had requested—through messages carried by mutual friends—was that he be told with sufficient warning to provide for his family's safety.

The only official authorized to maintain contacts with Pablo Escobar's attorneys—provided a written record was kept—was the director of Criminal Investigation, Carlos Eduardo Mejía. He was responsible by law for arranging the operative details of the surrender, and the security and living conditions in prison.

Minister Giraldo Angel personally reviewed the possible options. He had been interested in the high-security block at Itagüí ever since Fabio Ochoa's surrender the previous November, but Escobar's lawyers objected because it was an easy target for car bombs. He also found acceptable the idea of turning a convent in El Poblado—near the residential building where Escobar had escaped the explosion of two hundred kilos of dynamite, attributed to the Cali cartel—into a fortified prison, but the community of nuns who owned it did not wish to sell. He had proposed reinforcing the Medellín prison, but the Municipal Council opposed the plan in a plenary session. Alberto Villamizar, fearing that the surrender would be thwarted by lack of a prison, interceded with serious arguments in favor of the site proposed by Escobar in October: El Claret, the Municipal Rehabilitation Center for Drug Addicts, located twelve kilometers from Envigado's main park, on a property known as La Catedral del Valle, whose owner-of-record was one of Escobar's front men. The government studied the possibility of leasing the center and converting it into a prison, well aware that Escobar would not surrender if he could not resolve the problem of his own security. His lawyers demanded that the guards be Antioquian, and, fearing reprisals for the agents murdered in Medellín, that external security be in the hands of any armed force except the police.

The mayor of Envigado, who was responsible for completing the project, took note of the government's report and initiated the transfer of the prison, which had to be consigned to the Ministry of Justice according to the leasing contract both parties had signed. The basic construction displayed an elementary simplicity, with cement floors, tile roofs, and metal doors painted green. The administration area, in what had been the farmhouse, consisted of three small rooms, a kitchen, a paved courtyard, and a punishment cell. It had a dormitory measuring four hundred square meters, another large room to be used as a library and study, and six individual cells with private bathrooms. A common area in the center, measuring six hundred square meters, had four showers, a dressing room, and six toilets. The remodeling had begun in February, with seventy workers who slept in shifts at the site for a few hours a day. The rough topography, the awful condition of the access road, and the harsh winter obliged them to do without trucks and carriers, and to transport most of the furnishings by muleback. First among them were two fifty-liter water heaters, military cots, and some two dozen small tubular armchairs painted yellow. Twenty pots holding ornamental plants—araucarias, laurels, and areca palms—completed the interior decoration. Since the former rehabilitation center had no telephone lines, the prison's initial communications would be by radio. The final cost of the project was 120 million pesos, paid by the municipality of Envigado. Early estimates had calculated a period of eight months for the construction, but when Father García Herreros came on the scene, the pace of work was speeded up to a quick march.

Another obstacle to surrender had been the dismantling of Escobar's private army. He did not seem to consider prison a legal recourse but as protection from his enemies, and even from ordinary law enforcement agencies, but he could not persuade his troops to turn themselves in. He argued that he could not provide for the safety of himself and his family and leave his accomplices to the mercies of the Elite Corps. "I won't surrender alone," he said in a letter. But for many this was half a truth, since it is also likely that he wanted to have his entire team with him so he could continue to run his business from jail. In any case, the government preferred to imprison them along with Escobar. There were about a hundred crews that were not on permanent war footing but served as frontline reserve troops, easy to mobilize and arm in a few hours. It was a question of having Escobar disarm and bring to prison with him fifteen or twenty of his staunch captains.

In the few personal interviews that Villamizar had with the president, Gaviria's position was always to offer his personal efforts to free the hostages. Villamizar does not believe that the government held any negotiations other than the ones he was authorized to engage in, which were already foreseen in the capitulation policy. Former president Turbay and Hernando Santos—though they never expressed it, and were not unaware of the government's institutional difficulties—no doubt expected a minimum of flexibility from the president. His refusal to change the time limits established in the decrees, despite Nydia's insistence, entreaties, and protests, will continue to be a thorn in the hearts of the families who pleaded with him. And the fact that he did change them three days after Diana's death is something her family will never understand. Unfortunately—the president has said in private—by that time altering the date would not have stopped Diana's death or changed the way it happened.

Escobar never felt satisfied with only one avenue, and he never stopped trying to negotiate, with God and with the Devil, with every kind of legal or illegal weapon, not because he trusted one more than the other, but because he had no confidence in any of them. Even when he had secured what he wanted from Villamizar, he still embraced the dream of political amnesty, an idea that first surfaced in 1989 when the major dealers and many of their people obtained documents identifying them as members of the M-19 in order to find a place on the lists of pardoned guerrilla fighters. Commander Carlos Pizarro blocked their way with impossible demands. Two years later, Escobar tried it again through the Constituent Assembly, several of whose members were subjected to various kinds of pressure ranging from crude offers of money to the most serious intimidation.

But Escobar's enemies were also working at cross-purposes. This was the origin of a so-called narcovideo that caused an enormous, unproductive scandal. Presumably filmed in a hotel room with a hidden camera, it showed a member of the Constituent Assembly taking cash from an alleged lawyer for Escobar. The assembly member had been elected from the lists of the M-19 but in fact belonged to the paramilitary group that worked for the Cali cartel in its war against the Medellín cartel, and he did not have enough credibility to convince anyone. Months later, a leader of some private militias who turned in his weapons to the police said that his people had made that cheap soap opera in order to prove that Escobar was suborning members of the Assembly, and thereby invalidate amnesty or non-extradition.

One of the many new fronts that Escobar tried to open was his attempt to negotiate the release of Pacho Santos behind the back of Villamizar just as his efforts were beginning to bear fruit. In late April Escobar sent Hernando Santos a message through a priest he knew, asking that he meet with one of his attorneys in the church in Usaquén. It was—the message said—a matter of utmost importance regarding the release of Pacho. Hernando not only knew the priest but considered him a saint on earth, and so he went alone and arrived punctually at eight on the evening of the specified date. Inside the dim church the lawyer, almost invisible in the shadows, told him he had nothing to do with the cartels but that Pablo Escobar had paid for his education and he could not refuse him a favor. His mission was only to hand him two texts: a report from Amnesty International condemning the Medellín police, and the original copy of an article that had all the airs of an editorial attacking the abuses of the Elite Corps.

"I've come here with only your son's life in mind," said the lawyer. "If these articles are published tomorrow, by the day after tomorrow Francisco will be free."

Hernando read the manuscript with a political eye. It listed the incidents denounced so often by Escobar, but with bloodcurdling details that were impossible to prove. It was written with gravity and subtle malice. The author, according to the lawyer, was Escobar himself. In any case, the style seemed to be his.

The document from Amnesty International had already appeared in other newspapers, and Hernando Santos had no problem in publishing it again. The editorial, however, was too serious to publish with no evidence. "If he sends me proof, we'll print it right away even if they don't let Pacho go," said Hernando. There was nothing more to discuss. The lawyer, aware that his mission was over, took advantage of the opportunity to ask Hernando how much Guido Parra had charged for his mediation.

"Not a cent," replied Hernando. "Money was never mentioned."

"Tell me the truth," said the lawyer, "because Escobar controls the accounts, he controls everything, and he needs that information."

Hernando repeated his answer, and the meeting ended with formal goodbyes.

PERHAPS THE ONLY person at this time who was convinced that matters were close to resolution was the Colombian astrologer Mauricio Puerta—an attentive observer of national life by means of the stars—who had reached some surprising conclusions regarding Pablo Escobar's astrological chart.

Escobar had been born in Medellín on December 1, 1949, at 11:50 a.m. He was, therefore, a Sagittarius with Pisces in the ascendant, with one of the worst conjunctions: Mars and Saturn in Virgo. His tendencies were cruel authoritarianism, despotism, insatiable ambition, rebelliousness, turbulence, insubordination, anarchy, lack of discipline, attacks on authority. And an ineluctable outcome: sudden death.

Beginning on March 30, 1991, he had Saturn at five degrees for the next three years, and this meant that only three alternatives defined his future: the hospital, the cemetery, or prison. A fourth option—the monastery—did not seem applicable in his case. In any event, the period was more favorable for settling the terms of a negotiation than for closing a definitive deal. In other words: His best option was the conditional surrender proposed by the government.

"Escobar must be very worried if he's so interested in his chart," said one reporter. For as soon as he heard about Mauricio Puerta's reading, he wanted his analysis down to the smallest detail. But two messengers sent by Escobar never reached their destination, and one disappeared forever. Then Puerta arranged a well-publicized seminar in Medellín to make himself available to Escobar, but a series of strange difficulties made the meeting impossible. Puerta interpreted these as a defensive strategy by the stars to prevent anything from interfering with a destiny that was now inexorable.

Pacho Santos's wife also received supernatural revelations from a clairvoyant who had predicted Diana's death with amazing clarity, and had told her with equal certainty that Pacho was alive. In April they happened to meet again in a public place, and the clairvoyant murmured as she passed by:

"Congratulations. I can see his homecoming."

THESE WERE the only encouraging signs when Father García Herreros sent his cryptic message to Pablo Escobar. How he made that providential determination, and what the sea of Coveñas had to do with it, is something that still intrigues the nation. Yet how he happened to think of it is even more intriguing. On Friday, April 12, 1991, he visited Dr. Manuel Elkin Patarroyo—the inspired inventor of the malaria vaccine—to ask him to set up a clinic, in the area of the "God's Minute" charity, for the early detection of AIDS. In addition to a young priest from his community, he was accompanied by an old-style Antioquian, a great friend who advised him on earthly matters. By his own decision, this benefactor, who has asked that his name not be mentioned, not only had built and paid for Father García Herreros's private chapel, but also had made voluntary contributions to his social service projects. In the car that was taking them to Dr. Patarroyo's Institute of Immunology, he felt a kind of urgent inspiration.

"Listen, Father," he said. "Why don't you do something to move this thing along and help Pablo Escobar turn himself in?"

He said it with no preliminaries and no conscious motive. "It was a message from above," he would say later in the way he always refers to God, with the respect of a servant and the familiarity of a *compadre*. The father reacted as if an arrow had pierced his heart. He turned ashen. Dr. Patarroyo, who did not know him, was later struck by the energy shining from his eyes, and by his business sense, but to his Antioquian companion he seemed changed. "It was like Father was floating," he has said. "During the interview the only thing on his mind was what I had said, and when we left I thought he looked so excited that I began to worry." This is why he took the father away for the weekend to rest at a vacation house in Coveñas, a popular Caribbean resort that swarms with thousands of tourists and is the terminus of a pipeline bringing in 250,000 barrels of crude oil every day.

The father did not have a moment's peace. He hardly slept; he would leave the table in the middle of meals and take long walks along the beach at all hours of the day or night. "Oh sea of Coveñas," he shouted into the roar of the surf. "Can I do it? Should I do it? You who know everything: Will we not die in the attempt?" At the end of his tormented walks he would come into the house with absolute confidence, as if he had in reality received answers from the sea, and discuss every detail of the project with his host.

On Tuesday, when they returned to Bogotá, he could see the entire plan, and this gave him back his serenity. On Wednesday he returned to his routine: He got up at six, showered, put on his black cassock with the clerical collar, and over that his invariable white poncho, and brought his affairs up-to-date with the assistance of Paulina Garzón de Bermúdez, who had been his indispensable secretary for half her lifetime. The subject of his program that night had nothing to do with the obsession that drove him. On Thursday morning, just as he had promised, Dr. Patarroyo sent an affirmative reply to his request. The priest had no lunch. At ten to seven he reached the studios of Inravisión, where he broadcast his program, and in front of the cameras he improvised his direct message to Escobar. These were sixty seconds that changed the little life that still remained to him. When he came home he was greeted by a basket full of telephone messages from all over the country, and an avalanche of reporters who from that night on would not let him out of their sight until he had accomplished his goal of leading Pablo Escobar by the hand into prison.

The final process had begun but the outcome was uncertain because public opinion was divided between the masses of people who believed the good father was a saint, and the unbelievers who were convinced he was half-mad. The truth is that his life revealed him to be many things, but not that. He had turned eighty-two in January, would complete fifty-two years as a priest in August, and seemed to be the only well-known Colombian who had never dreamed of being president. His snowy head and the white poncho over his cassock complemented one of the most respected images in the country. He had written verses that he published in a book at the age of nineteen, and others, also composed in his youth, under the pen name Senescens. He was awarded a forgotten prize for a volume of stories, and forty-six decorations for his charitable projects. In good times and bad he always had his feet planted firmly on the ground, led the social life of a layman, told and listened to jokes of any color, and at the moment of truth revealed what he always had been under his cattleman's poncho: a dyed-in-the-wool Santanderean.

He lived in monastic austerity in the vicarage of San Juan Eudes Church, in a room riddled with leaks that he refused to repair. He slept on wooden planks without a mattress or pillow, and with a coverlet made of colored scraps of cloth cut in the shape of little houses that some charitable nuns had sewn for him. He refused a down pillow that someone once offered him because it seemed contrary to the will of God. He wore the same shoes until someone gave him a new pair, and did not replace his clothing and his eternal white poncho until someone provided him with new ones. He ate little, though he liked good food and appreciated fine wines, but would not accept invitations to expensive restaurants for fear people would think he was paying. In one restaurant he saw an elegant woman with a diamond the size of an almond on her finger.

"With a ring like that," he walked up to her and said, "I could build 120 houses for the poor."

She was too stunned to answer, but the next day she sent him the ring with a cordial note. It did not pay for 120 houses, of course, but the father built them anyway.

Paulina Garzón was a native of Chipatá, Santander del Sur, and had come to Bogotá with her mother in 1961, at the age of fifteen, with a letter of recommendation stating she was an expert typist. She was, in fact, though she did not know how to speak on the phone, and her shopping lists were indecipherable because of her calamitous spelling, but she learned both things well so that the priest would hire her. At twenty-five she married and had a son—Alfonso—and a daughter—María Constanza—who today are both systems engineers. Paulina arranged her life so that she could continue to work for Father García Herreros, who gave her more and more duties and responsibilities until she became so indispensable that she traveled with him in Colombia and abroad, but always accompanied by another priest. "To avoid gossip," Paulina explains. In the end she accompanied him everywhere, if only to put in and take out his contact lenses, something he never could do by himself.

In his final years the priest lost his hearing in his right ear, became irritable, and lost patience with the gaps in his memory. Little by little he had discarded classical prayers and improvised his own, which he said aloud and with a visionary's inspiration. His reputation as a lunatic grew along with the popular belief that he had a supernatural ability to talk with the waters and control their direction and movement. The understanding he showed toward Pablo Escobar recalled something he had said about the return of General Gustavo Rojas Pinilla, in August 1957, to be tried by Congress: "When a man turns himself over to the law, even if he is guilty, he deserves profound respect." Almost at the end of his life, at a Banquet for a Million that had been very difficult to organize, a friend asked what he would do now and he gave the answer of a nineteen-year-old: "I want to lie down in a meadow and look at the stars."

The day following his television message, Father García Herreros came to the Itagüí prison—unannounced and with no prior arrangements—to ask the Ochoa brothers how he could be useful in arranging Escobar's surrender. The Ochoas thought he was a saint, with only one problem that had to be taken into account: For more than forty years he had communicated with his audience through his daily sermon, and he could not conceive of any action that did not begin by telling the public about it. The decisive factor for the Ochoas, however, was that don Fabio thought he was a providential mediator—first, because with him Escobar would not feel the reluctance that kept him from seeing Villamizar, and second, because his image as a holy man could convince the entire Escobar crew to turn themselves in.

Two days later, at a press conference, Father García Herreros revealed that he was in contact with those responsible for the abduction of the journalists, and expressed his optimism that they would soon be free. Villamizar did not hesitate for a moment, and went to see him at "God's Minute." He accompanied him on his second visit to the Itagüí prison, and on the same day the costly, confidential process began that would culminate in the surrender. It began with a letter dictated by the priest in the Ochoas' cell and copied by María Lía on the typewriter. He improvised it as he stood in front of her, using the same manner, the same apostolic tone, the same Santanderean accent as in his one-minute homilies. He invited Escobar to join him in a search for the road that would bring peace to Colombia. He announced his hope that the government would name him as guarantor "that your rights, and those of your family and friends, will be respected." But he warned him not to ask for things the government could not grant. Before concluding with "affectionate greetings," he stated what was in reality the practical purpose of the letter: "If you believe we can meet in a place that is safe for both of us, let me know."

Escobar answered three days later, in his own hand. He agreed to surrender as a sacrifice for peace. He made it clear that he did not expect a pardon, was not asking for criminal prosecution but disciplinary action against the police wreaking havoc in the slums, and did not renounce his determination to respond with drastic reprisals. He was prepared to confess to any crime, though he knew with certainty that no judge, Colombian or foreign, had enough evidence to convict him, and he trusted that his adversaries would be subjected to the same strict procedures. However, despite the father's most fervent hope, he made no reference to his proposal to meet with him.

Father García Herreros had promised Villamizar that he would control his informative impulses, and at first he kept his word, but his almost boyish spirit of adventure was greater than his power to control them. The expectations created were so great, and there was so much coverage in the press, that from then on he could not make a move without a train of reporters and mobile television and radio crews following him right up to his front door.

AFTER FIVE MONTHS of working in absolute secret, under the almost sacramental silence imposed by Rafael Pardo, Villamizar thought that the easy talk of Father García Herreros put the entire operation at perpetual risk. This was when he requested and received help from the people closest to the father—beginning with Paulina—and was able to go forward with preparations for certain actions without having to inform the priest ahead of time.

On May 13 he received a message from Escobar in which he asked him to bring the father to La Loma and keep him there for as long as necessary. He said it might be three days or three months, because he had to review in person and in detail every stage of the operation. The possibility even existed that it could be canceled at the last minute if there were any doubts at all about security. Fortunately, the father was always available in a matter that had cost him so much sleep. At five o'clock on the morning of May 14, Villamizar knocked at his front door and found him working in his study as if it were the middle of the day.

"Come, Father," he said, "we're going to Medellín."

At La Loma the Ochoa sisters were prepared to entertain the father for as long as necessary. Don Fabio was not there, but the women in the house would take care of everything. It was not easy to distract him because the father knew that a trip as sudden and unplanned as this one could only be for something very serious.

The long breakfast was delicious, and the father ate well. At about ten, making an effort not to be too melodramatic, Martha Nieves told him that Escobar would be seeing him sometime soon. He gave a start, became very happy, but did not know what to do until Villamizar made the reality clear to him.

"It's better for you to know from the very beginning, Father," he said. "You may have to go alone with the driver, and nobody knows where he'll take you, or for how long."

The father turned pale. He could barely hold the rosary between his fingers as he paced back and forth, reciting his invented prayers aloud. Each time he passed the windows he looked toward the road, torn between terror that the car coming for him would appear, and fear that it would not come at all. He wanted to make a phone call but then realized the danger on his own. "Fortunately, there's no need for telephones when you talk to God," he said. He did not want to sit at the table during lunch, which was late and even more appetizing than breakfast. In the room that had been prepared for him, there was a bed with a passementerie canopy worthy of a bishop. The women tried to convince him to lie down for a while, and he seemed to agree. But he did not sleep. He was restive as he read Stephen Hawking's *A Brief History of Time*, a popular book that attempted to demonstrate with mathematical calculations that God does not exist. At about four he came to the room where Villamizar was dozing.

"Alberto," he said, "we'd better go back to Bogotá."

It was difficult to dissuade him, but the women succeeded with their charm and tact. At dusk he had another relapse, but by this time there was no escape. He knew the grave risks involved in traveling at night. When it was time to go to bed he asked for help in removing his contact lenses, since Paulina was the one who took them out and put them in for him, and he did not know how to do it alone. Villamizar did not sleep, because he accepted the possibility that Escobar might consider the dark of night as the safest time for their meeting.

The priest did not sleep at all. Breakfast at eight the next morning was more tempting than the day before, but he did not even sit at the table. He was in despair over his contact lenses, and no one had been able to help him until, after many tries, the woman who ran the farm managed to put them in. In contrast to the first day, he did not seem nervous or driven to pace back and forth, but sat with his eyes fixed on the road where the car would appear. He stayed there until impatience got the better of him and he jumped up from his chair.

"I'm leaving," he said, "this whole thing is as phony as a rooster laying eggs."

They persuaded him to wait until after lunch. The promise restored his good humor. He ate well, chatted, was as amusing as he had been in his best times, and at last said he would take a siesta.

"But I'm warning you," he said, his index finger wagging. "As soon as I wake up, I'm leaving."

Martha Nieves made a few phone calls, hoping to obtain some additional information that would help them to keep the priest there after his nap. It was impossible. A little before three they were all dozing in the living room when they were awakened by the sound of an engine. There was the car. Villamizar jumped up, gave a polite little knock, and pushed open the priest's door.

"Father," he said, "they've come for you."

The father was half-awake and struggled out of bed. Villamizar felt deeply moved, for he looked like a little bird without its feathers, his skin hanging from his bones and trembling with terror. But he recovered immediately, crossed himself, grew until he was resolute and enormous. "Kneel down, my boy," he ordered. "We'll pray together." When he stood he was a new man.

"Let's see what's going on with Pablo," he said.

Villamizar wanted to go with him but did not even try, since it had already been agreed that he would not, but he did speak in private to the driver.

"I'm holding you accountable for the father," he said. "He's too important a person. Be careful what you people do with him. Be aware of the responsibility you have."

The driver looked at Villamizar as if he were an idiot, and said:

"Do you think that if I get in a car with a saint anything can happen to us?"

He took out a baseball cap and told the priest to put it on so nobody would recognize his white hair. He did. Villamizar could not stop thinking about the fact that Medellín was a militarized zone. He was troubled by the idea that they might stop the father, that he would be hurt, or be caught in the cross fire between the killers and the police.

The father sat in front next to the driver. While everyone watched as the car drove away, he took off the cap and threw it out the window. "Don't worry about me, my boy," he shouted to Villamizar, "I control the waters." A clap of thunder rumbled across the vast countryside, and the skies opened in a biblical downpour.

THE ONLY KNOWN version of Father García Herreros's visit to Pablo Escobar was the one he recounted when he returned to La Loma. He said the house where he was received was large and luxurious, with an Olympic-size pool and various kinds of sports facilities. On the way they had to change cars three times for reasons of security, but they were not stopped at the many police checkpoints because of the heavy, pounding rain. Other checkpoints, the driver told him, were part of the Extraditables' security service. They drove for more than three hours, though the probability is that he was taken to one of Pablo Escobar's residences in Medellín, and the driver made a good number of detours so the father would think they were far from La Loma.

He said he was met in the garden by some twenty men carrying weapons, and that he chastised them for their sinful lives and their reluctance to surrender. Pablo Escobar was waiting for him on the terrace. He was dressed in a casual white cotton outfit and had a long black beard. The fear confessed to by the father from the time of his arrival at La Loma, and then during the uncertainty of the drive, vanished when he saw him.

"Pablo," he said, "I've come so we can straighten this out."

Escobar responded with similar cordiality and with great respect. They sat in two of the armchairs covered in flowered cretonne in the living room, facing each other, their spirits ready for the kind of long talk old friends have. The father drank a whiskey that helped to calm him, while Escobar sipped at fruit juice as if he had all the time in the world. But the expected duration of the visit shrank to forty-five minutes because of the father's natural impatience and Escobar's speaking style, as concise and to the point as in his letters.

Concerned about the priest's lapses in memory, Villamizar had told him to take notes on their conversation. He did, but went even further, it seems. Citing his poor memory as the reason, he asked Escobar to write down his essential conditions, and when they were written he had him modify or cross them out, saying they were impossible to meet. This was how Escobar minimized the obsessive subject of removing the police he had accused of atrocities, and concentrated instead on security in the prison where he would be confined.

The priest recounted that he had asked Escobar if he was responsible for the assassinations of four presidential candidates. His oblique response was that he had not committed all the crimes attributed to him. He assured the father he had not been able to stop the killing of Professor Low Mutra on April 30 on a street in Bogotá, because the order had been given a long time before and there was no way to change it. As for the release of Maruja and Pacho, he avoided saying anything that might implicate him as the responsible party, but did say that the Extraditables kept them in normal conditions and in good health, and that they would be re-leased as soon as terms for the surrender had been arranged. Re-garding Pacho in particular, he said with utmost seriousness: "He's happy with his captivity." Finally, he acknowledged President Gaviria's good faith, and expressed his willingness to reach an agreement. That paper, written on at times by the father, and for the most part corrected and clarified in Escobar's own hand, was the first formal proposal for his surrender.

The father had stood to take his leave when one of his contact lenses fell out. He tried to put it back in, Escobar helped him, they asked for assistance from his staff, all to no avail. The father was desperate. "It's no use," he said. "The only one who can do it is Paulina." To his surprise, Escobar knew who she was and where she was at that moment.

"Don't worry, Father," he said. "If you like we can bring her here."

But the father had an unbearable desire to go home, and he preferred to leave not wearing his lenses. Before they said goodbye, Escobar asked him to bless a little gold medal he wore around his neck. The priest did so in the garden, besieged by the bodyguards.

"Father," they said, "you can't leave without giving us your blessing."

They kneeled. Don Fabio Ochoa had said that the mediation of Father García Herrero would be decisive for the surrender of Escobar's men. Escobar must have agreed, and perhaps that was why he kneeled with them, to set a good example. The priest blessed them all and also admonished them to return to a lawful life and help to establish peace.

It took just six hours. He returned to La Loma at about eight-thirty, under brilliant stars, and leaped from the car like a fifteen-year-old schoolboy.

"Take it easy, my boy," he said to Villamizar, "no problems here, I had them all on their knees."

It was not easy to calm him down. He was in an alarming state of excitation, and no palliative, and none of the Ochoa sisters' tranquilizing infusions, had any effect. It was still raining, but he wanted to fly back to Bogotá right away, announce the news, talk to the president, conclude the agreement without further delay, and proclaim peace. They managed to get him to sleep for a few hours, but in the middle of the night he was walking around the darkened house, talking to himself, reciting his inspired prayers, until sleep got the better of him at dawn.

When they reached Bogotá at eleven o'clock on the morning of May 16, the news was thundering across the radio. Villamizar met his son Andrés at the airport and embraced him with emotion. "Don't worry, son," he said. "Your mother will be out in three days." Rafael Pardo was less easy to convince when Villamizar called.

"I'm truly happy, Alberto," he said. "But don't hope for too much."

For the first time since the abduction, Villamizar went to a party given by friends, and no one could understand why he was so elated over something that was, after all, no more than a vague promise, like so many others made by Pablo Escobar. By this time Father García Herreros had been interviewed by all the news media—audio, visual, and print—in the country. He asked people to be tolerant with Escobar. "If we don't defraud him, he will become the great architect of peace," he said. And added, without citing Rousseau: "Deep down all men are good, although some circumstances can make them evil." And surrounded by a tangled mass of microphones, he said with no reservation:

"Escobar is a good man."

El Tiempo reported on Friday, May 17, that the father was the bearer of a private letter that he would give to President Gaviria on the following Monday. In reality, these were the notes he and Escobar had written together during their interview. On Sunday, the Extraditables issued a communiqué that almost went unnoticed in the clamor of news: "We have ordered the release of Francisco Santos and Maruja Pachón." They did not say when. The radio, however, took it as a fait accompli and crowds of excited reporters began to stand guard at the captives' houses.

It was over: Villamizar received a message from Escobar in which he said he would not release Maruja Pachón and Francisco Santos that day but the next Monday, May 20—at seven in the evening. But on Tuesday, at nine in the morning, Villamizar would have to go back to Medellín for Escobar's surrender.

11

MARUJA HEARD the Extraditables' communiqué at seven o'clock on the evening of Sunday, May 19. It did not mention a time or a date for their release, and considering how the Extraditables operated, it could happen either in five minutes or two months later. The majordomo and his wife burst into the room, ready for a party.

"It's over!" they shouted. "We have to celebrate."

Maruja had a hard time convincing them to wait for a direct official order from one of Pablo Escobar's emissaries. The news did not surprise her, for in the past few weeks there had been unmistakable signs that things were going better than she had supposed when they made the disheartening promise to carpet the room. More and more friends and popular actors had appeared on recent broadcasts of "Colombia Wants Them Back." Her optimism renewed, Maruja followed the soap operas with so much attention that she thought she could find coded messages even in the glycerine tears of impossible loves. The news from Father García Herreros, which grew more spectacular every day, made it clear that the unbelievable was going to happen.

Maruja wanted to put on the clothes she had been wearing

when she arrived, foreseeing a sudden release that would have her appearing in front of the cameras dressed in a captive's melancholy sweatsuit. But the lack of new developments on the radio, and the disappointment of the majordomo who had expected the official order before he went to bed, put her on guard against playing the fool, if only to herself. She took a large dose of sleeping pills and did not wake until the following day, Monday, with the frightening impression that she did not know who she was, or where.

VILLAMIZAR HAD NOT been troubled by any doubts, for the communiqué from Escobar was unequivocal. He passed it on to the reporters, but they ignored it. At about nine, a radio station announced with great fanfare that Señora Maruja Pachón de Villamizar had just been released in the Salitre district. The reporters left in a stampede, but Villamizar did not move.

"They would never let her go in an isolated place like that, where anything could happen to her," he said. "It'll be tomorrow, for sure, and in a place that's safe."

A reporter barred his way with a microphone.

"What's surprising," he said, "is the confidence you have in those people."

"It's his word of honor," said Villamizar.

The reporters he knew best stayed in the hallways of the apartment—and some were at the bar—until Villamizar asked them to leave so he could lock up for the night. Others camped in vans and cars outside the building, and spent the night there.

On Monday Villamizar woke to the six o'clock news, as he always did, and stayed in bed until eleven. He tried to use the phone as little as possible, but there were constant calls from reporters and friends. The news of the day continued to be the wait for the hostages.

FATHER GARCÍA HERREROS had visited Mariavé on Thursday to tell her in confidence that her husband would be released the following Sunday. It has not been possible to learn how he obtained the news seventy-two hours before the first communiqué from the Extraditables, but the Santos family accepted it as fact. To celebrate they took a picture of Hernando with Mariavé and the children and published it on Saturday in *El Tiempo*, hoping that Pacho would understand it as a personal message. He did: As soon as he opened the paper in his captive's cell, Pacho had a clear intuition that his father's efforts had come to a successful conclusion. He spent an uneasy day waiting for the miracle, slipping innocent-seeming ploys into his conversation with the guards to see if he could catch them in an indiscretion, but he learned nothing. Radio and television, which had reported nothing else for several weeks, did not mention it at all that Saturday.

Sunday began the same way. It seemed to Pacho that the guards were tense and uneasy in the morning, but as the day wore on they made a gradual return to their Sunday routine: a special lunch of pizza, movies and taped television programs, some cards, some soccer. Then, when they least expected it, the newscast "Criptón" opened with the lead story: The Extraditables had announced the release of the last two hostages. Pacho jumped up with a triumphant shout and threw his arms around the guard on duty. "I thought I'd have a heart attack," he has said. But the guard responded with skeptical stoicism.

"Let's wait till we get confirmation," he said.

They made a rapid survey of other news programs on radio and television, and found the communiqué on all of them. One was transmitting from the editorial room at *El Tiempo*, and after eight months Pacho began to feel again the solid ground of a free life: the rather desolate atmosphere of the Sunday shift, the usual faces in their glass cubicles, his own work site. Following another repetition of the announcement of their imminent release, the television program's special correspondent waved the microphone and—like an ice cream cone—put it up to the mouth of a sports editor and asked:

"What do you think of the news?"

Pacho could not control the reflexive response of a chief editor.

"What a moronic question!" he said. "Was he expecting them to say I should be held for another month?"

As always, the radio news was less rigorous but more emotional. Many reporters were concentrating on Hernando Santos's house, broadcasting statements from every person who crossed their path. This increased Pacho's nervous tension, for it did not seem unreasonable to think he might be released that same night. "This was the start of the longest twenty-six hours of my life," he has said. "Each second was like an hour."

The press was everywhere. Television cameras moved back and forth from Pacho's house to his father's, both of which had been overflowing since Sunday night with relatives, friends, curious onlookers, and journalists from all over the world. Mariavé and Hernando Santos cannot remember how many times they went from one house to the other, following each unforeseen turn in the news, until Pacho was no longer certain which house was which on television. The worst thing was that at each one the same questions were asked over and over again, and the trip between the houses became intolerable. There was so much confusion that Hernando Santos could not get through the mob crowding around his own house, and had to slip in through the garage.

The off-duty guards came in to congratulate Pacho. They were so happy at the news that he forgot they were his jailers, and it turned into a party of *compadres* who were all the same age. At that moment he realized that his goal of rehabilitating his guards would be frustrated by his release. They were boys from the Antioquian countryside who had emigrated to Medellín, lost their way in the slums, and killed and were killed with no scruples. As a rule they came from broken homes where the father was a negative figure and the mother a very strong one. They were used to working for very high pay and had no sense of money.

When at last he fell asleep, Pacho had a horrifying dream that he was free and happy but suddenly opened his eyes and saw the ceiling unchanged. He spent the rest of the night tormented by the mad rooster—madder and closer than ever—and not knowing for certain where reality lay.

At six in the morning on Monday, the radio confirmed the news with no indication of the hour of their possible release. After countless repetitions of the original bulletin, it was announced that Father García Herreros would hold a press conference at noon following a meeting with President Gaviria: "Oh God," Pacho said to himself. "Don't let this man who has done so much for us screw it up at the last minute." At one in the afternoon they told him he would be freed, but he was not told anything else until after five, when one of the masked bosses said in an unemotional way that—in line with Escobar's feeling for publicity—Maruja would be released in time for the seven o'clock news, and he in time for the newscasts at nine-thirty.

MARUJA'S MORNING had been more pleasant. A low-ranking boss came into the room at about nine and said she would be released that afternoon. He also told her some of the details of Father García Herreros's efforts, perhaps by way of apology for an injustice he had committed on a recent visit when Maruja asked if her fate was in the hands of Father García Herreros. He had answered with a touch of mockery:

"Don't worry, you're much safer than that."

Maruja realized he had misinterpreted her question, and she was quick to clarify that she always had great respect for the father. It is true that at first she had ignored his television sermons, which at times were confusing and impenetrable, but after the first message to Escobar she understood that he was involved in her life, and she watched him night after night, paying very close attention. She had followed the steps he had taken, his visits to Medellín, the progress of his conversations with Escobar, and had no doubt he was on the right path. The boss's sarcasm, however, caused her to wonder if the father had less credit with the Extraditables than might be supposed from his public statements to journalists. The confirmation that she would soon be freed through his efforts made her feel happier.

After a brief conversation regarding the impact their release would have on the country, she asked about the ring that had been taken from her in the first house on the night of her abduction.

"Not to worry," he said. "All your things are safe."

"But I am worried," she said, "because it wasn't taken here but in that first house, and we never saw the man again. It wasn't you, was it?"

"Not me," he said. "But I already told you to take it easy, your things are safe. I've seen them."

The majordomo's wife offered to buy Maruja anything she needed. Maruja asked for mascara, lipstick, eyebrow pencil, and a pair of stockings to replace the ones that had been torn on the night she was kidnapped. Later the majordomo came in, troubled by the lack of new information regarding her release, afraid there had been a last-minute change in plans, as so often happened. Maruja, however, was calm. She showered, and dressed in the same clothing she had worn on the night of her abduction, except for the cream-colored jacket, which she would put on when she went out.

For the entire day the radio stations kept interest alive with speculations on the waiting hostages, interviews with their families, unconfirmed rumors that were canceled out the next minute by even more sensational ones. But nothing definite. Maruja listened to the voices of her children and friends with an anticipatory jubilation threatened by uncertainty. Again she saw her redecorated house, her husband conversing easily with a crowd of journalists who were growing tired of waiting. She had time to study the decorative details that had bothered her so much the first time, and her frame of mind improved. The guards took a break from their frenetic cleaning to watch and listen to the newscasts, and they tried to keep her spirits up but had less and less success as the afternoon wore on.

PRESIDENT GAVIRIA woke without the help of an alarm clock at five on the morning of his forty-first Monday in office. He got up without turning on the light so as not to disturb Ana Milena—who sometimes went to bed later than he did—and when he had shaved, showered, and dressed for the office, he sat in a folding chair that he kept outside the bedroom, in a cold, gloomy hallway, in order to hear the news without waking anyone. He listened to the radio newscasts on a pocket-size transistor that he held up to his ear and played at very low volume. He glanced through the papers, from the headlines to the advertisements, and tore out items to be dealt with later with his secretaries, advisers, and ministers. On one occasion he had found an article on something that was supposed to be taken care of and was not, and sent it to the appropriate minister with a single question scrawled in the margin: "When the hell is the ministry going to resolve this mess?" The solution was instantaneous.

The only news that day was the imminent release of the hostages, and that included his meeting with Father García Herreros to hear his report on the interview with Escobar. The president reorganized his day so that he would be available at a moment's notice. He canceled some meetings that could be postponed, and adjusted others. His first was with the presidential advisers, which he opened with his schoolboy's comment:

"Okay, let's finish this assignment."

Several of the advisers had just returned from Caracas, where they had talked on Friday with the reticent General Maza Márquez. In the course of the conversation the press adviser, Mauricio Vargas, had expressed his concern that no one, inside or outside the government, had a clear idea of where Pablo Escobar was really heading. Maza was sure he would not surrender because he trusted nothing but a pardon from the Constituent Assembly. Vargas replied with a question: What good would a pardon do for a man sentenced to death by his own enemies and by the Cali cartel? "It might help him, but it's not exactly a complete solution," he concluded. Escobar was in urgent need of a secure prison for himself and his people under the protection of the state.

The advisers raised the issue because of the fear that Father García Herreros would come to the twelve o'clock meeting with an unacceptable, eleventh-hour demand, without which Escobar would not surrender and not release the journalists. For the government, it would be an almost irreparable fiasco. Gabriel Silva, the adviser on foreign affairs, made two self-protective recommendations: first, that the president not attend the meeting alone, and second, that he issue as complete a communiqué as possible as soon as the meeting was over in order to forestall speculation. Rafael Pardo, who had flown to New York the day before, agreed by telephone.

The president received Father García Herreros at a special noon meeting. On one side were the priest, two clerics from his community, and Alberto Villamizar with his son Andrés; on the other, the president with his private secretary, Miguel Silva, and Mauricio Vargas. The presidential palace information services took photos and videos to give to the press if things went well. If not, at least the evidence of their failure would not be left up to the media.

The father, very conscious of the significance of the moment, told the president the details of his meeting with Escobar. He had no doubt at all that Escobar was going to turn himself in and free the hostages, and he backed up his words with the notes the two of them had written. For reasons of security that Escobar himself had outlined, his only condition was that the prison be the one in Envigado, not Itagüí.

The president read the notes and returned them to the father. He was struck by the fact that Escobar did not promise to release the prisoners but agreed only to raise the issue with the Extraditables. Villamizar explained that this was one of Escobar's many precautions: He had never admitted to holding the hostages so it could not be used as evidence against him.

The father asked what he should do if Escobar asked him to be present at his surrender. The president agreed that he should go. When the father raised doubts concerning the safety of the operation, the president replied that no one could provide better guarantees than Escobar for the safety of his own operation. Finally, the president indicated to the father—whose companions seconded the idea—that it was important to keep public statements to a minimum in order to avoid the damage that an inopportune word might create. The father agreed and even made a veiled final offer: "I've wanted to be of service in this, and I am at your disposal if you need me for anything else, like making peace with the other priest." It was clear to everyone that he was referring to the Spanish priest, Manuel Pérez, commander of the National Army of Liberation. The meeting took twenty minutes, and there was no official communiqué. Faithful to his promise, Father García Herreros displayed exemplary restraint in his statements to the press.

MARUJA WATCHED his news conference and learned nothing new. The television newscasts again showed reporters waiting at the houses of the hostages, which may well have been the same images shown the day before. Maruja also repeated the previous day's routine minute by minute, and had more than enough time to watch the afternoon soap operas. Damaris, energized by the official announcement, had granted her the privilege of choosing the menu for lunch, like condemned prisoners on the eve of their execution. Maruja said, with no touch of irony, that anything would be fine except lentils. But time grew short, Damaris could not go shopping, and there were only lentils with lentils for their farewell lunch.

For his part, Pacho put on the clothes he had been wearing the day of the kidnapping—these were too tight, since a sedentary life and bad food had made him put on weight—and sat down to listen to the news and smoke one cigarette after the other. He heard all kinds of stories about his release. He heard the corrections, the outright lies of his colleagues made reckless by the tension of waiting. He heard that he had been incognito in a restaurant, but the man eating there turned out to be one of his brothers.

He reread the editorials, the commentaries, the reports he had written on current events so he would not forget his trade, thinking he might publish them as a document of his captivity when he was freed. There were more than a hundred of them. He read one to his guards that had been written in December, when the traditional political class began its rantings against the legitimacy of the Constituent Assembly. Pacho lashed out at them with an energy and independence that were undoubtedly the product of his thinking in captivity: "We all know how you get votes in Colombia, and how countless parliamentarians won their elections," he said in an editorial note. He said that buying votes was rampant throughout the country, especially along the coast, that raffling off home appliances in exchange for electoral favors was the order of the day, and that many elected officials paid for their election through other kinds of political corruption, like charging fees over and above their public salaries and parliamentary compensation. And this was why, he said, the same people were always elected, and they, "faced with the possibility of losing their privileges, are now in an uproar." And he concluded with criticism that included himself: "The impartiality of the media—including *El Tiempo*—which was making progress after a long, hard struggle, has vanished."

The most surprising of his notes, however, was the one he wrote on the reactions of the political class when the M-19 won more than 10 percent of the vote for the Constituent Assembly. "The political aggression against the M-19," he wrote, "the strictures (or rather, discrimination) against it in the media, show how far we are from tolerance and how far we still have to go in modernizing what matters most: our minds." He said that the political class had celebrated electoral participation by the former guerrillas only to seem democratic, but when the votes amounted to more than 10 percent they turned to denunciations. And he concluded in the style of his grandfather, Enrique Santos Montejo ("Calibán"), the most widely read columnist in the history of Colombian journalism: "A very specific and traditional sector of Colombians killed the tiger and were frightened by its skin." Nothing could have been more surprising in someone who since elementary school had stood out as a precocious example of the romantic Right.

He tore up all his notes except for three that he decided to keep, for reasons he has not been able to explain. He also kept the rough drafts of the messages to his family and the president, and of his will. He would have liked to take the chain they had used to confine him to the bed, hoping that the artist Bernardo Salcedo could make a sculpture with it, but he was not allowed to keep it in case there were incriminating prints on it.

Maruja, however, did not want any memento of that hideous past, which she intended to erase from her life. But at about six that evening, when the door began to open from the outside, she realized how much those six months of bitterness were going to affect her. Since the death of Marina and the departure of Beatriz, this had been the hour of liberations or executions: the same in both cases. With her heart in her mouth she waited for the sinister ritual sentence: "We're going, get ready." It was the "Doctor," accompanied by the second-in-command who had been there the night before. They both seemed rushed.

"Now, now!" the "Doctor" urged Maruja. "Move it!"

She had imagined the moment so often that she felt over-whelmed by a strange need to gain some time, and she asked about her ring.

"I sent it with your sister-in-law," said the low-ranking boss.

"That's not true," Maruja replied with absolute calm. "You told me you had seen it after that."

More than the ring, what she wanted then was to embarrass him in front of his superior. But the "Doctor" pretended not to notice because of the pressure of time. The majordomo and his wife brought Maruja the bag that held her personal effects and the gifts that various guards had given her during her captivity: Christmas cards, the sweatsuit, the towel, magazines, a book or two. The gentle boys who had guarded her in the final days had nothing to give but medals and pictures of saints, and they asked her to pray for them, not to forget them, to do something to get them out of their bad life.

"Anything you want," said Maruja. "If you ever need me, get in touch with me and I'll help you."

The "Doctor" could do no less: "What can I give you to re-member me by?" he said, rooting through his pockets. He took out a 9mm shell and handed it to Maruja.

"Here," he said, not really joking. "The bullet we didn't shoot you with."

It was not easy to free Maruja from the embraces of the ma-jordomo and Damaris, who raised her mask as high as her nose to kiss her and ask that she not forget her. Maruja felt a sincere emo-tion. This was, after all, the end of the longest, most awful time of her life, and its happiest moment.

They covered her head with a hood that must have been the dirtiest, most foul-smelling one they could find. They put it on with the eye holes at the back of her head, and she could not avoid recalling that this was how they put the hood on Marina when they killed her. She was led, shuffling her feet in the darkness, to a car as comfortable as the one used for the abduction, and they sat her in the same spot, in the same position, and with the same precautions: her head resting on a man's knees so she could not be seen from the outside. They warned her that there were several police checkpoints, and if they were stopped Maruja had to take off the hood and behave herself.

AT ONE THAT AFTERNOON, Villamizar had eaten lunch with his son Andrés. At two-thirty he lay down for a nap, and made up for lost sleep until five-thirty. At six he had just come out of the shower, and was dressing to wait for his wife, when the telephone rang. He picked up the extension on the night table and said no more than "Hello?" An anonymous voice interrupted: "She'll arrive a few minutes after seven. They're leaving now." He hung up. The announcement was unexpected and Villamizar was grateful for it. He called the porter to make sure his car was in the garden, and the driver ready.

He put on a dark suit and a light tie with a diamond pattern to welcome his wife. He was thinner than ever, for he had lost nine pounds in six months. At seven he went to the living room to talk to the journalists while Maruja was arriving. Four of her children were there, and Andrés, their son. Only Nicolás, the musician in the family, was missing, and he would arrive from New York in a few hours. Villamizar sat in the chair closest to the phone.

BY THIS TIME Maruja was five minutes away from her release. In contrast to the night of the abduction, the drive to freedom was rapid and uneventful. At first they had taken an unpaved road, making the kinds of turns not recommended for a luxury car. Maruja could tell from the conversation that in addition to the man beside her, another was sitting next to the driver. She did not think that any of them was the "Doctor." After fifteen minutes they had her lie on the floor and stopped for about five minutes, but she did not know why. They came out onto a large, noisy avenue filled with heavy seven o'clock traffic, then turned with no difficulties onto another avenue. After no more than forty-five minutes altogether, they came to a sudden stop. The man next to the driver gave Maruja a frantic order:

"Now, get out, move."

The man sitting beside her tried to force her out of the car. Maruja struggled.

"I can't see," she shouted.

She tried to take off the hood but a brutal hand stopped her. "Wait five minutes before you take it off," he shouted. He shoved her out of the car. Maruja felt the vertigo of empty space, and terror, and thought they had thrown her over a cliff. Solid ground let her breathe again. While she waited for the car to drive away, she sensed she was on a street with little traffic. With great care she raised the hood, saw the houses among the trees with lights in the windows, and then she knew the truth of being free. It was 7:29, and 193 days had passed since the night she had been abducted.

A solitary automobile came down the avenue, made a U-turn, and stopped across the street, just opposite Maruja. Like Beatriz before her, she thought it could not be a coincidence. That car had to have been sent by the kidnappers to make sure her release was completed. Maruja went up to the driver's window.

"Please," she said, "I'm Maruja Pachón. They just let me go."

She only wanted someone to help her find a taxi. But the man let out a yell. Minutes earlier, listening to news on the radio about their imminent release, he had wondered: "Suppose I run into

Francisco Santos and he's looking for a ride?" Maruja longed to see her family, but she let him take her to the nearest house to use the telephone.

The woman in the house and her children all cried out and embraced her when they recognized her. Maruja felt numb, and everything that happened around her seemed like one more deception arranged by her kidnappers. The man who had taken her to the house was named Manuel Caro, and he was the son-in-law of the owner, Augusto Borrero, whose wife, a former activist in the New Liberalism Party, had worked with Maruja in Luis Carlos Galán's electoral campaign. But Maruja was seeing life from the outside, as if she were watching a movie screen. She asked for *aguardiente*—she never knew why—and drank it in one swallow. Then she telephoned her house, but had trouble remembering the number and misdialed twice. A woman answered right away: "Who is it?" Maruja recognized the voice and said, without melodrama:

"Alexandra, darling."

Alexandra shouted:

"Mamá! Where are you?"

Alberto Villamizar had jumped up from his chair when the phone rang but Alexandra, who was passing by, picked it up first. Maruja had begun to give her the address, but Alexandra did not have paper or pencil nearby. Villamizar took the receiver and greeted Maruja with stunning casualness:

"What do you say, baby. How are you?"

Maruja answered in the same tone:

"Fine, sweetheart, no problems."

He did have paper and pencil ready. He wrote down the address as Maruja gave it to him, but felt that something was not clear and asked to speak to somebody in the family. Borrero's wife gave him the missing details.

"Thanks very much," said Villamizar. "It's not far. I'm leaving now."

He forgot to hang up: The iron self-control he had maintained during the long months of tension suddenly melted away. He ran down the stairs two at a time and dashed across the lobby, followed by an avalanche of reporters armed to the teeth with their battle gear. Others, moving in the opposite direction, almost trampled him in the doorway.

"Maruja's free," he shouted. "Let's go."

He got into the car and slammed the door so hard he startled the dozing driver. "Let's go pick up the señora," Villamizar said. He gave him the address: Diagonal 107, No. 27-73. "It's a white house on the parallel road west of the highway," he said. But he said it so fast the driver became confused and started off in the wrong direction. Villamizar corrected him with a sharpness that was foreign to his character.

"Watch what you're doing," he shouted, "we have to be there in five minutes! If we get lost I'll cut off your balls!"

The driver, who had suffered the awful dramas of the abduction along with him, did not turn a hair. Villamizar caught his breath and directed him along the shortest, easiest roads, for he had visualized the route as he was given directions on the phone to be certain he would not get lost. It was the worst time for traffic, but not the worst day.

Andrés had pulled out behind his father, along with his cousin Gabriel, following the caravan of reporters who cut a path through traffic with fake ambulance sirens. Even though he was an expert driver, he became stuck in traffic, and could not move. Villamizar, on the other hand, arrived in the record time of fifteen minutes. He did not have to look for the house because some of the reporters who had been in his apartment were already arguing with the owner to let them in. Villamizar made his way through the noisy crowd. He did not have time to greet anyone, because the owner's wife recognized him and pointed to the stairs.

"This way," she said.

Maruja was in the main bedroom, where they had taken her to

freshen up while she waited for her husband. When she went in she had come face-to-face with a grotesque stranger: her reflection in the mirror. She looked bloated and flabby from nephritis, her eyelids swollen, her skin pasty and dry after six months of darkness.

Villamizar raced up the stairs, opened the first door he came to, and found himself in the children's room filled with dolls and bicycles. Then he opened the door facing him, and saw Maruja sitting on the bed in the checked jacket she had worn when she left the house on the day of her abduction, and freshly made up for him. "He came in like thunder," Maruja has said. She threw her arms around his neck, and their embrace was intense, long, and silent. The clamor of the reporters, who had overcome the owner's resistance and stormed into the house, broke the spell. Maruja gave a start. Villamizar smiled in amusement.

"Your colleagues," he said.

Maruja felt consternation. "I spent six months without looking in a mirror," she said. She smiled at her reflection, and it was not her. She stood erect, fluffed the hair pulled back at the nape of her neck, did what she could to make the woman in the mirror resemble the image of herself she had six months earlier. She failed.

"I look awful," she said, and showed her husband her swollen, misshapen fingers. "I didn't realize because they took my ring."

"You look perfect," Villamizar said.

He put his arm around her shoulder and walked her to the living room.

The reporters attacked with cameras, lights, and microphones. Maruja was dazzled. "Take it easy, guys," she said. "It'll be easier to talk in the apartment." Those were her first words.

THE SEVEN O'CLOCK news said nothing, but President Gaviria learned minutes later when he checked the radio that Maruja Pachón had been freed. He drove to her house with Mauricio

Vargas, but earlier they had left an official announcement of the release of Francisco Santos, which they expected at any moment. Mauricio Vargas had read it into the journalists' tape recorders on the condition they not broadcast it until they received official notification.

At this time Maruja was on her way home. A short while before she arrived, a rumor began to circulate that Pacho Santos had been freed, and the reporters unleashed the dog of the official announcement, which rushed out, barking with jubilation, over every station.

The president and Mauricio Vargas heard it in the car and celebrated the idea of having prerecorded it. But five minutes later the report was retracted.

"Mauricio," exclaimed Gaviria, "what a disaster!"

All they could do, however, was hope that events would occur as announced. In the meantime, since the overflowing crowd made it impossible for them to stay in Villamizar's apartment, they went up one floor to the apartment of Aseneth Velásquez to wait for Pacho's true release after his three false ones.

PACHO SANTOS HAD heard the announcement of Maruja's release, the premature announcement of his own, and the government's blunder. At that moment the man who had spoken to him in the morning came into his room, and led him by the arm, without a blindfold, down to the first floor. He saw that the house was empty, and one of his guards, convulsing with laughter, informed him they had moved out the furniture in a truck to avoid paying the last month's rent. They all said goodbye with huge hugs, and thanked Pacho for everything he had taught them. Pacho's reply was sincere:

"I learned a lot from you too."

In the garage they gave him a book to hold up to his face, as if he were reading, and intoned the warnings. If they ran into the police he had to jump out of the car so they could get away. And most important of all: He must not say he had been in Bogotá, but somewhere three hours away along a terrible highway. They had a gruesome reason: His captors knew Pacho was astute enough to have formed an idea of where the house was located, and he could not reveal it because the guards had lived openly in the neighborhood, taking no precautions at all, during the long days of his captivity.

"If you tell," the man in charge of his release concluded, "we'll have to kill all the neighbors to keep them from identifying us later on."

Across from the police kiosk at the intersection of Avenida Boyacá and Calle 80, the car stalled. They tried to start it again two, three, four times, but it did not turn over until the fifth attempt. They were all in a cold sweat. They drove two more blocks, took away the book, and let Pacho out on the corner with three 2,000-peso bills for the taxi. He took the first one that passed, and its young, amiable driver refused to charge him, and with blasts of the horn and joyful shouts cut a path through the mob waiting outside Pacho's house. The yellow journalists were disappointed: They had been expecting an emaciated, defeated man after 244 days of captivity, and instead they saw a Pancho Santos rejuvenated in spirit and body, and fatter, more reckless, more in love with life than ever. "They returned him exactly the same," declared his cousin Enrique Santos Calderón. Another cousin, infected by the family's jubilant mood, said: "He needed another six months."

BY NOW MARUJA was in her house. She had come home with Alberto, pursued by the mobile units that drove alongside them, preceded them, transmitting directly through all the snarled traffic. The drivers who were following the news on the radio recognized them as they passed and leaned on their horns in greeting, until the ovation spread all along the route.

Andrés Villamizar had tried to go back home when he lost sight of his father, but his driving was so merciless that the engine shook loose and a rod broke. He left his automobile in the care of the police at the nearest kiosk, and stopped the first car that passed: a dark-gray BMW driven by a sympathetic executive who had been listening to the news. Andrés told him who he was and why he needed help, and asked him to get as close to his house as he could.

"Get in," said the man, "but I warn you, if you're lying I'll make things hard for you."

At the corner of Carrera Séptima and Calle 80, he happened to see a friend driving an old Renault. Andrés continued on with her, but the car ran out of steam on the Circunvalar hill. Andrés squeezed into the last white Jeep from the National Radio Network (RCN).

The hill leading to the house was blocked by cars and a crowd of neighbors who had poured into the street. Maruja and Villamizar decided to leave the car and walk the last hundred meters, and without noticing it they got out at the same spot where she had been abducted. The first face Maruja recognized in the excited crowd was María del Rosario Ortiz, the originator and director of "Colombia Wants Them Back," which for the first time since its creation did not broadcast that night for lack of a subject. Then she saw Andrés, who had jumped out of the Jeep and was trying to get to his house just as a tall, determined police officer ordered the street closed. Andrés, in a moment of pure inspiration, looked him in the eye and said in a firm voice:

"I'm Andrés."

The officer knew nothing about him but let him pass. Maruja recognized him while he was running toward her and they embraced to the sound of applause. Patrol cars had to open a path for

them. Maruja, Alberto, and Andrés began to climb the hill with
full hearts, and were overcome by emotion. For the first time they
burst into the tears that all three had wanted to hold back. And
who could blame them: As far as the eye could see, a second crowd
of good neighbors had hung flags from the windows of the tallest
buildings and, with a springtime of white handkerchiefs and an
immense ovation, saluted the jubilant adventure of her return
home.

EPILOGUE

AT NINE the next morning, as planned, Villamizar landed in Medellín with less than an hour's sleep. The night had been a boisterous celebration of resurrection. At four in the morning, when they were finally alone in the apartment, Maruja and he were so elated by the day's events that they stayed in the living room until dawn exchanging belated news. At the La Loma hacienda he was welcomed with the usual banquet, but this time baptized with the champagne of liberation. It was a brief respite, however, because now the one in a hurry was Pablo Escobar, hiding somewhere in the world without the protection of the hostages. His new emissary was very tall and loquacious, a pure blond with a long golden mustache who was called the Monkey and had full authority to negotiate the surrender.

By order of President César Gaviria, the entire legal debate with Escobar's lawyers had been carried out through Dr. Carlos Eduardo Mejía, who reported to the justice minister. For the physical surrender, Mejía would represent Rafael Pardo for the government's side, and the other side would be represented by Jorge Luis Ochoa, the Monkey, and Escobar himself from the shadows.

Villamizar continued to be an active intermediary with the government, and Father García Herreros, who was a moral guarantor for Escobar, would remain available in the event of a major crisis.

Escobar's haste in having Villamizar come to Medellín the day after Maruja's release gave the impression that his surrender would be immediate, but it was soon evident that for him there were still a few diversionary tactics remaining. Everyone's greatest concern, Villamizar more than anyone, was that nothing happen to Escobar before he turned himself in. They had reason to worry: Villamizar knew that Escobar, or his survivors, would take it out of his hide if they even suspected him of not keeping his word. Escobar himself broke the ice when he telephoned him at La Loma and said without any preamble:

"Dr. Villa, are you happy?"

Villamizar had never seen or heard him, and he was struck by the absolute serenity of the voice that had no trace of his mythical aura. "I thank you for coming," Escobar continued without waiting for a reply, his earthly state revealed by his harsh shantytown diction. "You're a man of your word and I knew you wouldn't fail me." And then he came to the point:

"Let's start to arrange how I'll turn myself in."

In reality, Escobar already knew how he was going to turn himself in, but perhaps he wanted to review it again with a man in whom he had placed all his confidence. His lawyers and the director of Criminal Investigation, at times face-to-face and at times through the regional director, and always in coordination with the justice minister, had discussed every last detail of the surrender. When the legal questions stemming from each of their distinct interpretations of the presidential decrees had been clarified, the issues had been reduced to three: the prison, the staffing of the prison, and the role of the police and the army.

The prison—in the former Rehabilitation Center for Drug Addicts in Envigado—was almost finished. Villamizar and the Monkey visited it at Escobar's request on the day following the release of Maruja and Pacho Santos. Piles of rubble in the corners and the devastating effects of that year's heavy rains gave it a somewhat depressing appearance. The technical problems of security had been resolved. There was a double fence, 2.8 meters high, with fifteen rows of five-thousand-volt electrified barbed wire and seven watch towers, in addition to the two that guarded the entrance. These two installations would be further reinforced, as much to keep Escobar from escaping as to prevent anyone from killing him.

The only point that Villamizar found to criticize was an Italian-tiled bathroom in the room intended for Escobar, and he recommended changing it—and it was changed—to more sober decoration. The conclusion of his report was even more sober: "It seemed to me a very prisonlike prison." In fact, the folkloric splendor that would eventually shock the nation and compromise the government's prestige came later, from the inside, with an inconceivable program of bribery and intimidation.

Escobar asked Villamizar for a clean telephone number in Bogotá on which they could discuss the details of his physical surrender, and Villamizar gave him the number of his upstairs neighbor, Aseneth Velásquez. He thought no phone could be safer than hers, called at all hours of the day and night by writers and artists lunatic enough to unhinge the strongest-minded. The formula was simple and innocuous: An anonymous voice would call Villamizar's house and say, "In fifteen minutes, Doctor." Villamizar would go upstairs to Aseneth's apartment and Pablo Escobar himself would call a quarter of an hour later. On one occasion he was delayed in the elevator and Aseneth answered the phone. A raw Medellinese voice asked for Dr. Villamizar.

"He doesn't live here," said Aseneth.

"Don't worry about that," said the voice with amusement. "He's on his way up."

The person speaking was Pablo Escobar, live and direct, but Aseneth will know that only if she happens to read this book, for on that day Villamizar tried to tell her out of basic loyalty, and she—who is no fool—covered her ears.

"I don't want to know anything about anything," she said. "Do whatever you want in my house but don't tell me about it."

By this time Villamizar was traveling to Medellín several times a week. From the Hotel Intercontinental he would call María Lía, and she would send a car to take him to La Loma. On one of his early trips Maruja had gone with him to thank the Ochoas for their help. At lunch the question of her emerald and diamond ring came up, for it had not been returned to her on the night she was released. Villamizar had also mentioned it to the Ochoas, and they had sent a message to Escobar, but he did not reply. The Monkey, who was present, suggested giving her a new one, but Villamizar explained that Maruja wanted the ring for sentimental reasons, not for its monetary value. The Monkey promised to take the problem to Escobar.

Escobar's first call to Aseneth's house had to do with a "God's Minute" on which Father García Herreros accused him of being an unrepentant pornographer, and warned him to return to God's path. No one could understand his about-face. Escobar thought that if the priest had turned against him it must have been for a very significant reason, and he made his surrender conditional on an immediate public explanation. The worst thing for him was that his men had agreed to turn themselves in because of the faith they had in the father's word. Villamizar brought him to La Loma, and there the father made all kinds of explanations to Escobar by telephone. According to these, when the program was recorded an editing error made him say what in fact he had never said. Escobar taped the conversation, played it for his troops, and averted a crisis.

But there was still more. The government insisted on combined army and national guard patrols for the exterior of the prison, on cutting down the adjoining woods to make a firing range, and on its right to have the guards selected from a list compiled by a tripartite commission representing the central government, the municipality of Envigado, and the Prosecutor General's Office, since the prison was both municipal and national. Escobar opposed having guards close by because his enemies could murder him in the prison. He opposed combined patrols because—his lawyers claimed—no military forces were permitted inside a jail, according to the Law on Prisons. He opposed cutting down the nearby forest because it would permit helicopter landings and because he assumed a firing range was an area where prisoners would be the targets, until he was convinced that in military terms, a firing range is nothing more than a field with good visibility. And that, in fact, was the great advantage of the Rehabilitation Center—for the government and for the prisoners—because from anywhere in the building one had a clear view of the valley and the mountains, allowing more than enough time to respond to an attack. Then, at the last minute, the national director of Criminal Investigation wanted to build a fortified wall around the prison in addition to the barbed-wire fence. Escobar was furious.

On Thursday, May 30, *El Espectador* published a report—attributed to very reliable official sources—on the terms for surrender allegedly set by Escobar at a meeting between his lawyers and government spokesmen. The most sensational of these—according to the article—was the exile of General Maza Márquez and the dismissals of General Miguel Gómez Padilla, commander of the National Police, and General Octavio Vargas Silva, commander of the Police Office of Judicial Investigation (DIJIN).

PRESIDENT GAVIRIA met with General Maza Márquez in his office to clarify the origin of the report, which persons connected to the government had attributed to him. The interview lasted for half an hour, and knowing both men, it is impossible to imagine which of the two was more impassive. The general, in his soft, slow baritone, gave a detailed account of his inquiries into the case. The president listened in absolute silence. Twenty minutes later they said goodbye. The next day, the general sent the president an official six-page letter that repeated in minute detail what he had said, and documented their conversation.

According to his investigations—the letter said—the source of the report was Martha Nieves Ochoa, who had given it days before as an exclusive to the legal reporters at *El Tiempo*—the only ones who had it—and they could not understand how it had been published first in *El Espectador*. The general stated that he was a fervent supporter of Pablo Escobar's surrender. He reiterated his loyalty to his principles, obligations, and duties, and concluded: "For reasons known to you, Mr. President, many persons and entities are intent upon destabilizing my career, perhaps with the aim of placing me in a situation of risk that will allow them to carry out their plans against me."

Martha Nieves Ochoa denied being the source of the article, and did not speak of the matter again. Three months later, however—when Escobar was already in prison—Fabio Villegas, the secretary general to the president, asked General Maza to his office on behalf of the president, invited him into the Blue Room and, walking from one end to the other as if he were out for a Sunday stroll, communicated the president's decision to have him retire. Maza left convinced that this was evidence of an agreement with Escobar that the government had denied. In his words, "I was negotiated."

In any case, before this occurred, Escobar had let Maza know that the war between them had ended, that he had forgotten everything and was serious about his surrender: He was stopping the attacks, disbanding his men, and turning in his dynamite. As proof he sent him a list of hiding places for seven hundred kilos of explosives. Later, from prison, he would continue to disclose to the brigade in Medellín a series of caches totaling two tons. But Maza never trusted him.

Impatient over the delay in his surrender, the government appointed a man from Boyacá—Luis Jorge Pataquiva Silva—as director of the prison instead of an Antioquian, as well as twenty national guards from various departments, none from Antioquia. "In any event," said Villamizar, "if they want to bribe someone it makes no difference if he's from Antioquia or somewhere else." Escobar, weary of all the twisting and turning, barely discussed it. In the end it was agreed that the army and not the police would guard the entrance, and that exceptional measures would be taken to ease Escobar's fear that his food in prison might be poisoned.

The National Board of Prisons, on the other hand, adopted the same regulations regarding visits that applied to the Ochoa brothers in the maximum security block of Itagüí prison. The time for waking up was seven in the morning; the time for being confined and placed under lock and key in one's cell was eight in the evening. Escobar and his prison mates could have women visitors every Sunday, from eight in the morning until two in the afternoon; men could visit on Saturdays, and minors on the first and third Sunday of every month.

In the middle of the night on June 9, troops from the battalion of military police in Medellín relieved the cavalry unit that was guarding the sector, began to assemble an impressive security array, cleared the surrounding mountains of people who did not live in the area, and assumed total control of earth and heaven. There were no more excuses. Villamizar let Escobar know—with utmost sincerity—that he was grateful to him for Maruja's release, but was not prepared to take any more risks just so he could keep putting off his surrender. And he sent him a serious message: "From now on I'm not responsible." Escobar made his decision in two days, with one final condition: that the prosecutor general also be present at the surrender.

An unexpected problem could have caused a new delay: Escobar did not have an official identification document that would prove he was in fact the man giving himself up. One of his lawyers raised the issue with the government and requested official citizenship papers for him, not taking into account that Escobar, hunted by every armed force in the country, would have to go in person to the appropriate office of the Civil Registry. The emergency solution was that he would identify himself with his fingerprints and an old identification card he had once used and had notarized, declaring at the same time that he could not produce the card because it had been lost.

THE MONKEY woke Villamizar when he phoned at midnight on June 18 to tell him to go upstairs to take an urgent call. It was very late, but Aseneth's apartment resembled a happy inferno, with the accordion of Egidio Cuadrado and his *vallenatos* combo. Villamizar had to elbow his way through a frenetic jungle of elite cultural gossip. Aseneth, in typical fashion, blocked his path.

"I know now who's calling you," she said. "Be careful, because one false step and they'll have your balls."

She let him into her bedroom just as the phone rang. In the uproar that filled the house, Villamizar could barely make out what was most essential:

"Ready: Come to Medellín first thing tomorrow."

RAFAEL PARDO arranged for a Civil Aeronautics plane to be available at seven o'clock for the official committee that would witness the surrender. Villamizar, fearful of leaks, was at Father García Herreros's house by five. He found him in the oratory, the inevitable poncho over his cassock, just as he finished saying mass.

"Well, Father, let's go," he said. "We're flying to Medellín because Escobar's ready to surrender."

Traveling in the plane with them were Fernando García Herreros, one of the father's nephews who acted as his occasional assistant; Jaime Vázquez, from the Council on Public Information; Dr. Carlos Gustavo Arrieta, the prosecutor general for the republic; and Dr. Jaime Córdoba Triviño, the special prosecutor for human rights. At Olaya Herrera airport, in the center of Medellín, María Lía and Martha Nieves Ochoa were waiting for them.

The official committee was taken to the capitol building of the department of Antioquia. Villamizar and the father went to María Lía's apartment to have breakfast while last-minute arrangements were made for the surrender. There he learned that Escobar was already on his way, traveling by car and on foot to avoid the frequent police checkpoints. He was an expert in those evasive strategies.

Once again the father's nerves were on edge. One of his contact lenses fell out, he stepped on it, and was so exasperated that Martha Nieves had to take him to San Ignacio Opticians, where they solved his problem with a pair of normal glasses. The city teemed with rigorous checkpoints, and they were stopped at almost all of them, not to be searched but so the men could thank the good father for everything he was doing for Medellín. In that city where everything was possible, the best-kept secret in the world was already public knowledge.

The Monk came to María Lía's apartment at two-thirty, dressed for a day in the country with a light jacket and soft-soled shoes.

"Ready," he said to Villamizar. "Let's go to the capitol building. You take your car and I'll take mine."

He drove off alone. María Lía drove Villamizar, Father García Herreros, and Martha Nieves in her car. The two men got out at the capitol building. The women waited outside. The Monkey, no longer a cold, efficient technician, was trying to hide inside his own skin. He put on dark glasses and a golfer's hat, and kept in the background, behind Villamizar. Someone who saw him walking in with the priest rushed to telephone Rafael Pardo to say that Escobar—very blond, very tall and elegant—had just surrendered at the capitol building.

As they were preparing to leave, the Monkey received a call on his two-way radio informing him that a plane was heading for the airspace over the city. It was a military ambulance carrying several soldiers wounded in a clash with guerrillas in Urabá. It was getting late and the authorities were troubled, because the helicopters could not fly as dusk was falling, and delaying the surrender until the next day would be calamitous. Villamizar called Rafael Pardo, who rerouted the flight and repeated his categorical order that the sky be kept clear. As he waited for this to be settled, he wrote in his personal diary: "Not even birds will fly over Medellín today."

The first helicopter—a six-passenger Bell 206—took off from the roof of the capitol building a little after three, with the prosecutor general and Jaime Vázquez, Fernando García Herreros, and Luis Alirio Calle, a radio journalist whose enormous popularity was one more guarantee for Pablo Escobar's peace of mind. A security official would show the pilot the direct route to the prison.

The second helicopter—a twelve-passenger Bell 412—took off ten minutes later, when the Monkey received the order on his two-way radio. Villamizar flew with him and the father. As soon as they had taken off, they heard a report on the radio that the government's position had suffered a defeat in the Constituent Assembly, where non-extradition of nationals had just been approved by a vote of fifty-one to thirteen, with five abstentions, in a preliminary ballot that would be ratified later. Though there were no indications it had been planned, it was almost childish not to think Escobar had known ahead of time and had waited for that precise moment to surrender.

The pilots followed the Monkey's directions to the site where they would pick up Pablo Escobar and take him to prison. It was a very short flight, and at so low an altitude the directions seemed the kind you would give in a car: Take Eighth, keep going, turn right, more, a little more, to the park, that's it. Behind a grove of trees there suddenly appeared a splendid mansion surrounded by the bright colors of tropical flowers, with a soccer field as smooth as an enormous billiard table in the middle of El Poblado's traffic.

"Put it down over there," the Monkey said, pointing. "Don't turn off the engine."

Villamizar did not realize until they were right over the house that at least thirty armed men were waiting all around the field. When the helicopter landed on the grass, some fifteen bodyguards moved away from the group and walked uneasily to the helicopter in a circle around a man who was in no way inconspicuous. He had hair down to his shoulders, a very thick, rough-looking black beard that reached to his chest, and skin browned and weathered by a desert sun. He was thick-set, wore tennis shoes and a light-blue cotton jacket, had an easy walk and a chilling calm. Villamizar knew who he was at first sight only because he was different from all the other men he had ever seen in his life.

After saying goodbye to the nearest bodyguards with a series of powerful, rapid embraces, Escobar indicated to two of them that they should climb in the other side of the helicopter. They were Mugre and Otto, two of the men closest to him. Then he climbed in, paying no attention to the blades turning at half-speed. The first man he greeted before he sat down was Villamizar. He extended his warm, well-manicured hand and asked with no change in his voice:

"How are you, Dr. Villamizar?"

"How's it going, Pablo?" he replied.

Then Escobar turned to Father García Herreros with an amiable smile and thanked him for everything. He sat next to his two bodyguards, and only then did he seem to realize that the Monkey was there. Perhaps he had expected him only to give directions to Villamizar without getting into the helicopter.

"And you," Escobar said, "in the middle of this right to the end."

Nobody could tell if he was praising or berating him, but his tone was cordial. The Monkey, as confused as everyone else, shook his head and smiled.

"Ah, Chief!"

Then, in a kind of revelation, it occurred to Villamizar that Escobar was a much more dangerous man than anyone supposed, because there was something supernatural in his serenity and self-possession. The Monkey tried to close the door on his side but did not know how and the co-pilot had to do it. In the emotion of the moment, no one had thought to give any orders. The pilot, tense at the controls, asked a question:

"Do we take off now?"

Then Escobar let slip the only sign of his repressed anxiety.

He gave a quick order: "What do you think? Move it! Move it!"

When the helicopter lifted off from the grass, he asked Villamizar: "Everything's fine, isn't it, Doctor?" Villamizar, not turning around to look at him, answered with all his heart: "Everything's perfect." And that was all, because the flight was over. The helicopter flew the remaining distance almost grazing the trees, and came down on the prison soccer field—rock-strewn, its goalposts broken—next to the first helicopter, which had arrived a quarter of an hour earlier. The trip from the residence had taken less than fifteen minutes.

The next two minutes, however, were the most dramatic of all. Escobar tried to get out first, as soon as the door was opened, and found himself surrounded by the prison guards: some fifty tense, fairly bewildered men in blue uniforms who were aiming their weapons at him. Escobar gave a start, lost his control for a moment, and in a voice heavy with fearsome authority he roared:

"Lower your weapons, damn it!"

By the time the head of the guards gave the same order, Escobar's command had already been obeyed. Escobar and his companions walked the two hundred meters to the house where the prison officials, the members of the official delegation, and the first group of Escobar's men, who had come overland to surrender with him, were all waiting. Also present were Escobar's wife and his mother, who was very pale and on the verge of tears. As he passed he gave her an affectionate little pat on the shoulder and said: "Take it easy, Ma." The director of the prison came out to meet him, his hand extended.

"Señor Escobar," he introduced himself. "I'm Luis Jorge Pataquiva."

Escobar shook his hand. Then he raised his left pant leg and took out the pistol he was carrying in an ankle holster. It was a magnificent weapon: a Sig Sauer 9mm with a gold monogram inlaid on the mother-of-pearl handle. Escobar did not remove the clip but took out the bullets one by one and tossed them to the ground.

It was a somewhat theatrical gesture that seemed rehearsed, and it had its intended effect as a show of confidence in the warden whose appointment had caused so much concern. The following day it was reported that when he turned in his pistol Escobar had said to Pataquiva: "For peace in Colombia." No witness remembers this, least of all Villamizar, who was still dazzled by the beauty of the weapon.

Escobar greeted everyone. The special prosecutor held on to his hand as he said: "I am here, Señor Escobar, to make certain your rights are respected." Escobar thanked him with special deference. Then he took Villamizar's arm.

"Let's go, Doctor," he said. "You and I have a lot to talk about."

He led him to the end of the outside gallery, and they chatted there for about ten minutes, leaning against the railing, their backs to everyone. Escobar began by thanking him in formal terms. Then, with his awesome calm, he expressed regret for the suffering he had caused Villamizar and his family, but asked him to understand that the war had been very hard on both sides. Villamizar did not miss this opportunity to solve three great mysteries in his life: why they had killed Luis Carlos Galán, why Escobar had tried to kill him, and why he had abducted Maruja and Beatriz.

Escobar denied all responsibility for the first crime. "The fact is that everybody wanted to kill Dr. Galán," he said. He admitted being present at the discussions when the attack was decided, but denied taking part or having anything to do with what happened. "A lot of people were involved in that," he said. "I didn't even like the idea because I knew what would happen if they killed him, but once the decision was made I couldn't oppose it. Please tell doña Gloria that for me."

As for the second, he was very explicit: A group of friends in congress had convinced him that Villamizar was uncontrollable and stubborn and had to be stopped somehow before he succeeded in having extradition approved. "Besides," he said, "in that war we were fighting, just a rumor could get you killed. But now that I know you, Dr. Villamizar, thank God nothing happened to you."

As for Maruja's abduction, his explanation was simplistic. "I was kidnapping people to get something and I didn't get it, nobody was talking to me, nobody was paying attention, so I went after doña Maruja to see if that would work." He had no other reasons, but did drift into a long commentary about how he had gotten to know Villamizar over the course of the negotiations until he became convinced he was a serious, brave man whose word was as good as gold, and for that he pledged his eternal gratitude. "I know you and I can't be friends," he said. But Villamizar could be sure that nothing would happen to him or anybody in his family again.

"Who knows how long I'll be here," he said, "but I still have a lot of friends, so if any of you feels unsafe, if anybody tries to give you a hard time, you let me know and that'll be the end of it. You met your obligations to me, and I thank you and will do the same for you. You have my word of honor."

Before they said goodbye, Escobar asked Villamizar, as a final favor, to try to calm his mother and wife, who were both on the verge of hysteria. Villamizar did, without much hope of success, since both were convinced that the entire ceremony was nothing but a sinister trick on the part of the government to murder Escobar in prison. Finally Villamizar went into the director's office and dialed 284 33 00, the number of the presidential palace, which he knew by heart, and asked them to find Rafael Pardo no matter where he might be.

He was in the office of Mauricio Vargas, the press adviser, who answered the phone and passed Pardo the receiver without saying a word. Pardo recognized the grave, quiet voice, but this time it had a glowing aura.

"Dr. Pardo," said Villamizar, "I'm here with Escobar in prison."

Pardo—perhaps for the first time in his life—heard the news without passing it through the filter of doubt.

"How wonderful!" he said.

He made a rapid remark that Mauricio Vargas did not even try to interpret, hung up the phone, and walked into the president's office without knocking. Vargas, who is a born reporter twenty-four hours a day, suspected that Pardo's hurry, and the amount of time he spent in the office, meant that something important had happened. His nervous excitement could not tolerate a wait of more than five minutes. He went into the president's office without being announced, and found him laughing out loud at something Pardo had just said. Then he heard the news. Mauricio thought with pleasure about the army of journalists who would burst into his office any minute now, and he looked at his watch. It was 4:30 in the afternoon. Two months later, Rafael Pardo would be the first civilian named defense minister after fifty years of military ministers.

PABLO EMILIO ESCOBAR GAVIRIA had turned forty-one in December. According to the medical examination required when he entered prison, his state of health was that of "a young man in normal physical and mental condition." The only unusual observation was congestion in the nasal mucous membranes and something that looked like a plastic surgery scar on his nose, but he said he had been injured as a boy during a soccer game.

The document of voluntary surrender was signed by the national and regional directors of Criminal Investigation, and the special prosecutor for human rights. Escobar endorsed his signature with his thumbprint and the number of his lost identification card: 8.345.766, Envigado. The secretary, Carlos Alberto Bravo, added at the bottom of the document: "Having affixed his signature to this document, Señor Pablo Emilio Escobar requested that Dr. Alberto Villamizar Cárdenas also affix his signature to same, said signature appearing below." Villamizar signed, though he was never told in what capacity.

When this process had been completed, Pablo Escobar took his leave of everyone and walked into the cell where he would live as involved as ever in his business affairs, and also have the power of the state protecting his domestic tranquillity and security. Starting the next day, however, the very prisonlike prison described by Villamizar began to be transformed into a five-star hacienda with all kinds of luxuries, sports installations, and facilities for parties and pleasures, built with first-class materials brought in gradually in the false bottom of a supply van. When the government learned about the scandal 299 days later, it decided to transfer Escobar to another prison with no prior announcement. Just as incredible as the government's needing a year to find out what was going on was the fact that Escobar bribed a sergeant and two terrified soldiers with a plate of food and escaped on foot with his bodyguards through the nearby woods, under the noses of the functionaries and troops responsible for the transfer.

It was his death sentence. According to his subsequent statement, the government's action had been so strange and precipitous that he did not think they were really going to transfer him but kill him or turn him over to the United States. When he realized the enormity of his error, he undertook two parallel campaigns to have the government repeat the favor of imprisoning him: the greatest terrorist bombing offensive in the history of the country, and his offer to surrender without conditions of any kind. The government never acknowledged his proposals, the country did not succumb to the terror of the car bombs, and the police offensive reached unsustainable proportions.

The world had changed for Escobar. Those who could have helped him save his life again had no desire or reason to. Father García Herreros died of kidney failure on November 24, 1992, and Paulina—with no job and no savings—retired so far into a peaceful autumn with her children and good memories that today no one at "God's Word" even mentions her. Alberto Villamizar, named ambassador to Holland, received several messages from Escobar, but it was too late now for everything. His immense fortune, estimated at 3 billion dollars, was for the most part drained by the cost of the war or spent disbanding the cartel. His family found no place in the world where they could sleep without nightmares. Having become the biggest prey in our history, Escobar could not stay more than six hours in one spot, and in his crazed flight he left behind him a trail of dead innocents, and his own bodyguards murdered, captured, or gone over to the forces of his enemies. His security services, and even his own almost animal instinct for survival, lost the sharp edge of former days.

On December 2, 1993—one day after his forty-fourth birthday—he could not resist the temptation of talking on the phone with his son Juan Pablo who, with his mother and younger sister, had just returned to Bogotá following Germany's refusal to admit them. Juan Pablo, who was now more alert than his father, warned him after two minutes not to talk anymore because the police would trace the call. Escobar—whose devotion to his family was proverbial—ignored him. By this time the trace had established the exact phone in the Los Olivos district in Medellín that he was using. At 3:15 in the afternoon, an inconspicuous group of twenty-three special plainclothes police cordoned off the area, took over the house, and began to force the door to the second floor. Escobar heard them. "I'm hanging up," he said to his son on the telephone, "because something funny's going on here." Those were his last words.

VILLAMIZAR SPENT the night of the surrender in the noisiest, most dangerous clubs in the city, drinking man-size glasses of *aguardiente* with Escobar's bodyguards. The Monkey, drunk as a lord, told anyone who would listen that Dr. Villamizar was the only person the Chief had ever apologized to. At two in the morning he stood up and with no preliminaries said goodbye with a wave of his hand.

"So long, Dr. Villamizar," he said. "I have to disappear now, and we may never see each other again. It was a pleasure knowing you."

Villamizar, besotted with drink, was dropped off at La Loma at dawn. In the afternoon, the only topic of conversation on the plane to Bogotá was Pablo Escobar's surrender. Villamizar was one of the best-known men in the country that day, but no one recognized him in the crowded airports. The newspapers had indicated his presence at the prison but had published no photographs, and the real extent of his decisive participation in the entire capitulation process seemed destined for the shadows of secret glories.

Back home that afternoon, he realized that daily life was returning to normal. Andrés was studying in his room. Maruja was waging a difficult, silent war against her phantoms in order to become herself again. The Tang Dynasty horse was back in its usual place, between her prized mementos of Indonesia and her antiquities from half the world, rearing its front legs on the sacred table where she wanted it to be, in the corner where she dreamed of seeing it during the interminable nights of her captivity. She had returned to her offices at FOCINE in the same car—the bullet scars on the windows erased—from which she had been abducted, with a new, grateful driver in the dead chauffeur's seat. In less than two years she would be named education minister.

Villamizar, with no job and no desire to have one, with the bad taste of politics in his mouth, chose to rest for a time in his own way, making small household repairs, taking his leisure sip by sip with old drinking companions, doing the shopping himself so that he and his friends could enjoy the pleasures of the local cuisine. It was the perfect frame of mind for reading in the afternoon and growing a beard. One Sunday at lunch, when the mists of memory had already begun to rarefy the past, someone knocked at the door. They thought Andrés had forgotten his keys again. The servants had the day off, and Villamizar opened the door. A young man in a sports jacket handed him a small package wrapped in gift paper and tied with a gold ribbon, and then disappeared down the stairs without saying a word or giving him time to ask any questions. Villamizar thought it might be a bomb. In an instant he was shuddering with the nausea of the abduction, but he untied the bow and unwrapped the package with his fingertips, away from the dining room where Maruja was waiting for him. It was a case made of imitation leather, and inside the case, nestled in satin, was the ring they had taken from Maruja on the night she was abducted. One diamond chip was missing, but it was the same ring.

Maruja was stunned. She put it on, and realized she was recovering her health faster than she had imagined because now it fit her finger.

"How incredible!" she said with a hopeful sigh. "Somebody ought to write a book."